Our Schools
and
Our Future
. . . Are We Still at Risk?

The Hoover Institution gratefully acknowledges
the following individuals and foundations for their
significant support of the

Initiative
on
American Public Education

KORET FOUNDATION

TAD AND DIANNE TAUBE

LYNDE AND HARRY BRADLEY FOUNDATION

BOYD AND JILL SMITH

JACK AND MARY LOIS WHEATLEY

FRANKLIN AND CATHERINE JOHNSON

JERRY AND PATTI HUME

DORIS AND DONALD FISHER

BERNARD LEE SCHWARTZ FOUNDATION

ELIZABETH AND STEPHEN BECHTEL JR. FOUNDATION

The Hoover Institution
gratefully acknowledges generous support from

TAD AND DIANNE TAUBE

TAUBE FAMILY FOUNDATION

KORET FOUNDATION

Founders of the program on
American Institutions and Economic Performance

And Cornerstone gifts from

SARAH SCAIFE FOUNDATION

Our Schools
and
Our Future

. . . Are We Still at Risk?

EDITED BY
Paul E. Peterson

MEMBERS OF THE TASK FORCE
ON K–12 EDUCATION
John E. Chubb
Williamson M. Evers
Chester E. Finn Jr.
Eric A. Hanushek
Paul T. Hill
E. D. Hirsch Jr.
Caroline M. Hoxby
Terry M. Moe
Paul E. Peterson
Diane Ravitch
Herbert J. Walberg

HOOVER INSTITUTION PRESS
Stanford University   Stanford, California

www.hoover.org

Hoover Institution Press Publication No. 516
Copyright © 2003 by the Board of Trustees of the
    Leland Stanford Junior University

First printing 2003
09   08   07   06   05   04   03   9   8   7   6   5   4   3   2   1

Manufactured in the United States of America
The paper used in this publication meets the minimum requirements
of American National Standard for Information Sciences—Permanence
of Paper for Printed Library Materials, ANSI Z39.48-1984. ⊗

Library of Congress Cataloging-in-Publication Data
Our schools and our future : are we still at risk? / edited by
Paul E. Peterson ; contributing authors, John E. Chubb . . . [et al.]
        p.   cm.
    "An assessment by the Koret Task Force on K–12 Education"—Cover.
    ISBN 0-8179-3921-0 — ISBN 0-8179-3922-9 (pbk.)
    1. Education—United States.   2. Educational change—United States.
I. Peterson, Paul E.   II. Chubb, John E.
LA217.2 .O87   2003
370'.973—dc21   2002191907

Contents

Foreword

Some years ago, Tad Taube and I met on several occasions to discuss the quality of schooling provided to America's children, particularly those in low-income situations. Tad is president of the Koret Foundation, a philanthropic organization that, in recent years, has focused on ways of improving the quality of public education in the United States. Tad also serves on the Board of Overseers of the Hoover Institution and is a member of the board's Executive Committee. In this capacity, he encouraged Hoover to find ways of mobilizing its intellectual resources to help achieve the critically important policy objective of improving public education in the United States.

With Tad's encouragement, and the strong support of the board of the Koret Foundation, the Institution embarked on the *Initiative on American Public Education*. The purposes include presenting key facts on the current condition of American education, contributing to the debate over ways in which it might be improved, and developing proposals for education reform. The centerpiece of the initiative has been the formation of a task force of educational experts who are well regarded within the education community and who have a broad understanding of the country's capacity for school reform. The Board of Directors of the Koret Foundation, interested in supporting this effort, provided crucial resources that allowed for the establishment of the Koret Task Force on K–12 Education, a group of eleven scholars, namely, John E. Chubb, Williamson M. Evers, Chester E. Finn Jr., Eric A. Hanushek, E. D. Hirsch Jr., Paul T. Hill, Caroline M. Hoxby, Terry M. Moe, Paul E. Peterson, Diane Ravitch, and Herbert J. Wal berg. (Their titles and affiliations are provided elsewhere in this volume.)

The Koret Task Force on K–12 Education has proven to be more productive than even the most optimistic of us had anticipated. Since it formally convened in 1999, it has developed a strong collegial spirit and a willingness to work cooperatively on behalf of a common goal. Its work has culminated in a variety of publications. It has issued three books, *A Primer on America's Schools* (Hoover Institution Press, 2001), edited by Terry Moe; *School Accountability* (Hoover Institution Press, 2002), edited by Williamson M. Evers and Herbert J. Walberg; and *Choice with Equity* (Hoover Institution Press, 2002), edited by Paul T. Hill. Koret Task Force members also serve as editors, contributors, and members of the editorial board of a new journal, *Education Next: A Journal of Opinion and Research*, which the Hoover Institution publishes and which is available by subscription, at bookstores throughout the country, and on the Internet at www.educationnext.org. Koret Task Force members have also prepared numerous interpretative essays that have appeared in newspapers, journals, and magazines throughout the country. In recognition of these accomplishments, the task force received the prestigious Koret Prize in April 2002.

The Koret Task Force once again breaks new ground with the publication of *Our Schools and Our Future: . . . Are We Still At Risk?* The Koret Task Force, in this volume, reviews the state of American education twenty years after the original report on the quality of America's schools by the National Commission on Educational Excellence, appointed by President Ronald Reagan's secretary of education, Terrel H. Bell. As Paul Peterson discusses in the preface that follows, A *Nation at Risk* identified a rising tide of mediocrity in American education and asked Americans to halt that rise by renewing their commitment to quality education. Examining the progress—or lack thereof—during the ensuing years, the Koret Task Force has produced its own updated report on the condition of American education and the steps needed to make significant progress in the future. Included with this jointly authored report are essays on more specific topics prepared by individual members of the task force, providing documentation for the findings and recommendations made in the comprehensive statement itself. In *Our Schools and Our Future: . . . Are We Still at Risk?* the Koret Task Force renews the call for excellence but also asks the country to bring accountability, choice, and transparency into the structure and operation of its public schools. Only by taking such steps can public education achieve the excellence the National Commission demanded.

Many individuals have made essential contributions to this undertaking. In particular, I wish to thank Patricia Baker, Marshall Blanchard, David Davenport, Peggy Dooley, Christie Harlick, Laura Huggins, Tyce Palmaffy, Joan Saunders, Richard Sousa, and Ann Wood for their outstanding efforts.

John Raisian
Director
Hoover Institution

Contributors

Mary Beth Celio is a statistician with the University of Washington's Center on Reinventing Public Education, and the demographer for the Archdiocese of Seattle. Her recent work focuses on the achievement gap between white and minority students. She also works on urban education reform and accountability, and her recent publications include *Fixing Urban Schools* and a U.S. Department of Education report on charter school accountability.

John E. Chubb is chief education officer and one of the founders of Edison Schools, a private manager of public schools, including many charter schools. Edison Schools today operates 136 schools in twenty-two states, with approximately 75,000 students. He is the coauthor (with task force member Terry M. Moe) of *Politics, Markets, and America's Schools*, a seminal work that argues for the introduction of free-market principles within the American education system. He also is a distinguished visiting fellow at the Hoover Institution.

Paul Clopton is a biomedical statistician for the Department of Veterans Affairs in San Diego, California, conducting research studies for the VA and the faculty of the School of Medicine of the University of California at San Diego. He has coauthored more than seventy medical research publications and developed analytic software used by NASA and other research organizations. Clopton also is a cofounder of Mathematically Correct, a national mathematics-education advocacy organization. For the state of California, he has served as a member of the Mathematics Content Review Panel for the California Standards Tests, the Mathematics Curriculum Framework Committee, the Mathematics Instructional Materials Advisory Panel, and the Education Technology Advisory Committee. He also has coauthored reviews of textbooks, standards, and testing systems, and he serves as a consultant to states and districts around the country on curricular and testing policies.

Williamson M. Evers, a research fellow at the Hoover Institution, serves on the White House Commission on Presidential Scholars and served in 2001–2002 on the National Educational Research Policy and Priorities Board. He also is a member of the panels that write mathematics and history questions for California's statewide testing system and served as a commissioner of the California State Commission for the Establishment of Academic Content and Performance. He is coeditor of *School Accountability*, a 2002 publication by the Koret Task Force. He also is the editor of and contributor to *What's Gone Wrong in America's Classrooms* and the coeditor of *School Reform: The Critical Issues*.

Chester E. Finn Jr. is a senior fellow at the Hoover Institution and chairman of Hoover's Koret Task Force on K–12 Education. He also is president and a trustee of the Thomas B. Fordham Foundation. Formerly a professor of education and public policy at Vanderbilt University, he also served as assistant secretary for research and improvement and counselor to the secretary of the U.S. Department of

Education. With William J. Bennett and John Cribb, he recently authored *The Educated Child: A Parent's Guide from Preschool through Eighth Grade*, and he currently serves as the senior editor for *Education Next*.

Kacey Guin is a graduate student at the University of Washington's Daniel J. Evans School of Public Affairs and a staff member at the Center on Reinventing Public Education. Her graduate thesis focuses on the effects of rapid teacher turnover on school effectiveness.

Eric A. Hanushek is the Paul and Jean Hanna Senior Fellow at the Hoover Institution. His works on education policy include *Improving America's Schools: The Role of Incentives, Making Schools Work: Improving Performance and Controlling Costs*, and *Educational Performance of the Poor: Lessons from Rural Northeast Brazil*. His current research involves understanding the role of teachers, programs, and funding in determining student achievement.

Paul T. Hill is a research professor and acting dean in the Daniel J. Evans School of Public Affairs and director of the Center on Reinventing Public Education, all at the University of Washington. The center develops and helps communities adopt alternative governance systems for public K–12 education. His most recent publication is *Charter Schools and Accountability in Public Education*. He edited *Choice with Equity*, an assessment by the Koret Task Force, and he also contributed a chapter to *Private Vouchers*, a groundbreaking study edited by Terry Moe. He also is a distinguished visiting fellow at the Hoover Institution.

E. D. Hirsch Jr. is a professor of education and humanities emeritus at the University of Virginia and a distinguished visiting fellow at the Hoover Institution. He is the author of several books on education issues, including *The Schools We Need and Why We Don't Have Them* and a series beginning with *What Your Kindergartner Needs to Know* that continues through each elementary grade, concluding with *What*

Your Sixth Grader Needs to Know. He is the founder and president of the Core Knowledge Foundation.

Caroline M. Hoxby is a professor of economics at Harvard University and director of the Economics of Education Program at the National Bureau of Economic Research. She also is a distinguished visiting fellow at the Hoover Institution. She is the editor of *The Economics of School Choice* and the forthcoming book *College Choices.* She also is the author of several influential papers on education policy, including "Does Competition among Public Schools Benefit Students and Taxpayers," "The Effects of Class Size and Composition on Student Achievement: New Evidence from Natural Population Variation," and "Not All School Finance Equalizations Are Created Equal."

Terry M. Moe is a senior fellow at the Hoover Institution and a professor of political science at Stanford University. He is the author of *Schools, Vouchers, and the American Public,* the coauthor (with task force member John E. Chubb) of *Politics, Markets, and America's Schools,* and the editor of *A Primer on America's Schools.* He also edited *Private Vouchers,* the first book to chronicle the growing support for school vouchers for low-income children.

Paul E. Peterson is a senior fellow at the Hoover Institution as well as the Henry Lee Shattuck Professor of Government and director of the Program on Education Policy and Governance at Harvard University. He is the editor in chief of *Education Next* and an author or editor of numerous books on U.S. education, including *The Education Gap: Vouchers and Urban Schools; Earning and Learning: How Schools Matter; Learning from School Choice; The Politics of School Reform: 1870– 1940;* and *School Politics Chicago Style.*

Diane Ravitch, a research professor at New York University, holds the Brown Chair in Education Policy at the Brookings Institution. She also is a distinguished visiting fellow at the Hoover Institution. She is a member of the National Assessment Governing Board, to which she was appointed by Secretary of Education Richard Riley. From 1991 to 1993, she served as assistant secretary of education and counselor to Secretary of Education Lamar Alexander. A historian of American education, she is the author of many books, including *The Great School Wars*, *The Troubled Crusade*, *Left Back: A Century of Failed School Reforms*, and *The Language Police: How Pressure Groups Restrict What Students Learn*.

Herbert J. Walberg, research professor of education and psychology emeritus and University Scholar at the University of Illinois at Chicago, has edited more than sixty books and written approximately 350 articles on educational productivity and human accomplishment. He is one of ten U.S. members of the International Academy of Education and a fellow of several scholarly associations in the United States and abroad. He is coeditor of *School Accountability*, a 2002 publication by the Koret Task Force. He also is a distinguished visiting fellow at the Hoover Institution.

Preface

In 1983, the National Commission on Excellence in Education, appointed by Ronald Reagan's first secretary of education, Terrel M. Bell, announced to the nation that its "educational institutions seem to have lost sight of the basic purposes of schooling, and of the high expectations and disciplined effort needed to attain them." In its report, *A Nation at Risk*, the commission expressed concern that the quality of the "intellectual, moral and spiritual strengths of our people" was endangered. United States schools, once the envy of the world, had been overtaken by competitors abroad. In one of its most quoted phrases, the commission spoke of a "rising tide of mediocrity that threatens our very future as a Nation and a people."

At first glance, the metaphor—a rising tide of mediocrity—seems odd, even inapt. Do tides just rise? Don't they ebb and flow? When they flow, don't good things typically happen? Perhaps a sleeping bather may on occasion be unpleasantly surprised, but flowing tides refresh tide pools, float boats stuck at the bottom, and leave children entranced as they watch surf pound against headlands.

To be sure, shorelines struck by hurricanes at high tide may suffer harsh erosion. But how can mediocrity be equated with a tropical storm? It better characterizes those dreary days marked by overcast sky, falling drizzle, and becalmed sails.

But if the metaphor at first seems peculiar, it has acquired new meaning with the passage of time. As the globe has warmed, the slow rise in ocean levels has come to be feared. As glaciers and ice caps melt, Louisiana is losing land to the sea by the square mile and barrier islands on the Atlantic coast are gradually slipping beneath the watery surface—as the tide seeps in.

Mediocrity can seep into our educational system in just this same insidious way—imperceptibly, an inch at a time, without definitive scientific proof of its causes or consequences. Vested interests can deny it. The media can ignore it. Scholars can try to document it, even if never to everyone's satisfaction. The public can sense it but not quite understand what to do about it.

It is just this kind of slowly creeping mediocrity that the Koret Task Force on K–12 Education finds on the twentieth anniversary of the report issued by the National Commission on Excellence in Education. Mediocrity is still on the rise, despite the need, now more than ever, for intellectual and moral strength. Far from stemming the rising tide, the recommendations of the National Commission were only selectively adopted, providing reform more symbolic than substantive.

In this volume we include the Koret Task Force report as well as individual analyses prepared by each of its eleven members. The report and the accompanying essays argue that the National Commission did a better job of diagnosis than prescription. It focused on the right issue—educational excellence—but provided an inadequate set of solutions. The commission thought time, money, formal standards, and dedication could alone stop the rising tide. Not so, say the Koret report and essays that follow. As well as money and dedication, we need systemic change that will hold schools accountable, give parents more choices, and provide citizens with a transparent system whose accomplishments they can assess. Only if these structural changes are put into place will the public find it worthwhile to invest more resources in our country's schools.

The Koret report can be read on its own terms. But the power and persuasiveness of the report are magnified by the detailed assessments in the chapters that follow. The chapters in the first part of the book describe the major changes that have occurred since the National Commission first found the nation at risk. In the opening chapter, Diane Ravitch places the National Commission on Excellence in Education in historical context, explaining both its significance and its limitations. In chapter 2, I show that there is little sign of gains in student learning over the past three decades. Despite the efforts of the National Commission, mediocrity still abounds in American education. Caroline M. Hoxby identifies in chapter 3 the changes that did occur subsequent to the commission report: School expenditures rose, teacher pay climbed, and classes were reduced in size. But there is little sign that all these expensive undertakings had much payoff—and most other changes were more symbolic than substantive. In the two concluding essays to Part I, Paul Hill, Kacey Guin, and Mary Beth Celio identify the continuing inequities in America's schools, while Eric A. Hanushek draws out the implications for long-term economic growth.

The second part of the book explains why so much happened and so little improvement took place. Terry M. Moe identifies the powerful interests opposed to school reform, Chester E. Finn Jr. explains why teacher policy veered in a direction quite different from that recommended by the National Commission, Williamson M. Evers and Paul Clopton show how the efforts to encourage students to take more academic courses were offset by curricular and textbook changes that softened the rigor of these courses, and E. D. Hirsch decries educational inattention to the acquisition of basic facts and information during the elementary years. Part III examines two reforms—accountability and choice—that were hatched in the aftermath of the National Commission report. Although these fledglings have only begun to spread their wings, the task force recommends they be given a chance to fly. After reading these essays, I hope you will agree.

Paul E. Peterson

. . . ARE WE STILL AT RISK?

Our Schools
and
Our Future
. . . Are We Still at Risk?

FINDINGS AND
RECOMMENDATIONS OF
THE KORET TASK FORCE
ON K–12 EDUCATION

Twenty years ago, the National Commission on Excellence in Education (Excellence Commission) delivered a thunderbolt in the form of a report called *A Nation at Risk*. With the hindsight that two decades can provide, it is clear that this report awakened millions of Americans to a national crisis in primary and secondary education. *A Nation at Risk* bluntly and forcefully pinpointed the problems facing our public schools and insisted that their solution would require a new commitment to education quality, on the part of school administrators, teachers, parents, and students. Though the Excellence Commission did not consider some of the far-reaching reforms that would later become an important part of the national discourse, it did help set the stage for such reforms by pointing to worrisome signs of weakness and decay in our school system.

That system did not suddenly crash in the early eighties. The declines, shortcomings, and inadequacies so starkly set forth in *A Nation at Risk* had been accumulating for many years. But until the Excellence Commission documented and framed them as grave problems in urgent need of attention, many Americans—especially those within the field of education—had supposed that the schools were doing an adequate job and that, whatever its shortcomings, the system was sufficient to meet the country's needs.

The Excellence Commission called an abrupt halt to this smug contentment. It admonished the nation in forceful, martial language that America faced a momentous problem, one that threatened its national security, and its economic vitality. Not since the late fifties, when Sputnik startled the nation with the possibility that the Soviet Union was surpassing us in science and mathematics, had there been such alarm over the academic weakness of U.S. schools.

Within a few years after Sputnik, the sense of urgency had faded and the focus of reform had turned away from academic performance. Well-intended efforts to address racial segregation, meet the needs of handicapped youngsters, compensate for disadvantage, and provide bilingual schooling for immigrants eclipsed concern about student achievement. They also produced much red tape, litigiousness, and contentious battles over means and ends. Teacher organizations, at the same time, asserted their right to bargain collectively and to strike, which brought them unprecedented power over schools and school systems, even as other interest groups and bureaucratic rigidities made it ever harder to change public education. In other words, the Sputnik-inspired commitment to improving the education system had clearly lost priority—as had student achievement. SAT scores peaked in 1964 and declined thereafter, reaching their nadir about the time *A Nation at Risk* was unleashed.

Yet twenty years following the alarm sounded by *A Nation at Risk*, the commitment has not faded. Thanks to the report's eloquence and official standing in Washington, D.C., it reinforced and dramatized concerns expressed by a simultaneous outpouring of other reports, studies, and manifestos all pointing to the fact that American students were not learning enough and U.S. schools were not performing well enough to meet international competition The Excellence Commission caught a wave of concern about education quality that was beginning to sweep the nation—and that has not yet receded. It effectively recast many people's thinking about education, from the focus on resources, services, and mindless innovation that had absorbed us during the sixties and seventies to the emphasis on achievement, performance, and excellence that remains central today. It redefined our principal challenge in education: where once it was to provide equal access, now it is to promote successful learning among students from all different backgrounds. And it laid bare the truths that equity without excellence is an empty achievement and quantity without quality is an unkept promise. But while its reverberations are still being felt, solid and conclusive reforms in American primary and secondary education remain elusive.

What the Excellence Commission Said

The commission organized its findings within four broad topics: content, expectations, time, and teaching. Under these headings, *A Nation at Risk* issued a twenty-four-count indictment of American primary and secondary education as the members of the Excellence Commission found it in 1983. The spirit of these indictments can be sensed from the following excerpts:

> Secondary school curricula have been homogenized, diluted, and diffused to the point that they no longer have a central purpose. In effect, we have a cafeteria-style curriculum in which the appetizers and desserts can easily be mistaken for the main course. . . .
>
> The amount of homework for high school seniors has decreased

. . . and grades have risen as average student achievement has been declining.

In thirteen states, 50 percent or more of the units required for high school graduation may be electives chosen by the student. Given this freedom . . . many students opt for less demanding personal service courses, such as bachelor living.

A study of the school week in the United States found that some schools provided students only seventeen hours of academic instruction. . . . In . . . other industrialized countries, it is not unusual for academic high school students to spend eight hours a day at school, 220 days per year.

Too many teachers are being drawn from the bottom quarter of graduating high school and college students. . . . Half of the newly employed mathematics, science, and English teachers are not qualified to teach those subjects. . . .

The Excellence Commission made four major recommendations and thirty-two "implementing recommendations." Though these did not call for sweeping reform of the education system itself, they demanded higher standards of performance. These are the four major recommendations.

- High school graduation requirements should be strengthened so that all students acquire a solid foundation in five "new basics": English, mathematics, science, social studies, and computer science.

- Schools and colleges should adopt higher and measurable standards for academic performance.

- The amount of time students devote to learning should be significantly increased.

- The teaching profession should be strengthened by raising standards for training, entry, and professional growth.

The Response

It did not take long for A *Nation at Risk*'s analysis and central findings to win acceptance among the general public, editorial writers, business leaders, governors, and other elected officials at the national, state, and local levels. Ten years following its release, Excellence Commission member and Nobel Prize–winning chemist Glenn Seaborg wrote, "It is now apparent that the precollege educational crisis and the urgent need for educational reform are broadly perceived as being a top priority." Today, twenty years after its release, nearly everyone in the United States who attends to such matters, save for a few Panglosses within the education profession, recognizes that A *Nation at Risk* accurately described our flagging academic performance, underperforming schools, and underachieving children and the insidious threat they posed to our national welfare, long-term economic strength, cultural vitality, and civic competence.

While A *Nation at Risk* arguments may have been widely embraced, that did not necessarily translate into positive action. In fact, many of the reforms that were implemented in the aftermath of A *Nation at Risk* did not even track the Excellence Commission's advice. In his 1993 reflection, Seaborg noted, "Overall, the lack of progress in implementing the recommendations of . . . A *Nation at Risk* has been discouraging." Agreeing with the A *Nation at Risk* critique and finding the will to make the changes it called for were obviously two different animals.

Familiar strategies were tried first: new programs, more money, and tighter regulations. Among the changes were some the Excellence Commission had urged—such as stiffer high school graduation requirements—as well as many it had not. Yet these produced little in the way of improved outcomes. Test scores are at basically the same level today as in 1970. Students do no more homework today than they did twenty years ago. Remediation remains the fastest-growing activity on many college campuses. Graduation rates have actually declined—less than three-fourths of our young people now earn high school diplomas, though this slippage is often masked by the suggestion that "equivalency certificates" amount to the same thing. Employers and professors remain dissatisfied with young people's readiness for work and for higher education. And international assessment results reveal that American seventeen-year-olds know far less math and science than their peers in most other modern nations.

As it became clear in the late eighties that more of the same was not yielding acceptable gains even as anxiety about United States education performance deepened, energized governors and business leaders started to make the education-reform crusade their own. They launched bolder strategies, no doubt inspired by *A Nation at Risk* but often breaking new policy ground. By 1990, the country was setting national education goals, giving birth to novel school designs, breaking up big high schools, and revamping the National Assessment of Educational Progress to get better information. The first Bush administration briefly tried to create national academic standards but the effort to do this from Washington soon fizzled. Within a few years, however, prodded by the Clinton administration's Goals 2000 program, almost every state was setting its own standards, establishing its own assessments, and devising its own accountability systems. By the mid-nineties, a number of innovations were also visible in the organization of the education delivery system itself: Charter schools were spreading, vouchers were being tried, and private firms were beginning to operate public schools on an outsourced basis.

Why Did *A Nation at Risk* Produce So Much Change and So Little Improvement?

First, the Excellence Commission's diagnosis was incomplete. It paid scant attention to the K–8 years, seeing them as providing a reasonably successful level of basic skills, when in fact many children were failing to gain the fundamental knowledge they would need to continue learning in subsequent years.

Second, the Excellence Commission was either too obtuse or too naïve to take on the basic functioning and political control of the system itself. It seemingly believed that the public education system of the day, given higher standards, better trained teachers, and more time on task, would move the schools and their pupils toward loftier levels of performance. In a word, it trusted the system to do the right thing once that system was duly chastised and pointed in the right direction.

We now know that this was unrealistic, that the Excellence Commission failed to confront essential issues of power and control. It seemed not to realize that the system lacked meaningful accountability and tangible incentives to improve, that it exhibited the characteristic flaws of a command-and-control enterprise, that it enjoyed a virtual monopoly, and that the system itself would have to change at its core if it was to produce fundamentally different results. The Excellence Commission never penetrated to that core. It accepted the system as it was, with all the anachronisms inherent in a political mechanism created in the mid-nineteenth century.

We now know that powerful forces of inertia—three in particular—proved far stronger and more stubborn than the Excellence Commission could have foreseen in 1983.

1. A *Nation at Risk* underestimated the resistance to change from the organized adult interests of the K–12 public education system, centering upon the two big national teacher unions and their state and local affiliates as well as administrators, colleges of education, state bureaucracies, school boards, and many others. These groups see any changes beyond the most marginal as threats to their own jealously guarded power, influence, and monopoly. Moreover, they are permanent features on the education landscape, whereas the Excellence Commission detonated its report, then disappeared,

with no real heirs or successors to shepherd its recommendations through the political minefields.

2. *A Nation at Risk* underestimated the tenacity of the "thought-world" of the nation's colleges of education, which see themselves as owners of the nation's schools and the minds of educators, free to impose their ideas on future teachers and administrators regardless of evidence about their effectiveness. Some of the Excellence Commission's own expert advisers were advocates of these ideas, in effect poisoning the report from within and leading to recommendations that worked against the very goals it set out to achieve.

3. *A Nation at Risk* also underestimated the large number of Americans, particularly in middle-class suburbs, who believe that their schools are basically sound and academically successful. This misapprehension arises mainly from the dearth of honest, standards-based information from objective outside sources concerning the true performance levels of our schools, an immense data void that the Excellence Commission failed to address.

In counterweight to these forces of inertia, the past two decades have also seen the development of powerful new forces for reform that should strengthen America's ability to improve its schools as we head into the future. These include

- the public's surprisingly durable belief that education reform is one of the most critical issues facing the nation—a belief heartily shared by impatient business leaders and elected officials. Although this sense of urgency seems inconsistent with the oft-reported complacency of parents about their own child's school, satisfaction levels do not run deep. A majority of American parents believe that private schools are more effective than their children's public schools and say they would move their children if they could.

- growing and sustained support for both standards-based and choice-based education reforms, which has the potential to leverage changes that are farther-reaching than those envisioned by A *Nation at Risk*, though both reform strategies face staunch resistance from established education interests.

- minority parents' increasing anger and disenchantment with failing inner-city school systems. These parents are less willing to listen to promises that things will get better if they continue to trust the system and drench it with resources.

Findings of the Koret Task Force

The members of this task force have studied American education for many years. We come from several disciplines and have different interests. But we come together in unanimous support of the ten findings and three major recommendations that follow. These encompass the most important lessons we have learned about American K–12 education over the two decades since A *Nation at Risk*.

1. *U.S. education outcomes, measured in many ways, show little improvement since 1970.* The trends that alarmed the Excellence Commission have not been reversed. Though small gains can be seen in some areas (especially math), they amount to no more than a return to the achievement levels of thirty years ago. And while the United States runs in place, other nations are overtaking us. In the past, we could always boast that America educates a larger proportion of its school-age children than other lands, but this is no longer true. Many countries now match and exceed us in years of school attained by their youth, and they are surpassing us as well in what is actually learned during those years.

2. *The U.S. economy has fared well during the past two decades not because of the strong performance of its K–12 system, but because of a host of coping and compensating mechanisms.* These include

an endlessly forgiving (and generously remediating) higher education system; the presence within the United States of most of the world's top universities; huge efforts at research and development (leading, for example, to notable productivity gains that owe little to workers' skills); a hard-working populace and an adaptable immigration policy; a society that encourages second chances and invites new ideas; and the world's largest and best-functioning free market economy. Yet even as we have racked up successes in economic and foreign policy domains, we have also seen unmistakable evidence of civic erosion, cultural decline, and moral wavering.

3. *We've made progress in narrowing resource gaps between schools, communities, states, and groups, but the achievement gaps that vex us remain nearly as wide as ever.* This is because the problems that A *Nation at Risk* highlighted particularly affect schools that serve disadvantaged children, and these problems have not been successfully addressed. Minority youngsters are far less apt to complete school and college, and their average academic performance is markedly lower. On some measures, minority twelfth-graders score about the same as white eighth-graders, who themselves are not scoring well. The bottom line: America's primary-secondary education system not only remains mediocre, but its failure to reform also has strikingly inequitable consequences for poor and minority children.

4. *The preponderance of school reform efforts since* A Nation at Risk *has concentrated on augmenting the system's resources, widening its services, and tightening its regulation of school practices.* This has not proven to be a trustworthy path to improved educational performance.

5. *Higher-quality teachers are key to improving our schools, but the proper gauge to measure that quality has nothing to do with paper credentials or more resources and everything to do with classroom*

effectiveness. Across-the-board raises for all teachers, good and bad alike, do not strengthen pupil learning. And stricter regulation of teacher preparation and accreditation only creates shortages and bottlenecks that reduce the supply of capable new instructors for U.S. schools.

6. *Bold reform attempts have been implemented in limited and piece-meal fashion, despite their potential to improve student learning.* It has been demonstrated in several states that "accountability," or standards-based, reform, when done persistently and carefully, can boost achievement, especially among minority and disadvantaged youngsters. And "choice-based" reform has shown promise and is in great demand, as witnessed by the growth of the charter school movement, the rise in home schooling, and parental and community support for scholarship and voucher programs.

7. *Standards-based reform has not achieved its full potential. Though promising, it is hard to get right.* States find it difficult to gain consensus on a coherent set of substantial and ambitious academic standards, to align their tests with those standards, and to get strong accountability systems working. Standards and tests are essential for parents and policy makers to identify faltering schools and gauge the effectiveness of different programs, but they do not themselves solve the problems that they illumine. Moreover, the steps taken so far in the name of accountability fall, for the most part, only upon children, not on the adults in the system.

The No Child Left Behind (NCLB) Act may help by mobilizing federal muscle to push states and districts in the right direction. But Washington has scant leverage over states and districts. NCLB has long, slow timelines—and few sanctions when states and districts do not meet those timelines. It imposes few real consequences on educators whose schools fail. It is likely, therefore, to make the biggest difference in places that share its goals and have the greatest capacity to attain them and to accomplish least in those places—probably the neediest places—where officials may not much care or simply do not know how to go about achieving the goals.

8. *Choice-based reforms have not had a fair test.* Most evidence to date suggests that they can boost student learning and parental satisfaction, but constraints have kept them from being fully tried. Opponents have hamstrung school-choice programs at every turn: fighting voucher demonstrations in legislative chambers and courtrooms; limiting per-pupil funding so tightly that it's impractical for new schools to come into being; capping the number of charter schools; and regulating and harassing them into near-conformity with conventional schools.

   These barriers have kept choice-based reforms from receiving the proper trials they deserve, which is significant on two counts: first, by ensuring that only half-baked versions have been adopted, opponents have made it easier to claim that the reforms were tried but they failed; second, profound changes in a system—the kind of changes that choice would bring to bear—cannot arise overnight. Market systems, in particular, take time to develop.

9. *Americans need better, more timely information about student performance, not only at the national and international levels, but also for individual schools, pupils, and teachers.* We need more and clearer data about what schools do, where they spend their money, and what results they're producing. Currently, the only audits of the system's performance are conducted by those running the system or by organizations that depend upon them for future business, including colleges of education and testing firms. As the country has recently and painfully observed in the business world, such audits are simply unsatisfactory from the standpoint of the system's stakeholders and clients.

10. *We need a thoroughgoing reform of elementary and middle schooling.* Though our high schools require attention, preschool and K–

8 education are far from what they need to be. These are the years
when children gain fundamental knowledge about their country
and their world, about science and literature, about art and civics.
This calls for close attention to K–8 curricula as well as to the
curricular aspects of prekindergarten education and for purposeful
steps to help prepare all children to succeed in kindergarten and
beyond.

Our Recommendations

In the years since A *Nation at Risk*, the incremental changes that
passed for reform have not improved school performance or student
achievement. We conclude that fundamental changes are needed in
the incentive structures and power relationships of schooling itself.
Those changes are anchored to three core principles: *accountability,
choice, and transparency.*

By *accountability*, we mean that every school or education pro-
vider—at least every one that accepts public dollars—subscribes to a
coherent set of rigorous, statewide academic standards, statewide assessments of student and school performance, and statewide systems
of incentives and interventions tied to academic results in relation to
those standards.

- *Clear goals.* Every state needs a coherent set of challenging academic standards and curricular guidelines, subject by subject and
  grade by grade, standards that are not confined to basic skills and
  the three R's but that incorporate such other vital studies as
  history, science, geography, civics, and literature. Every state also
  needs a coherent and corresponding set of proficiency levels to be
  attained by all children in these subjects, levels that encompass
  essential knowledge as well as necessary skills.

- *Accurate measures.* Every state needs tests and other assessments
  that accurately gauge the performance of individual children,

schools, and school systems in relation to its standards. These assessments should form the basis for evaluating the educational value added by each school, and incentives should be linked to how much schools contribute to student learning. The National Assessment of Educational Progress functions as a fine external yardstick by which to gauge the rigor of a state's standards and the performance of its pupils—and could do the same at the district level if current statutory limits were eased.

- *Consequences.* Every state needs an accountability system in which the consequences—both welcome and dire—fall not just upon students but also upon responsible adults. Success should be rewarded. Failing schools should be closed, reconstituted, taken over by other authorities, outsourced to private operators, or their students given the right—and full funding—to leave for better schools. This does not mean just to other public schools in their own district—the limp compromise Congress wrote into No Child Left Behind—but the capacity to transfer to any school, anywhere. Taxpayers should no longer be forced to pay for ineffective schools.

- *Replacing failed schools.* Every state should include school and district takeover provisions in its accountability systems and should strive to reconstitute failing schools within the public system or contract out their management to alternative providers, both for-profit and not-for-profit. Takeovers and outsourcing provide states and districts with potential remedies and alternatives for their failed schools while stimulating competition among potential providers—all of whom must be held to account for their own results.

By *choice* we mean that parental decisions rather than bureaucratic regulation should drive the education enterprise. Open competition among ideas and methods, with people free to abandon weak schools for stronger ones, is the surest way to make major progress. The concept that underlies charter schools—freedom of operation in return for evidence of satisfactory results—makes sense at every level of education. It is the central doctrine of modern management: Operators of a production unit enjoy sweeping autonomy to run their unit as they think best but are strictly held to account for the bottom line. In education, that bottom line is denominated primarily in terms of student learning and parental satisfaction. The education system's clients must be free to select other providers that teach their children more effectively and in accord with family and community priorities as well as core American values.

- *Charter schools.* Given that one aim of the charter-school movement is to improve the public education system, every state should allow charter schools a full and fair chance to show what they can do to provide high-quality education options to children and families. States should exempt charter schools from local district veto and numerical caps. They should provide charter schools with full per-pupil funding and capital funds to support facility costs. Charters should not be subject to teacher certification requirements or mandatory collective bargaining. In turn, schools that do not add substantial academic value to their pupils—and do not satisfy their clients—should lose their charters and close.

- *Voucher experiments.* Every state should explore additional forms of school choice, pushing far beyond the boundaries of within-district public school choice. More states should give vouchers a proper test in selected communities, in tandem with strenuous efforts to renew the public schools of those communities. These experiments should be rigorously and objectively evaluated—as should every education innovation. Sponsoring such experiments and evaluations is a key role for the federal government in primary-secondary education.

- *Full funding for high-risk students.* Children who pose difficult challenges to schools should, under a choice regimen, command added resources to pay for their education. Disadvantaged, disabled, and limited-English-proficiency pupils should carry with them substantially larger amounts of funding than "regular" students, both to make them more attractive to schools and to assist schools with the added costs of teaching them well.

- *Teacher quality and incentives.* The principle of choice should extend to teachers and administrators as well. Training, recruitment, licensing, and compensation should be redesigned to offer wider opportunities for able, willing individuals. A person who is knowledgeable in a subject should be given the right to teach it, with actual classroom effectiveness then used as the primary gauge of competence. Performance in the classroom should be the chief determinant of whether teachers are retained and promoted. Effective teachers should be paid more than ineffective ones. Those who teach fields in which there is a scarcity of teachers should be paid more than those who teach fields oversupplied with teachers. And teachers and administrators who take on challenging assignments should be paid more than teachers who opt for easier situations.

By *transparency* we mean that those who seek complete information about a school or school system (excluding personal information about individuals) should readily be able to get it. This information should be provided in forms and formats that enable users to easily compare one school, system, or state with another.

- *Solid information.* Parents, teachers, and policy makers need to know exactly how their children and schools are performing and how their money is being spent. This requires for each school (1) a clear statement of standards and objectives, (2) a detailed curriculum, (3) the indicators it uses to track progress toward its goals, (4) evidence of its progress to date, and (5) a budget presented in ways that link expenditures to programs and goals.

- *Reports on progress.* Academic achievement should be reported in *absolute* terms (how students are performing vis-à-vis the school's standards), in *value-added* terms (how much more they know at the end of the school year), and in *comparative* terms (in relation to district, state, or national standards or to the performance of other schools and students).

- *Ready access.* All this information should be available on a well-tended school or school system Web site where it can easily be accessed by staff, parents, and policy makers—and by journalists, researchers, taxpayers, and rival schools. Today's technologies make this far easier than in the past. Private firms and nonprofit organizations now offer high-quality systems where vital education data is clearly presented and can be carefully analyzed.

- *Nationwide reporting.* Though the primary burden of transparency rests on individual schools, school systems, and states, Washington also bears a responsibility. America is overdue for a thorough upgrading of federal education-data gathering and analysis, primarily housed at the National Center for Education Statistics, as well as for needed strengthening and expansion of—and enhanced independence for—the National Assessment of Educational Progress.

Accountability, choice, and transparency are the essential trinity of principles by which to reconstruct America's schools. Each must be in place for the others to work. In combination, they transform the education system's priorities, power relationships, and incentive structures.

Accountability means that all of those in the education system—the child, the teacher, the school, and district leaders—know what they must produce in the way of results, how they will be measured, and what will happen if they do or do not attain the desired results.

Choice brings freedom, diversity, and innovation to how education is provided, who provides it, and what options are available to families.

Transparency yields the information needed to assure both top-down accountability and a viable marketplace of methods and ideas.

Taken together, the result of these three will be a reinvigorated yet very different public education system, a new constitutional arrangement with power distributed where it belongs, checks and balances among those who wield that power, and incentives that pull toward—rather than away from—achievement, productivity, freedom, and accountability.

This new system will rekindle Americans' confidence in public education and this should lead to a greater public willingness—once people understand how and why additional resources will make a difference—to invest more in education. Such new investments, in turn, could lead to even greater gains, such as abler people entering and staying in the teaching field; better preschooling; better technology and textbooks; and better performance in the classroom.

The rebirth of this confidence, however, requires the radical overhaul we have outlined here.

Conclusion

The National Commission on Excellence in Education concluded its historic 1983 report by noting that "Children born today can expect to graduate from high school in the year 2000. . . . We firmly believe that a movement of America's schools in the direction called for by our recommendations will prepare these children for far more effective lives in a far stronger America."

But since those words were written, we have gained little by way of better education results. Twenty years of entering first-graders—

about eighty million children—have walked into schools where they have scant chance of learning much more than the youngsters whose plight troubled the Excellence Commission in 1983.

The Excellence Commission was alarmed by what it found. It used strong language. In its most often quoted passage, A *Nation at Risk* told us that "The educational foundations of our society are presently being eroded by a rising tide of mediocrity that threatens our very future as a nation and a people. What was unimaginable a generation ago has begun to occur—others are matching and surpassing our educational attainments. If an unfriendly foreign power had attempted to impose on America the mediocre educational performance that exists today, we might well have viewed it as an act of war. As it stands, we have allowed this to happen to ourselves."

Every word of that indictment is as true in 2003 as in 1983. The tide of mediocrity remains high. Other nations are surpassing our educational attainments. While our military strength remains unchallenged today, our continued strength as a nation depends on the educated intelligence of our people. As the world grows both more interconnected and at the same time more dangerous, the schools must do more to strengthen the foundations of citizenship and to ensure that young Americans understand the democratic values, ideals, and traditions of our society.

Our international economic competitiveness, while robust, is far shakier today than in many years, and the shrinking globe has made it vastly easier than in 1983 for investments and jobs to go anywhere on the planet that seems likeliest to succeed with them. Here, too, we must look to our schools to produce the highly educated citizenry on which America's future economic vitality depends.

We have learned, painfully, that when it comes to education reform, wishing doesn't make it happen. Trusting the system to change itself doesn't work. Adding resources without requiring reform is a false hope.

Issuing new commands and setting new goals doesn't make it

happen either, unless they are accompanied by a viable strategy for achieving them—a strategy built upon accountability, competition, and transparency. Education reform will only come about in the United States when the delivery system itself is reconstructed around clear principles, sound ideas, and learning-centered rules, incentives, and power relationships.

A nation that responded enthusiastically but irresolutely to the Excellence Commission's thoughtful yet modest recommendations in 1983 must now find the resolve to carry out a bottom-to-top reconstruction of its system of schooling. Can we do it? The stakes are huge, the challenge historic. We must begin today, in 2003, to make the changes that will transform American public education so that it can deliver on the democratic ideal of equal educational opportunity for students in 2013 and 2023. This is a promise that our nation has made to its children. For their sake, and for the sake of our country's future, it is a promise that we must keep.

PART ONE

"A NATION AT RISK": THEN AND NOW

I

A
Historic
Document

Diane Ravitch

With the perspective of two decades, it is now apparent that *A Nation at Risk* was the most important education reform document of the twentieth century. Upon its release in 1983 by the National Commission on Excellence in Education (Excellence Commission), it created a media sensation. Unlike most other such documents, which sank without a trace, *A Nation at Risk* captured national attention, shaping the terms of the debate about schooling for a generation after its publication.

Although the report received an unusual amount of press, its format followed a well-worn path. Across the twentieth century, American educators perfected the art of "reform by commission." Whenever it seemed important to rouse the public or fellow members of their profession to a particular course of action, educators formed a commission to write a report and call for what they saw as needed reforms. The first such commission—famously known as the Committee of Ten because it had ten prestigious members—made the first such statement in 1893, which was ever after known as the *Report of the Committee of Ten*. (Over the next two decades, there was also the Committee of Five, the Committee of Seven, and the Committee of Fifteen, but none was as renowned as the Ten.) The Ten addressed the question of whether the curriculum for college-bound students should be different from the curriculum for the great majority who did not intend to go to college. At the time, only a tiny proportion of youth ever attended high school or prepared for college. Nonetheless, the Ten called for strong academic preparation for all, on the grounds that a strong academic education was the best preparation for life regardless of one's future occupation.

After the remarkable attention paid to the Ten's report, educators regularly created commissions and issued reports, usually diametrically opposed to the recommendations of the Ten. For example, the most significant report of the early twentieth century, known as the *Cardinal Principles of Secondary Education* (released in 1918), declared that academic studies should be relegated to equal status with instruction in health, vocation, "worthy home-membership," citizenship, character, and "worthy use of leisure."[1] .

Such public statements by prominent educators became something of a ritual within the pedagogical profession. Over the decades, as more and more of them poured forth, keyed to the latest crisis in school or society, they gained less and less attention. The fact that so many of them were written by education professionals for other education professionals often made them incomprehensible to the larger public.

In *A Nation at Risk*, by contrast, the American public found a report that was written in plain English. Here was a report with a message that noneducators understood. The public's powerful response signaled that *A Nation at Risk* spoke to deeply held concerns; its calls for higher expectations and higher standards had clearly struck a chord. Unlike any such document in our national past, it reached far beyond the professionals and energized reforms that twenty years later have still not run their course.

* * *

An unintended effect of A *Nation at Risk* was that it salvaged the U.S. Department of Education. During his first presidential campaign, Ronald Reagan had promised to abolish the department, which had been created in the closing months of the Carter administration. Reagan believed that the department would inevitably expand the reach of the federal government into issues that he thought should be left to state and local officials. However, Reagan's secretary of education, Terrell Bell, did not agree with Reagan's plan (nor did Reagan have the votes in Congress to get rid of the department; indeed, no bill was ever formally filed in Congress). In his effort to demonstrate the power of the bully pulpit, Secretary Bell asked Reagan to appoint an independent commission to study the condition of American education. When the president declined to do so, Secretary Bell, in August 1981, created the National Commission on Excellence in Education as a cabinet-level activity. The favorable attention accorded the commission's report upon its release in April 1983 ended the debate about abolishing the department and guaranteed its political survival.

The Excellence Commission included several eminent educators, such as: the commission's chairman, David P. Gardner, president of the University of Utah and soon-to-be president of the University of California; Nobel laureate Glenn T. Seaborg of the University of California; Gerald Holton of Harvard University; and A. Bartlett Giamatti, president of Yale University.

Their report warned in vivid language that the nation's future prosperity was threatened by the woeful condition of American education. In its most memorable and oft-quoted phrase, the Excellence Commission wrote that the once-proud American education system was "being eroded by a rising tide of mediocrity that threatens our very future as a nation and a people." The commission further maintained, "If an unfriendly foreign power had attempted to impose on America the mediocre educational performance that exists today, we might well have viewed it as an act of war. As it stands, we have allowed this to happen to ourselves. . . . We have, in effect, been committing an act of unthinking, unilateral educational disarmament."[2]

A *Nation at Risk* was one of several critiques of American education released that same year, including the Twentieth Century Fund's *Making the Grade* and books by Ted Sizer, John Goodlad, Ernest Boyer, and myself. A *Nation at Risk*, however, was accorded the high-level prestige that the backing of the federal government and the presidency endow. Not only the press, but also political leaders, educators, and citizen groups reacted with alacrity to the report's recommendations. Across the nation, task forces, study groups, and committees sprang up to examine the implications of the report for states and school districts.

A *Nation at Risk* argued that the nation's future prosperity was imperiled by recent declines in student achievement. In the industrial era, it said, an educated elite was sufficient, but in the emerging "information age," knowledge, learning, and "skilled intelligence" were necessary for all. To demonstrate its claims, A *Nation at Risk* reviewed test score data drawn from national and international sources, including the SAT, the National Assessment of Educational Progress, the College Board achievement tests, and international tests. If achievement continued to decline, it implied, other nations—with better educated populations—would overtake the American economy and leave us behind.[3]

At the time, a few critics from the academic world complained that the report's diagnosis was far too gloomy and that its bellicose imagery was overstated. Over the years, academic critics continued to deride the data presented by the Excellence Commission and question its assertions about grade inflation and low standards (of course, they did not object to its recommendations for more spending). A decade later, they regarded the American economy's long boom and the Japanese economy's prolonged recession as proof of A *Nation at Risk*'s misguided rhetoric. How, after all, could the economy be so successful if it relied on allegedly poorly educated workers? Either there was no relation between the quality of education and economic success, or the education system was already good enough to produce enough skilled workers for a robust economy.[4]

In retrospect, it seems clear that the report's attempt to draw a straight line between the quality of the schools and the health of the economy was on shaky ground (see the chapter 5 essay by Eric Hanushek for a discussion of the relationship between education and economic growth). It would be ridiculous to claim that a nation's economic well-being is unaffected by the quality of education available to its citizens. But the connections are not as clear-cut as A *Nation at Risk* asserted, and there are many other factors, such as immigration of educated workers, opportunities for remediation, out-of-school learning opportunities, and the abundance of postsecondary institutions, that may compensate for the failings of the formal K–12 education system.

The Historical Context

A *Nation at Risk* was uniquely a document of the early 1980s. It was the leading edge of a wave of critiques, a reflection of a broad consensus about the damage done to students by low expectations. It appeared at precisely the moment when the public was ready for its message. The American economy was in recession, while the economies of Japan and several other Asian nations were booming. Since the early twentieth century, the tradition among educators in search of new funds or new programs (or both) has been to hitch education to whatever issue was the foremost national concern. The formula of this long-standing tradition went like this: Whatever the crisis was, new education programs would solve it. In the early decades of the century, when the industrial revolution was well under way, reformers insisted that the schools needed more vocational programs to meet the labor needs of American business. The rhetoric of education-as-panacea was trotted out during the Depression, the Second World War, the Atomic Age, and the Sputnik era. With new funds and pedagogical changes, promised educators, the schools would solve the crisis of the day.

The early eighties presented, in addition to an economic crisis, a heap of public discontent about schooling that had been accumulating since the sixties. At the time, numerous journalistic accounts reported that schools had abandoned most academic requirements, replacing them with frivolous, fluffy electives, like cooking for singles. Parents worried whether students were learning basic skills, especially when they saw allegations in the newspaper about high school graduates who couldn't read their own diploma. Many state legislatures re-sponded to this generalized concern by mandating minimum-com-petency tests to ensure that students were able to read, write, and figure.

The eighties was not the first decade to see intense criticism of low standards in the public schools. In the fifties, there were loud complaints by critics of anti-intellectualism like Arthur Bestor, Mor-timer Smith, Jacques Barzun, and others who eventually formed the Council for Basic Education. In the main, however, these critics were ignored because the American public continued to have a high opinion of its schools. Public schools, it was widely believed, were synonymous with the fate of our nation; they were a bedrock democratic institution that opened a pathway to merit regardless of social origins. Leaders of education dismissed the critics of the fifties as "enemies of the public schools," even though they were not (they were critics of fads and foolish ideas, not of public education). Nor did state and federal education officials pay attention to the complaints of the critics.[5]

The warm regard that public education enjoyed in American cul-ture began to dissipate in the late sixties and early seventies as radical critics hammered away at the public school system for whatever faults they discerned in American society. Jonathan Kozol's award-winning *Death at an Early Age* portrayed the Boston public schools as havens for sadistic, racist teachers; other critics painted equally gloomy pictures—of American public schools as racist and of teachers as rigid, insensitive, hostile to children, and ignorant about pedagogical innovation, among other things. The radical critics agreed that planned curricula, testing, textbooks, homework, and the other practices associated with schooling were instruments of oppression. Their goal was child liberation, the creation of permissive environments in which there was no authority and in which children learned because they wanted to and studied whatever interested them most. In one of the more temperate tracts of that era, a prominent critic, Charles Silberman, insisted that the public schools were not really malign, just mindless.[6]

Under attack from the left, educators sought to reinvent traditional schooling, trying innovations such as open education, schools "without walls," curricula relevant to student interests, and student-designed curricula. Schools of education embraced the innovations and identified themselves with the radical attacks on traditional teacher-led schooling and public education. The ferment excited those pedagogical leaders who agreed with its direction, but it was disheartening for teachers and parents who wanted schools and classrooms where adults were in charge. It also played havoc with curriculum, standards, grades, and other traditional elements of schooling.

By the mid-seventies, after nearly a decade of what seemed to be a cultural revolution in the schools, troubling reports began to emerge. In 1975, the *New York Times* reported that scores on the Scholastic Aptitude Test had been falling since the mid-sixties. The shock value of this information cannot be overestimated. Not only were average scores falling on both the verbal and mathematical tests, but the percentage of students scoring at high levels (over 600 and over 700) had fallen sharply.

In response to this disheartening news, the College Board, which was responsible for the SAT, created a blue-ribbon commission to examine the causes of the score decline. That group, called the Advisory Panel on the Scholastic Aptitude Test Score Decline, was headed by Willard Wirtz, former secretary of labor, and included such prominent educators as Harold Howe II, Ralph W. Tyler, Benjamin Bloom, and Robert L. Thorndike. Its report, *On Further Examination*, was virtually a rehearsal for *A Nation at Risk*. Most of the initial score decline from 1963 to 1970, the panel concluded, was caused by changes in the composition of the pool of test-takers, that is, by increases in the number of low-scoring students who took the college-entry test. However, after 1970, scores fell even faster than before, and little of that decline could be attributed to the changing demography of the test-taking population. Most of the post-1970 decline was the result of what the panel called "pervasive changes," changes in schools and society. Of the school-based causes, the panel regarded as most significant the fact that students were taking fewer basic academic courses and more nonacademic electives; studies from Massachusetts showed that schools had been adding such courses as Film Making even as course offerings in eleventh-grade English and world history were being eliminated. The panel also pointed out that "less thoughtful and critical reading is now being demanded and done" and that "careful writing has apparently about gone out of style." The panel cast blame on absenteeism, social promotion, less homework being assigned, and a general lowering of standards. Coming as they did from a blue-ribbon commission with impeccable educationist credentials, these charges set the stage for *A Nation at Risk* only six years later.[7]

In the late seventies, no one suggested that criticism of the quality of education was partisan or that it emanated from "enemies of the public schools." In the closing years of the administration of President Jimmy Carter, two presidentially appointed commissions lamented the state of instruction in specific subject areas. In 1979, a commission created to examine the teaching of foreign languages concluded that "Americans' incompetence in foreign languages is nothing short of scandalous, and it is becoming worse." High school enrollments in foreign-language study, it pointed out, had fallen from 24 percent of each grade in 1965 to 15 percent in the late seventies. Worse, only one of every twenty high school students ever studied a second year of a foreign language. Colleges had ceased to require foreign language study for admission, in response to campus revolts in the late sixties against such requirements, and high school students stopped taking foreign languages once they were no longer necessary for college admission. In 1980, another Carter-appointed commission lamented the condition of education in mathematics, science, and engineering; it pointed to lower standards in the schools and to the weakening of college entrance requirements as causes.[8]

High Expectations

These earlier studies and critiques by highly respectable agencies paved the way for A *Nation at Risk*. When the National Commission on Excellence in Education began its deliberations in 1981, the public was already disillusioned with the pedagogical faddism and extremism of the seventies. Schools that had torn down the walls between classrooms were rebuilding them; schools that had been built without walls were installing them. A "back to basics" movement prompted several state legislatures to adopt new testing requirements for high school graduation.

As it set to work, the Excellence Commission solicited papers from educators. One of the most influential was Clifford Adelman's study of high school transcripts from 1964 to 1981. Adelman, a researcher at the U.S. Department of Education, concluded that during this period there had been a "systematic devaluation of academic (and some vocational) courses." Students were spending less time in academic study and more time in nonacademic courses for which they received credit toward graduation. The curriculum in high school was "diffused and fragmented." The typical high school curriculum of the day was divided into three tracks: academic, vocational, and general. As graduation requirements diminished, enrollment in the general track—which was neither academic nor vocational—jumped from 12.0 percent in the late sixties to 42.5 percent by the late seventies. Consisting of courses like driver education, general shop, business math, remedial studies, consumer education, and home economics, the general track had become the dominant program in American high schools.[9]

One of the most important prescriptions advanced by A *Nation at Risk* was that schools should have high expectations for all children and should expect all to complete a reasonably demanding academic curriculum. This was a radical message. In the checkered history of reform-by-commission, only the 1893 Committee of Ten had made a similarly egalitarian claim on behalf of the intellectual capacity of all children. Seemingly unaware of the historical precedent, the authors of A *Nation at Risk* held that "All, regardless of race or class or economic status, are entitled to a fair chance and to the tools for developing their individual powers of mind and spirit to the utmost."[10]

Among educators, this message was translated to mean "All children can learn." This earnest maxim repudiated the long-established practice of separating children into different programs on the basis of their likelihood of going to college. "All children can learn" changed the rules of the game in American education; it shifted educational debate from discussions about access and resources to discussions about results. It was no longer enough to provide equal facilities; it became necessary to justify programs and expenditures in terms of whether students made genuine gains. The rhetoric and philosophy of "all children can learn" had a strong impact on educational issues as it became increasingly clear that educators not only had to set higher expectations, but also had to devise methods and incentives to get almost all students to learn more and exert greater effort. After A

Nation at Risk, states and school districts scrutinized their standards and curricula, changed high school graduation requirements, and insisted that students take more courses in academic subjects.

Many researchers challenged A *Nation at Risk*. Those who didn't like its conclusions objected in principle to the call for higher standards and a more academic curriculum. Others complained that the data were not sufficient to sustain the report's arguments. We now realize that the available data concerning the quality of education in the United States are limited and spotty. Despite the existence of a sizable education research industry, we still lack solid information about student achievement and effective pedagogy. The National Assessment of Educational Progress is the only consistent barometer of student achievement; however, its reports reveal little about the causes of differential achievement, and there are genuine questions about the motivation of high school seniors who take this no-stakes examination in which no one will ever know the scope of any individual test-taker. While the American public accepts the validity of almost any test results, testing experts do not. Indeed, testing experts are not happy with most extant tests. It seems fair to say that we need tests that accurately reflect the curriculum that is taught and that report results in a timely manner.

A *Nation at Risk*'s Achilles' heel, if a report may be said to have one, was its thesis of educational decline. Critics could rightly charge that the report had waxed nostalgic about an imaginary golden age. They could then blast this image by counter-claims that the schools were as good as ever, that any decline was a blip, and that a golden age never existed. We now know that the drop in test scores, which was real, actually ended about the time that A *Nation at Risk* was released. But to argue about whether there was a golden age or whether the schools were better in 1983 than in 1973 or 1963 or 1953 is pointless. The issues are the same as they were a half-century ago, when Arthur Bestor wrote:

> If we are to have improvement, we must learn to make comparisons, not with the wretchedly inadequate public schools of earlier generations, but with the very best schools, public or private, American or foreign, past or present, of which we can obtain any knowledge. . . . If some other nation designs a better military plane, our aeronautical engineers do not point smugly to the fact that our own aircraft are better than they were in 1920 or 1930 or 1940.[11]

The challenge before us is, as it has always been, to secure equal educational opportunity. Every American child should have the same opportunities for an excellent education. All should have the same chance to maximize their potential, to contribute to the common good, and to live a full and rewarding life. The real issue was and is whether the schools are good enough to prepare students for the challenges that will confront them. For the schools of 2003 to be better than the schools of 1983 is no great feat. For the schools of 2003 to be among the best in the world is what matters most for students today and for the future of American society.

Notes

1. National Education Association, *Cardinal Principles of Secondary Education: A Report of the Commission on the Reorganization of Secondary Education*, Bulletin No. 35 (Washington, D.C.: Bureau of Education, 1918), 5.
2. National Committee on Excellence in Education (Excellence Commission), *A Nation at Risk* (1983), 5.
3. Excellence Commission, *A Nation at Risk*, 7.
4. See Maris Vinovskis, "*A Nation at Risk* and the 'Crisis' in Education in the Mid-1980s," in *The Road to Charlottesville: The 1989 Education Summit* (Washington, D.C.: National Education Goals Panel, 1999), 10; see also David Tyack and Larry Cuban, *Tinkering Toward Utopia: A Century of Public School Reform* (Cambridge: Harvard University Press, 1995), 34.
5. Diane Ravitch, *The Troubled Crusade: American Education, 1945–1980* (New York: Basic Books, 1983), 70.

6. Jonathan Kozol, *Death at an Early Age: The Destruction of the Minds and Hearts of Negro Children in the Boston Public Schools* (Boston: Houghton Mifflin, 1967); Herbert Kohl, *36 Children* (New York: New American Library, 1967); Nat Hentoff, *Our Children Are Dying* (New York: Viking Press, 1966); James Herndon, *The Way It Spozed to Be* (New York: Simon and Schuster, 1968); James Herndon, *How to Survive in Your Native Land* (New York: Simon and Schuster, 1971); George Dennison, *The Lives of Children: The Story of the First Street School* (New York: Random House, 1969); John Holt, *How Children Fail* (New York: Pitman, 1964); George B. Leonard, *Education and Ecstasy* (New York: Delta, 1968); Charles B. Silberman, *Crisis in the Classroom* (New York: Random House, 1970). For a discussion of these books and trends, see Diane Ravitch, *The Troubled Crusade: American Education, 1945–1980* (New York: Basic Books, 1983), 228–66.

7. The Advisory Panel on the Scholastic Aptitude Test Score Decline, *On Further Examination* (New York; College Board, 1977), 26–27.

8. President's Commission on Foreign Language and International Studies, *Strength Through Wisdom: A Critique of U.S. Capability* (Washington, D.C.: U.S. Government Printing Office, 1980), 6; National Science Foundation and U.S. Department of Education, *Science and Engineering Education for the 1980s and Beyond* (Washington, D.C.: U.S. Government Printing Office, 1980), 3, 46–48.

9. Clifford Adelman, "Devaluation, Diffusion, and the College Connection: A Study of High School Transcripts, 1964–1981," prepared for the National Commission on Excellence in Education (Washington, D.C.: U.S. Department of Education, 1983).

10. Excellence Commission, *A Nation at Risk*, 8.

11. Arthur Bestor, *Educational Wastelands: The Retreat from Learning in Our Public Schools*, 2d ed. (Urbana: University of Illinois Press, 1985), 4–6.

2

Little Gain
in Student
Achievement

Paul E. Peterson

Except for what is learned at school, very little in American life has remained unchanged since A *Nation at Risk*. Homes are bigger, appliances niftier, and gardens more lush. E-mail, Websites, faxing, and cell phones have transformed communication. Recreational equipment has become so sophisticated that sports can reach new extremes.

Nor is it just technology that is improving. Most social indicators have also moved in a positive direction. The average child today is growing up in a more learning-friendly family environment than ever before. For instance, parents are, on average, more educated. In 1970, 52 percent of the population over age twenty-five had a high school diploma or its equivalent; by 1999, 83 percent did. The share of the population holding a college degree increased from 11 percent in 1970 to 25 percent in 1999. Families are smaller, allowing parents to con-

Samuel Abrams provided valuable research assistance for this essay. Thomas Polseno and Antonio Wendland provided staff assistance.

centrate more attention on each child. The percentage of families with three children or more declined from 36 percent in 1970 to 15 percent in 2000. True, immigration rates have risen and more children live in homes that are non-English-speaking (17 percent in 2000, compared with 8 percent in 1980). Likewise, more children do not live with both their parents (now 31 percent, versus 15 percent three decades ago). Yet the poverty rate has remained essentially unchanged, average income has risen steeply, welfare dependency has declined, the murder rate has attenuated, and drug dependence has abated. A much higher percentage of the population of very young children are enrolled in some kind of preschool program, an increase among four-year-olds from 29 percent to 69 percent between 1970 and 2000. On balance, the positive trends seem to outweigh the more problematic ones.

Despite all these favorable changes in society, few demonstrable achievement gains have been realized in elementary and secondary schools.

Upon issuing A *Nation at Risk*, the National Commission on Excellence in Education appeared to mobilize new focus and energy within America's schools. The report motivated calls for reform by governors, presidents, lawmakers, task forces, and national committees. Citizens regularly tell pollsters that education is, for them, a leading national issue. Yet, if one looks at what students learn in school, nothing much has altered for more than a third of a century.

We know this because we have a variety of yardsticks that help us track key trends in American education. The most familiar of these measuring devices is the SAT, the test given to those high schoolers planning to attend college. Also well regarded is the National Assessment of Educational Progress (NAEP), which administers tests in math, reading, science, and other subjects to a cross-section of all students nationwide at ages nine, thirteen, and seventeen. A more traditional measure of progress can be gleaned by looking at high school graduation rates, long used as an indicator of educational improvement in the United States. Finally, it is possible to compare U.S. students with their peers abroad. The International Association for the Evaluation of Educational Achievement (IEA) has administered tests in mathematics and science on several occasions since the early sixties, to samples of students in many countries at ages nine, thirteen, and seventeen. More recently, the Organization for Economic Cooperation and Development's (OECD) Program for International Student Assessment (PISA) and the International Adult Literacy Survey (IALS) have provided comparative estimates of literacy skills.

None of these measuring devices supplies, by itself, an indisputably exact measure of what is happening in American education. But when all yield similar results, it is unlikely that the overall findings can be attributed to peculiar defects in specific measuring rods. It is therefore especially significant that, no matter what instrument is used, the results are roughly the same: America's schools are stagnating, showing little improvement since A *Nation at Risk* was written. In fact, by some measures, educational performance has fallen below the standards set by previous generations.

To compare findings from a variety of assessments of American education, it is helpful to introduce a statistical concept, the standard deviation. This concept provides a measure of how much scores (or some other measured variable) are spread around their average. It allows one to place into a single metric results from different tests that contain unlike questions and employ alternative scoring conventions. It is not necessary here to describe all the properties of a standard deviation, but its magnitude needs characterization. Generally speaking, a full standard deviation (generally presented as 1.0 standard deviations) is very large. When it comes to the NAEP test, for example, a standard deviation is equivalent to roughly the four years of learning that take place between the fourth and eighth grades. If a group of fourth-graders score one standard deviation higher than average on the NAEP fourth-grade test, then they are performing as well as the average eighth-grader would have. Conversely, if low-performing eighth-graders score a standard deviation below average, then they score no better than the average fourth-grader would have.

A standard deviation change of 1.0 in test-score performance is estimated to raise annual earnings by 15 percent to 20 percent later in life.[1] Making an adjustment for all other factors that affect earnings, it is estimated that young adults in their late twenties who earn $30,000 a year could have earned $4,500 to $6,000 more if their test-score performance had been one standard deviation higher. Quite apart from dollars and cents, higher performance is correlated with happier lives, including a reduction in the risk of incarceration, welfare dependency, and the bearing of a child out of wedlock.[2]

There are other ways of characterizing the magnitude of a one standard deviation difference in test performance. Japanese middle schoolers scored about this much higher on the IEA math test than did their peers in America. The large size of this difference has prompted many to search for the secret of the Japanese success. If the Japanese-American comparison seems too abstract, consider a home-grown example, the black-white test-score gap, which in math is also approximately one standard deviation. A variety of explanations have been offered for the size of this gap—the legacy of slavery, poverty, family life, peer-group influence, school resources, low expectations, and minimal school choice for black students. If there is little agreement on which of these factors is most important, there is no doubt that the discrepancy itself is large.

Even a change in test scores of just half a standard deviation (also referred to as 50 percent of a standard deviation) constitutes a substantial change, particularly if the change occurs within a few years. Changes of as little as 10 percent of a standard deviation are usually considered quite small. But even small changes can become big ones if they accumulate over time. If test scores in America had increased by an average of 4 percent of a standard deviation each year over the twenty years since *A Nation at Risk* was written, today's scores, compounded over time, would have been nearly 120 percent of a standard deviation higher than in 1983. Had such small changes been occurring regularly, from year to year, the U.S. education system would have been recognized as a dynamic element in American society, just as innovative as many other sectors of the American economy.

But what really happened? By using the standard deviation as a statistical measure of changes over time, we are able to address this question by looking at overall trends in American educational outcomes, as measured by a range of surveys of student achievement and high school graduation rates.

SAT Scores

We first pick up the best-known ruler used to assess the state of American education—the SAT. The letters once stood for the Scholastic Aptitude Test, but its makers decided to drop any substantive meaning from the letters once it became apparent that the SAT measured cognitive skill attained at a point in time—not just some underlying propensity to learn. Despite its peculiar moniker, the SAT has several advantages as a measuring device. For one thing, it has been used to measure student performance for decades, during which time psychometricians have refined the test's precision.[3] For another, it is a high-stakes test. Performance on the SAT affects the likelihood that high schoolers will be admitted to the college of their choice and the probability that they will win a scholarship. Because real consequences flow from performance on this test, most students take it seriously, studying sample questions to familiarize themselves with the test's general format and approach. Private entrepreneurs claim they can raise a student's test scores, and in some cases they do, but usually not by more than a modest amount—unless the student makes the special kind of effort usually associated with genuine learning. In short, the SAT reveals how well students can demonstrate their command of a body of material on an occasion when high performance is expected.

It is not just students who take the test seriously. So does the College Entrance Examination Board, which recommends to colleges that they accept this test as a criterion for college admission, and the Educational Testing Service, the private firm that designs and administers the SAT. Questions are carefully prepared and pretested to ensure precise measurement of a student's demonstrated ability. Special efforts are taken to ensure accurate scoring and to guard against cheating. Items are closely held, and the test is administered under the direction of trained proctors.

Offsetting these advantages are certain limitations. The SAT is generally taken only by college-bound high schoolers. Indeed, not even all of these students take the test. Some colleges accept the American College Testing Assessment (ACT) instead.[4] And if a student plans to attend junior or community college, most of the time neither the SAT nor the ACT is demanded. Nor is the SAT a requirement for admission to many four-year colleges. In 2000, only 46 percent of high school seniors took the SAT.

To the extent that the percentage of seniors taking the test varies from year to year, scores can fluctuate for this reason alone, making it difficult to draw straightforward conclusions from changing SAT test scores. Critics of school reform often ascribe the drop in SAT scores to the fact that the share of high school seniors taking the test has been increasing during the post–World War II period, potentially diluting the skills of the test-taking pool. However, studies have found that the decline in SAT scores during the sixties and seventies was only partially caused by a change in the social composition of the test-taking pool. The percentage of high school seniors taking the test hovered at around 33 percent between 1972 and 1984, after which the share climbed to about 45 percent in 1990 and essentially leveled off. Meanwhile, the drop in SAT scores occurred during the seventies, when participation rates were stable. The modest revival in SAT scores occurred during the eighties, when participation rates were actually *rising*.[5] Figure 1 presents the trend in average SAT scores between

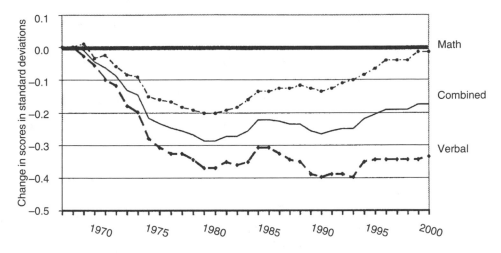

Fig. 1. SAT math, verbal, and combined scores, 1967–2001

Note: Initial score set to zero; subsequent scores constitute changes in standard deviations relative to scores in 1967. The standard deviation used in this table is the average standard deviation from years 1972–2001 (110.6 in verbal and 118.2 in math).

Source: College Entrance Examination Board, National Report on College-Bound Seniors.

1967 and 2001. In the figure, average SAT scores in 1967 are set at zero, allowing one to ascertain how much of a standard deviation the scores have changed in the years since 1967. If the score climbs above zero, students, on average, are doing better than students did in 1967. If the score is below zero, they are doing worse. All comparisons are calculated as percentages of a standard deviation.

The overall picture can be grasped by looking at the trend in combined math and verbal scores displayed in figure 1. These combined scores fell by nearly 30 percent of a standard deviation between 1967 and 1982, a serious sign of deterioration that helped prompt the writing of A *Nation at Risk*. Those who drafted this document can take heart—perhaps even credit—for halting a further decline. But the gains since 1982 are modest, only about 15 percent of a standard deviation, or less than one percent per year, leaving the country well below its standing in 1967.

When these combined scores are broken down separately into their math and verbal components, noticeable differences may be observed. The math decline was never as steep, just 20 percent of a standard deviation, and by 2001 it had fully recovered. Meanwhile average verbal scores collapsed by 35 percent of a standard deviation, and they have not recovered.

The more positive trend in math scores, compared with verbal scores, may or may not be related to the specific reforms promoted by A *Nation at Risk*. On the one hand, there is little sign that schools adequately addressed the shortage of qualified math and science teachers. As Caroline Hoxby reports in her essay "What Has Changed and What Has Not" (chapter 3), teachers were even less likely to have a degree in these subjects in 1999 than in 1982. On the other hand, more high school graduates were taking academically oriented math and science courses in 1999 than at the time A *Nation at Risk* was penned.

But if more academic courses in math had positive effects on student learning in this subject area, why did we not obtain a similar impact after A *Nation at Risk* from the introduction of more English courses that were given an academic label? The answer to this question remains elusive. Perhaps, as E. D. Hirsch Jr. suggests in his essay "Neglecting the Early Grades" (chapter 9), the replacement of phonics with whole word instruction in elementary school left high schoolers unequipped to read challenging material. Perhaps high school teachers have given up trying to provide rigorous instruction in reading comprehension, letting students focus instead on their own personal responses to the material. Perhaps the syntax and range of expression to which students are exposed in their textbooks has been unduly simplified. Perhaps instruction in math, with its more structured curriculum and clearer set of standards, has been kept relatively intact, though Paul Clopton and Williamson Evers suggest otherwise in their essay "The Curricular Smorgasbord" (chapter 8).

About such matters, one can only speculate. But this much is known: Even SAT math scores were no better in 2001 than in 1967. And when math and verbal SAT scores are considered together, they reveal a decline of nearly 20 percent of a standard deviation since 1967 and less than a 10 percent uptick since 1982. On the whole, there is little sign of substantial improvement. If the United States was at risk in 1982, it remains so now.

The National Assessment of Educational Progress

The SAT may not be the best tool for assessing the overall state of elementary and secondary schools in the United States. Less than half of all high school seniors took the test in 2001. Nor does the SAT tell us anything about what is happening to children at an earlier age. But if the SAT is a less than perfect measure of school performance, the National Assessment of Educational Progress (NAEP) should be the answer. After all, it is known as the nation's report card, the product of an official, government-administered survey of student learning located within the Department of Education's National Center for Education Statistics. The test is designed by the Educational Testing Service, the same firm that designs the SAT, ensuring, once again, that the skills of leading psychometricians are utilized in its preparation. And the NAEP surveys a representative sample of all students in school, not just those planning to go to college. NAEP math, science, and reading tests have been regularly administered to a representative sample of students at ages nine, thirteen, and seventeen since the early seventies.

Not every student takes the NAEP. Instead, a carefully identified representative sample of schools are selected for testing, and, within each school, designated students are invited to participate in testing sessions. Unlike the SAT, the test is a low-stakes test. Results are not reported by schools, nor are individual scores released. In fact, no one student answers all the questions on the NAEP, though it uses a sophisticated sampling frame that most psychometricians believe yields reliable results for the population that is sampled. The short test each student takes reduces test fatigue and constitutes less of an intrusion on the time of the school and the student.[6]

Nonetheless, the NAEP, too, has certain limitations. Most important, participation in the NAEP by individual schools has been voluntary. And even when a school agrees to participate, not every student does. Unfortunately, as can be seen in figure 2, participation rates have fallen noticeably since the 1970s, especially among older students.

The joint school-student participation rate for seventeen-year-olds dropped from 68 percent in 1973 to only 58 percent in 1999. For those at age thirteen, the drop over this time period was from 79 percent to 74 percent. If one assumes that low-performing schools are the most likely to refuse to participate and that low-performing students within schools are the most likely to be excused from participation or absent that day, then a decline in participation rates could by itself raise average score results, lending the false appearance that student performance was improving. Although the Educational Testing Service makes statistical adjustments in NAEP scores for nonparticipation by schools, the adjustments only take into account geographical and demographic characteristics of a school, such as whether it is in an urban or nonurban location and the share of a school's students who are minorities. These adjustments cannot correct for variation in school quality unrelated to these characteristics. Similarly, statistical adjustments are made for students, but apart from adjustments for school characteristics, the ethnic background of the student is the only student demographic characteristic for which an adjustment is made. No adjustment is made for any other variation in student performance unrelated to these characteristics. Among seventeen-year-olds, year-to-year changes in participation rates are sig-

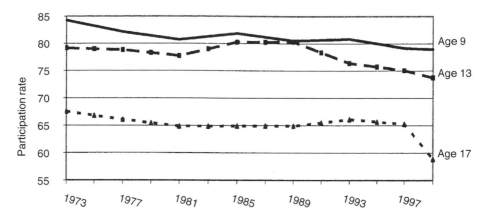

Fig. 2. Combined school-student participation rates in the National Assessment of Educational Progress (NAEP), 1973–1999

Note: Participation rates occasionally differed by science, math, and reading exams. The data points present the average participation rate for all three NAEP exams by age cohort. Participation rates are the probability that a student participates in a particular subject-matter testing-session times the probability that the original school selected participates.

Source: J. R. Campbell, C. M. Hombo, and J. Mazzeo, *NAEP 1999 Trends in Academic Progress: Three Decades of Student Performance.* (NCES #2000469, October 13, 2000).

nificantly correlated with year-to-year changes in average test score performance, suggesting that falling rates have inflated recent NAEP test scores.[7]

In other words, NAEP biases run in a direction exactly opposite of SAT biases. If potentially upward trends in American education could be underestimated by the SAT simply because SAT participation rates have risen, then such trends are likely to be exaggerated by the NAEP because its participation rates have been falling.

Bearing this in mind, let's examine the pattern of change in NAEP test scores of those aged seventeen, most of whom were in their last year of high school, about the time many were taking the SAT. As figure 3 shows, among this group of students, NAEP math scores climbed by about 10 percent of a standard deviation between 1973

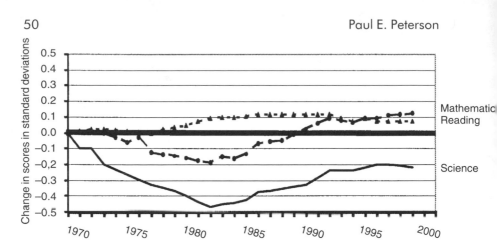

Fig. 3. Math, reading, and science scores on the National Assessment of Educational Progress (NAEP), seventeen-year-olds, 1970–1999

Note: Initial score set to zero; subsequent scores constitute changes in standard deviations relative to initial score. Initial science and math scores obtained in 1970; in reading, initial score obtained in 1973. The standard deviation used here is the average standard deviation from years 1970–1996 (45.4 in science, 31.4 in math, and 42.2 in reading).

Sources: NAEP test scores: J. R. Campbell, C. M. Hombo, and J. Mazzeo, *NAEP 1999 Trends in Academic Progress: Three Decades of Student Performance.* (NCES #2000469, October 13, 2000). NAEP standard deviation data: N. L. Allen, J. E. Carlson, and C. A. Zelenak, *The NAEP 1996 Technical Report.* (NCES #1999452, October 19, 2000).

and 1999. Over about the same time period, reading scores rose by about 8 percent. But given the 10 percentage point decline in participation rates, even this slight gain may be more apparent than real.

Science scores dropped by 20 percent, however. The downward shift occurred during the seventies, falling by as much as 50 percent of a standard deviation. Though they recovered subsequently, students in 1999 were still not performing as well in science as they had in the early seventies. And some of the apparent recovery may have been artificial, the simple by-product of falling participation rates. Taken as a whole, NAEP results for seventeen-year-olds, like the SAT scores, reveal a system unable to revive itself.

If one looks at thirteen-year-olds, the picture is only slightly brighter. Figure 4 shows that reading scores barely improved between 1970 and 1999, a gain so small it may simply be due to the slip in participation rates. Science scores dropped by 20 percent of a standard deviation during the seventies, recovered in the eighties, only to slip again in the nineties. In the end, they were about where they had been in 1970. While reading and science scores were essentially flat, math scores over roughly the same period were as much as 30 percent of a standard deviation higher. But in the three subjects taken together, not much of an upward trend in test score performance can be detected over the time period or as a result of the issuance of A *Nation at Risk* once declining participation rates are taken into account.

The brightest picture appears when one examines the youngest cohort, the nine-year-olds. As displayed in figure 5, these math scores rose by nearly 40 percent of a standard deviation between 1973 and 1999. However, reading and science gains were much smaller, only 5 percent and 10 percent of a standard deviation. Still, the 40 percent uptick in math among this youngest cohort is encouraging. Yet the gains in these early years are not sustained as the child continues into middle and high school.

Some have attributed the minimal sign of educational progress to negative changes in society, rather than to the school.[8] The most important factor that might be depressing student test performance is the rising number of immigrants from Third World countries. If these families have weak educational backgrounds and speak little English, their children may perform poorly on standardized tests. Perhaps the performance of immigrant children is offsetting the gains that American schools are otherwise realizing. To explore this possibility, we examined the trend in average test scores of white students, a group which contains only a few immigrants, most of whom have migrated from advanced industrialized societies whose schools are at least comparable with those in the United States. As can be seen in figure 6, trends in NAEP performance among seventeen-year-old white students track closely the overall trends reported above. The reading

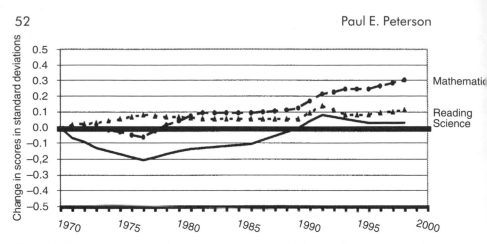

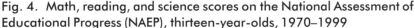

Fig. 4. Math, reading, and science scores on the National Assessment of Educational Progress (NAEP), thirteen-year-olds, 1970–1999

Note: Initial score set to zero; subsequent scores constitute changes in standard deviations relative to initial score. The standard deviation used here is the average standard deviation from years 1970–1996 (38.4 in science, 32.7 in math, and 36.8 in reading).

Sources: NAEP test scores: J. R. Campbell, C. M. Hombo, and J. Mazzeo, *NAEP 1999 Trends in Academic Progress: Three Decades of Student Performance.* (NCES #2000469, October 13, 2000). NAEP standard deviation data: N. L. Allen, J. E. Carlson, and C. A. Zelenak, *The NAEP 1996 Technical Report.* (NCES #1999452, October 19, 2000).

scores of seventeen-year-old white students rose slightly (10 percent of a standard deviation) before *A Nation at Risk* was issued but have not increased since. Math scores declined noticeably (20 percent of a standard deviation) before *A Nation at Risk* was issued, but have recovered so that they are now somewhat above their 1970 benchmark. Science scores fell sharply before *A Nation at Risk* and have recovered only about half of their losses. Taking the three subject areas together (and taking into account declining participation in NAEP testing sessions), the test scores of white seventeen-year-olds remained essentially flat over the last thirty years of the twentieth century. One cannot attribute educational stagnation to the influx of immigrants from Third World countries.[9]

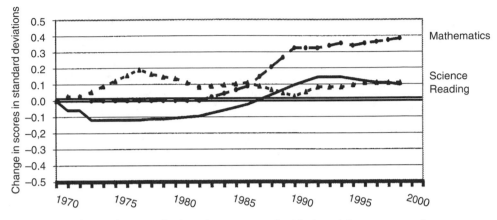

Fig. 5. Math, reading, and science scores on the National Assessment of Educational Progress (NAEP), nine-year-olds, 1970–1999

Note: Initial score set to zero; subsequent scores constitute changes in standard deviations relative to initial score. The standard deviation used here is the average standard deviation from years 1970–1996 (41.5 in science, 33.9 in math, and 36.8 in reading).

Sources: NAEP test scores: J. R. Campbell, C. M. Hombo, and J. Mazzeo, *NAEP 1999 Trends in Academic Progress: Three Decades of Student Performance.* (NCES #2000469, October 13, 2000). NAEP standard deviation data: N. L. Allen, J. E. Carlson, and C. A. Zelenak, *The NAEP 1996 Technical Report.* (NCES #1999452, October 19, 2000).

An optimist might interpret these results as showing that reforms recommended by *A Nation at Risk* are slowly taking hold, having their initial impact on younger students who will sustain—and perhaps accelerate—these gains as their schooling continues. Unfortunately, there is little basis for such optimism. The science scores of nine-year-olds shifted upward between 1986 and 1992, but these did not translate into gains when these students reached the age of thirteen. The math scores of nine-year-olds rose quite dramatically between 1986 and 1990, but the improvement for this cohort at age thirteen was much less. When the same cohort became seventeen in 1996, no gain could be detected. What had been achieved by age nine had been lost altogether by age seventeen.

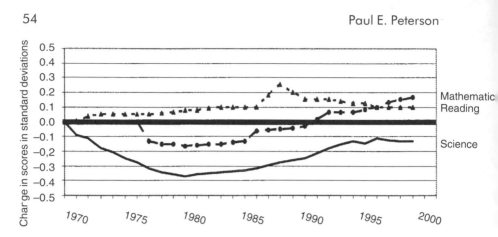

Fig. 6. Math, reading, and science scores on the National Assessment of Educational Progress (NAEP), white seventeen-year-olds, 1970–1999

Note: Initial score set to zero; subsequent scores constitute changes in standard deviations relative to initial score. The standard deviation used here is the average standard deviation from years 1970–1996 (45.4 in science, 31.4 in math, and 42.2 in reading).

Sources: NAEP test scores: J. R. Campbell, C. M. Hombo, and J. Mazzeo, *NAEP 1999 Trends in Academic Progress: Three Decades of Student Performance.* (NCES #2000469, October 13, 2000). NAEP standard deviation data: N. L. Allen, J. E. Carlson, and C. A. Zelenak, *The NAEP 1996 Technical Report.* (NCES #1999452, October 19, 2000).

To the pessimist, these results reveal a school system in decline. Although student performance could be depressed by today's greater prevalence of single-parent families, this should be more than offset by the higher levels of parents' educational attainment and smaller family sizes, the two most important family characteristics affecting a child's ability level. Were the deterioration in family life the main cause of educational stagnation, then one would expect to find the worst results among the youngest cohort, the nine-year-olds. But it is this young group that has actually shown the most improvement, perhaps as a result of the higher levels of their parents' educational attainment. As the child ages, however, schools are not adding to what has been learned by the age of nine.

In sum, NAEP scores do not show much more improvement in American education than SAT scores did. Gains apparent when a child is young are not sustained through high school. Those in their last year of schooling score about the same as those a generation and more earlier. If the National Assessment of Educational Progress is supposed to indicate the country's "progress," then the survey's title is quite ironic. It might be better termed the National Assessment of Educational Stagnation.

Graduation Rates

Thus far, we have examined trends in test score performance over time. Perhaps the landscape changes when one looks at real-world outcomes, such as high school graduation rates. Just as higher test scores positively affect a student's well-being later in life, so does the acquisition of a high school diploma. High school graduates are more likely to remain married and avoid incarceration. They are also less likely to bear children out of wedlock or become welfare-dependent. Even if test scores have not improved, perhaps a growing percentage of students are at least remaining in school. After all, the National Education Goals Panel, a group appointed in 1989 to push the *A Nation at Risk* agenda forward, established a 90 percent high school completion rate as a key objective to be reached by the end of the century.

Unfortunately, one cannot even report good news on this front. Not only have high school graduation rates failed to continue to move upward; they have actually declined since *A Nation at Risk* was written.

Surprisingly, the deterioration in the high school graduation rate has not been given the public attention the subject deserves—mainly because the accounting system regularly used to track the graduation rate is quite misleading. Displayed in figure 7 is information from the *Digest of Education Statistics,* the official record keeper on the state of American education. It shows an 86 percent graduation rate in

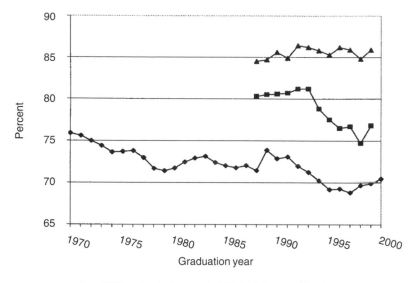

-▲- CPS estimated percent of 18- to 24-year-olds who are
not enrolled in high school or below and have a high
school diploma, GED, or other alternative high school
diploma.

-■- Current Population Survey (CPS) estimated percent of
18- to 24-year-olds who are not enrolled in high school
or below and have a high school diploma (not GED or
other alternative high school diploma)

-◆- Degree Ratio (multiplied by 100): The degree ratio is
the total number of high school graduates divided by
the total population of 17-year-olds.

Fig. 7. Estimated high school graduation rates
Note: CPS data indicating whether high school credentials were obtained through
a regular diploma or through an alternative route were first collected in 1988.
*Sources: The Digest of Education Statistics, 2001; CPS data from NCES Dropout
Rates in the United States, 2001.*

1998, the same percentage as in 1985. The 86 percent figure has been
accepted as accurate, repeated in numerous official reports, including
the one issued by the National Education Goals Panel. If it indicates
little progress in graduation rates, at least it shows no decline.

The statistic overstates what is being accomplished in U.S. high schools, however. The data themselves are collected by the Census Bureau in its annual Current Population Survey of 50,000 households. Each household is asked whether any member in the household between the ages of 18 and 24 has received a high school diploma, is currently in school, or has received the equivalent of a diploma. Approximately 86 percent of young people of this age are said to be high school graduates, so defined.

Relying on this source for information about the quality of the American high school has several problems. For one thing, Census Bureau surveys tend to undercount those households at greatest risk of having a high school dropout. Just as schools can't retain some at-risk students, so census takers cannot find them. It also counts as graduates those still in high school, even at age 18 or older.[10] Even more important, the metric treats the certificate of General Educational Development (GED) as equivalent to a high school diploma, when it is not.

A GED is awarded to students who can pass an examination that apparently demonstrates they have learned as much as is expected of a high school graduate. By law in thirty-five states, the GED is treated as if it were a high school diploma. As the GED has become increasingly promoted as the equivalent of a high school diploma, the number of certificates awarded has risen, climbing from 227,000 in 1971 to 419,000 in 1980 to 501,000 in 2001.

The rising tide of GED bearers is routinely counted in official statistics as part of the high school graduation rate. On the face of it, no test can be thought to be equivalent to a training program. Were it so, then GED recipients would be paid as well as high school graduates. But according to two studies that adjusted for other factors affecting wages, a regular high school diploma is worth 11 to 18 percent more than the GED.[11]

A case for the GED can still be made. For one thing, it provides some students with the opportunity to circumvent an unsuitable high school and still pursue further education. Also, there is some evidence that the GED, particularly when coupled with work training programs, can enhance earnings.[12] And older immigrants may use the GED as a way to get ahead in their new land. But the growth in the number of GEDs cannot be attributed simply to its utilization by older immigrants. The biggest growth in test-taking has been among nineteen-year-olds, who accounted for 42 percent of all test-takers in 2000 versus just 36 percent in 1990. As figure 8 shows, the numbers of teenagers taking the GED examination grew from around 120,000 in 1989 to around 220,000 in 2000.

Regardless of the merits of the GED, there is little reason to include recipients of a GED when one is assessing the progress made by U.S. high schools. GED programs of study are offered by community colleges, prisons, and private entrepreneurs. They constitute an alternative to, not a component of, the high school. For our purposes, then, GEDs should be excluded from estimates of trends in the graduation rate.

When one puts those holding a GED to one side, the declining state of the American high school becomes manifest. As can be seen in figure 7 (see page 56), Census Bureau estimates that the graduation rate for eighteen- to twenty-four-year-olds fell from 81 percent in 1990 to 77 percent in 1999.[13] Other indicators of high school graduation rates reveal a similar decline. If one calculates the rate by calculating the number graduating from public schools as a proportion of the number of public school students in eighth grade five years earlier, the public school graduation rate declined from more than 78 percent in 1991 to less than 75 percent in 2000.[14] This is a higher-bound estimate of public school graduation rates, however. Many eighth-graders in the private sector transfer into the public sector in their high school years, thereby boosting this estimate. Immigration of adolescents from abroad also boosts this measure of graduation rates. Perhaps a more precise measure is to calculate the number of all high school diplomas handed out each year as a percentage of all seventeen-year-olds. According to this measure the ratio of graduates to those in the appro-

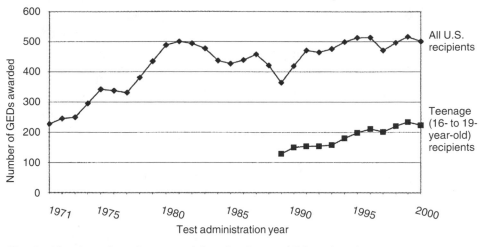

Fig. 8. Number of students receiving the General Educational Development certification, 1971–2001
Source: Digest of Education Statistics, 2001

priate age group fell from 77 percent in 1970 to 74 percent in 1990 and down to 70 percent in 1999—a drop of seven percentage points over the last third of the century (see figure 7, page 56). In other words, in a society where the demand for human capital has been constantly rising, America's schools have responded by turning out a smaller percentage of high school graduates. On the face of it, the nation, far from making progress, remains at risk. Not only are high schoolers not learning as much as their predecessors, a smaller percentage are completing their program of study. Looking at these same data, Paul Barton of the Educational Testing Service asks whether there has been a "closing of the education frontier."[15]

International Comparisons

We have seen few, if any, gains in American education over the past three decades. But how does the country compare with other advanced democracies? Does it remain the world's educational superpower? Is it just one of the pack? Or is it trailing most of the industrial world?

Historically, the U.S. education system has had an outstanding record. It was the first country to achieve universal elementary education, the first to expand its secondary system so as to include the vast majority of students, and the first to establish a broadly encompassing, highly competitive, and world-renowned system of higher education. As late as 1970, a higher percentage of U.S. young people completed their secondary education than did their peers in any other country in the world.

But by the late nineties, the United States no longer led the world in the quantity of secondary schooling received. Instead, the U.S. secondary school completion rate was only about average among the advanced industrial democracies that are members of the OECD, ranking behind Japan, Korea, Germany, France, Ireland, and other European countries (see figures 3 and 4 in the chapter 5 essay by Eric Hanushek, "The Importance of School Quality," for data on high school and college completion rates worldwide). Nor is it just in quantity that the United States lags other advanced industrial democracies. On quality indicators, too, its record is less than sterling.

The best information on school quality has been collected by the IEA, whose tests have been administered to countries throughout the world on several occasions, beginning in the sixties.[16] The IEA tests students only in math and science, forgoing tests of verbal skill, because the designers of the IEA tests thought language differences might invalidate international comparisons of verbal ability. The number of participating countries has changed over the years; during the mid-nineties, thirty-eight countries agreed to have their students tested. Most of the advanced democracies participate in the survey, and several developing countries do so as well.

Hanushek summarizes the results from the IEA surveys in chapter 5 of this volume. As can be seen in figure 1 of that chapter, U.S. average scores in math and science fall below those of the world leaders. In the mid-nineties, for example, the performance of U.S. students ranked closer to the international average (among participating nations) than to that of students in the highest-performing countries—Singapore, Korea, Japan, Belgium, Hong Kong, the Netherlands, and Austria. Nor are there signs of improvement in U.S. test score performance since the 1970s. Even though some fluctuation over time can be observed, average scores were almost exactly the same in the mid-nineties as they had been in the early seventies. In other words, as with the SAT and the NAEP, IEA tests reveal little sign of educational progress in the United States.

The U.S. standing in the world deteriorates the further along the students are in their educational careers. As can be seen in figure 5 in the Hanushek essay, the ranking of U.S. children at age nine is reasonably satisfactory. Admittedly, U.S. students, on average, scored about 60 percent of a standard deviation below the highest-performing country, Korea, and 20 percent behind the Netherlands, a higher-performing European country. But their overall standing is nonetheless higher than the international average. In other words, just as elementary school children's NAEP scores seemed to be improving, so it appears that their IEA scores reveal an elementary educational system that is functioning adequately, if not brilliantly.

But the standing of the United States slips downward to the international average among students taking the IEA at age thirteen. At this age, U.S. students are 50 percent—no longer just 20 percent—of a standard deviation behind their peers in the Netherlands. And they have fallen more than two-thirds of a standard deviation behind Korean and Japanese thirteen-year-olds, as well as a full standard deviation below world-leading Singapore.

The Unites States' place in the world deteriorates further in the last year of high school. Among seventeen-year-olds, the United States ranks at the bottom of participating countries, save for Lithuania, Cyprus, and South Africa. Although Japan, Korea, and Singapore are not in this survey, students in the Netherlands now outrank those in the United States by nearly a full standard deviation.

In other words, the IEA data, when examined separately by age group, yield results quite consistent with the NAEP data reported in a previous section: a U.S. education system that is somewhat strong at the elementary level, but weakens as students age and move through school. These results cannot be explained away, as some critics like to do, by claiming that the United States is testing, at age seventeen, a broader array of students than other nations are. IEA data analysts have adjusted for intercountry differences in participation rates. Though critics say the IEA corrections are less than perfect, it's not clear that this point, if valid, would be decisive. Among nations participating in the IEA assessments, the United States no longer has the largest percentage of students in school at age seventeen. As discussed earlier, the graduation rate in the United States now trails those of many other industrialized nations.

The IEA results are taken from tests of math and science ability and knowledge. But according to SAT and NAEP data, U.S. schools are doing even more poorly at inculcating verbal and reading skills. Is there any international evidence on this score? Until recently, no international testing student survey had been conducted in reading. But in 2000, the OECD's PISA conducted its own international survey of what they refer to as reading, math, and science literacy. They surveyed students at the age of fifteen in thirty-one countries, almost all of them advanced industrial democracies. As a supplement to the IEA's surveys, the PISA has many advantages. It provides information at age fifteen (rather than nine, thirteen, and seventeen, the age of students surveyed by the IEA), yielding data at another point in a student's progression through high school. By focusing on age fifteen, the PISA surveys students at an age when hardly any have dropped out of school and before students begin taking highly differentiated courses. Also, the PISA, as a distinct survey by another organization, can reveal whether the IEA's findings are robust, not simply the result of some unknown quirk in the IEA's methodology. Furthermore, by including math, science, and reading literacy in one survey, the PISA provides for direct comparisons across the three domains of knowledge.

Though PISA results differ from those reported by the IEA in some particulars, overall, the findings from the two international surveys are very similar: As can be seen in figure 9, the average combined scores of U.S. students in all three subjects fall at about the international average of all participating countries, more than 40 percent of a standard deviation behind Japan, Korea, and Finland, the highest-performing countries.

Figures 10 and 11 break out test score results by subject matter. In reading, the United States ranks fifteenth among the thirty-one participating countries, 45 percent of a standard deviation behind Finland, the highest-performing country. One might excuse U.S. performance on the grounds that English is a difficult language to learn, except for the fact that the United States was the lowest-scoring of all the English-speaking countries. Canada, New Zealand, Australia, the United Kingdom, and Ireland all ranked higher (in the order presented). So did Korea, Japan, Sweden, Austria, Belgium, Norway, and France.

In math, the United States scored slightly below the international average and 60 percent of a standard deviation behind Japan, the world leader (see figure 11). On this test, eighteen of thirty-one countries outranked the United States. Most of those with scores below the United States scores were developing countries in Eastern Europe or Latin America. Among well-established, industrial democracies, only Italian schools trailed those of the United States. On the science test, the United States performed only slightly better, this time outranked by thirteen other countries.

Still another international comparison, by the IALS, provides a way of assessing educational quality in the United States from a comparative vantage point. Unlike the IEA and PISA surveys, the IALS was administered not to students but to adults. It was given during the mid-nineties to a cross-section of those aged sixteen to sixty-five

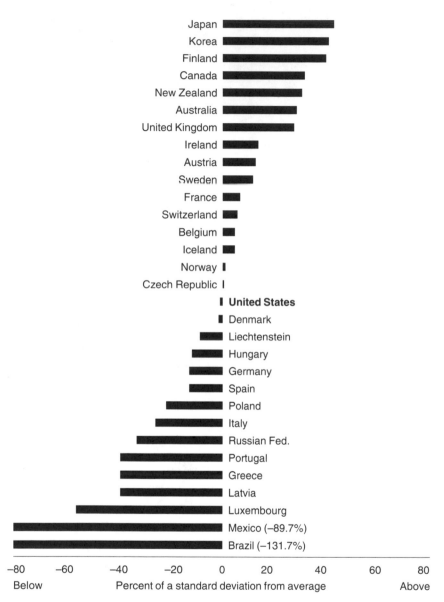

Fig. 9. Student combined test score performance on Program for International Student Assessment (PISA), 2000

Note: Percentage exceeds graph boundary.

Source: Organization for Economic Cooperation and Development, Program for International Student Assessment, Knowledge and Skills for Life, 2000.

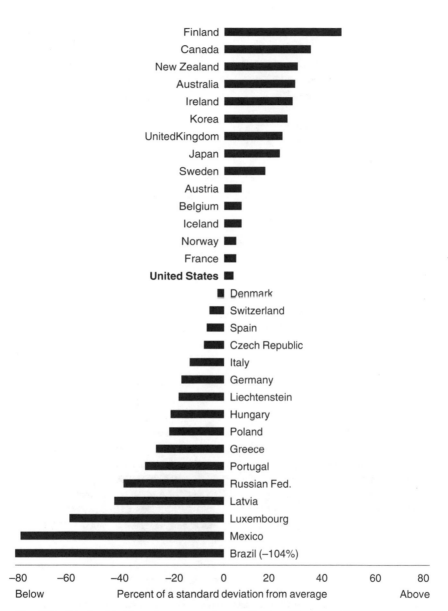

Fig. 10. Student test performance in reading on Program for International Student Assessment (PISA), 2000

Source: Organization for Economic Cooperation and Development, Program for International Student Assessment, Knowledge and Skills for Life, 2000.

Fig. 11. Student test performance in math and science on Program for International Student Assessment (PISA), 2000

Note: Percentage exceeds graph boundary.

Source: Organization for Economic Cooperation and Development, Program for International Student Assessment, Knowledge and Skills for Life, 2000.

in fourteen European and North American countries. On this test, American adults barely attained the international average set by these advanced democracies, says a report issued by the Educational Testing Service.

The United States ranked twelfth on the test, trailing Sweden, Norway, Denmark, Finland, the Netherlands, and Germany by significant margins. The news gets even worse. The United States is living on its past. Among the oldest group in the study (those aged fifty-six to sixty-five), U.S. prose skills stood in second place. These oldsters had attended school in the fifties, a time when U.S. schools were no-nonsense learning institutions, SAT scores reached heights to which they have never since returned—and Europeans were still trying to put together an educational system that could serve more than an elite cadre.

The younger the age group, the lower the place of the United States on this international list. Americans who went to school during the sixties captured a respectable bronze medal in literacy, while those schooled in the seventies ran a respectable race, so as to get fifth place. But those aged sixteen to twenty-five, that is, those who were wandering school hallways during the nineties, ranked fourteenth. The IALS records a simple, steady progression downward.

Apologists will find excuses for these outcomes, of course. The downward U.S. trajectory is due more to gains elsewhere than to slippage within the United States, some will say, as if we should then not care that it is happening. Or, it will be said, U.S. scores are pulled down by its immigrants and ethnic diversity, overlooking the fact that other countries have immigrants, too. Lifelong learning opportunities are greater in the United States than elsewhere, it will be claimed, so young folks will eventually reach the levels the oldest group has achieved. No matter that schools are bad; catch-up time will come later on.

But such excuses don't ring true, especially when the literacy test only confirms results from the IEA, the PISA, the NAEP, and the SAT.

All signs point to stagnation, perhaps even deterioration, in the quality of American schools.

Conclusions

What is the best way to assess the state of American elementary and secondary education? Should we look at the SAT scores of those high schoolers planning to go to college? Or the NAEP scores of all seniors? Or the PISA performance of fifteen-year-olds, an age when fewer students have left school? Or perhaps the NAEP scores of thirteen-year-olds? Or is it best to get an estimate at age nine? Should we rely on SAT or NAEP results, which look at U.S. trends over time? Or use IEA, PISA, and IALS surveys to compare the United States with other countries? Or should we place greater weight on high school graduation rates than test-score performance?

Any one of these measures may be defective. SAT scores may not have climbed as much as they would have, had participation rates not increased. NAEP scores might have been even lower, had participation rates not declined. There are several ways to measure the graduation rate, and, depending on how it is done, one can obtain somewhat different results. International assessments have their own challenges. Making sure that sampling techniques are equivalent requires great care and sophistication. In addition, reading and literacy assessments may unfairly equate languages that are noticeably different. Nor is this problem eliminated altogether when making science and math comparisons.

So no one measure should be accepted as providing the definitive assessment of American education. But when multiple measures yield similar results, the story they tell becomes ever more compelling. By all accounting devices available since the National Commission on Excellence in Education published A *Nation at Risk* twenty years ago, the United States has not responded adequately to the challenge set forth in the commission's report. The picture the statistics portray is not such an unrelieved span of gray that it could be taken as a modern artistic masterpiece. A tinge of blue appears here and there. Some gains at the elementary level can be detected. Math scores have not slipped much since the seventies—in fact they may have improved somewhat. But the overall effect is unmistakably grim. The United States has always trailed many other countries in math instruction, and there is no sign it has closed the gap. Verbal skills are even worse. Here there are multiple signs of a downward trend. Most disturbing, all signs of declining quality in test performance among high schoolers are accompanied by a decline in the percentage of students finishing high school. Students are walking away from public schools, choosing other ways of getting the apparent equivalent of a diploma. They seem to understand, better than anyone else, that the American schoolhouse is badly in need of repair.

Notes

1. The 15 percent estimate is drawn from Richard Murnane, John B. Willet, Yves Duhaldeborde and John H. Tyler (2000), "How Important Are the Cognitive Skills of Teenagers in Predicting Subsequent Earnings?" *Journal of Policy Analysis and Management*, Vol. 19 (4): 547–68. See also Duncan D. Chaplin, 1998, "Raising Standards: The Effects of High School Math and Science Courses on Future Earnings." *Virginia Journal of Social Policy and Law*, 6:1, 111–26. The 20 percent estimate is made by Susan E. Mayer and Paul E. Peterson, "The Costs and Benefits of School Reform," in Susan E. Mayer and Paul E. Peterson, eds., *Earning and Learning: How Schools Matter* (Brookings Institution Press, 1999), 341–54.
2. Sanders D. Korenman and Christopher Winship, "A Reanalysis of the Bell Curve," in Kenneth Arrow, Samuel Bowles, and Stephen Durlauf, eds., *Meritocracy and Economic Inequality* (Princeton: Princeton University Press, 2000), 137–78.
3. Unfortunately, the design of the SAT is being altered in important respects, so it is not clear whether it will remain a useful yardstick for measuring change in American schooling.

4. According to the American College Testing Assessment Web site, the test is an "examination designed to measure academic achievement in four major curriculum areas: English, mathematics, reading, and natural sciences. Materials covered on the four tests that make up the ACT Assessment correspond very closely to topics covered in typical high school classes." On this Web site, ACT, Inc., describes itself as an "independent, not-for-profit organization that provides more than a hundred assessment, research, information, and program management services in the broad areas of educational planning, career planning, and workforce development." ACT Incorporated Home Site. 2002. Accessed 5 July 2002. www.act.org.

5. For a comparison of the two trend lines, see David W. Murray, "Waiting for Utopia," *Education Next* (Summer 2002), 75. Also see Daniel Koretz, "What Happened to Test Scores, and Why?" *Educational Measurement: Issues and Practice* (Winter 1992), 7–11; Daniel Koretz, *Educational Achievement: Explanations and Implications of Recent Trends* (Congressional Budget Office, 1987).

6. The original purpose of this complicated testing design was to preclude measurement for any particular school, school district, or state. When originally proposed, state school officials were concerned that the NAEP would lead to national accountability standards that would intrude on state and local control. Diane Ravitch, *National Standards in American Education: A Citizen's Guide* (Brookings Institution Press, 1995), 70–71.

7. To see whether or not changing participation rates were correlated with test score performance, regression analyses were conducted in order to see whether participation rates were correlated with test score performance when controls were introduced for the year in which the test was administered, and, specifically, whether or not the testing date preceded or postdated the issuance of *A Nation at Risk*. We found a statistically significant impact of participation rates on the test score performance of seventeen-year-olds. For seventeen-year-olds, regression results were as follows: participation rate –63.439, annual trend 55.39, issuance of *Nation at Risk* report –181.15. Constant: 4417.27 Participation was significant at .1 level, one tail test. Other variables not significant. Number of observations: 27. Similar results were obtained from a regression that included a term that controlled for the interaction between the annual

trend and the issuance of A *Nation at Risk*. Although a negative relationship between participation rates and average test score performance is also observed for the younger cohorts, the relationship is not statistically significant in similar estimations of average test scores of nine-year-olds and thirteen-year-olds.

8. Richard Rothstein, "Out of Balance: Our Understandings of How Schools Affect Society and How Society Affects Schools," 30th Anniversary Conference: Traditions of Scholarship in Education, Spencer Foundation, Chicago, Illinois, January 2002. Available at Spencer Foundation Web site.

9. The trends among white students in the younger cohorts also track overall trends fairly closely. For white nine-year-olds, math scores are up by 40 percent of a standard deviation since 1970, with the gains coming after A *Nation at Risk* was issued. Math and science scores are also up slightly since 1970 (10 percent of a standard deviation). The change for thirteen-year-old white students is a gain between 1970 and 1999 of roughly 30 percent of a standard deviation in math, 15 percent of a standard deviation in reading, and 5 percent of a standard deviation in science. As with the nine-year-olds, the math gain occurs after 1982.

10. Although this inflates graduation rates, there is no reason to believe that the prevalence of older students remaining in high schools has changed over time.

11. Stephen Cameron and James Heckman, "The Nonequivalence of High School Equivalents," *Journal of Labor Economics*, 11, no. 1, (1993); Richard J. Murnane, John B. Willett, and Kathryn Parker Boudett," "Do High School Dropouts Benefit from Obtaining a GED?" *Educational Evaluation and Policy Analysis* 17(2), 1995, 133–47.

12. Murnane, Willett, and Boudett.

13. Duncan Chaplin, "Tassels on the Cheap: The GED and the Falling Graduation Rate," *Education Next* 2, no. 3 (Fall 2002), 24–29. Figures 6 and 7 are drawn from this essay.

14. For a full discussion and application of a variation on this estimation technique, see Jay P. Greene, *High School Graduation Rates in the United States*, Center for Civic Innovation at the Manhattan Institute and the Black Alliance for Educational Options, April 2002.

15. Paul Barton, "The Closing of the Education Frontier?" Policy Informa-

tion Report (Research and Development, Policy Information Center, Educational Testing Service, Princeton University, September 2002). Available at www.ets.org/research/pic.

16. Both the title of the TIMSS survey and the number of countries participating in the survey have changed over the decades.

3

What Has Changed and What Has Not

Caroline M. Hoxby

A *Nation at Risk*'s findings can be summarized succinctly: Its authors argued that American public education was being watered down, so that the typical 1982 high school graduate was *less* capable of mastering information and technology than the typical graduate from an earlier cohort. The report's authors, the National Commission on Excellence in Education (Excellence Commission), recognized that more students than ever were graduating from high school, but argued that it was not acceptable to let standards slip in order to graduate more students. Just the opposite, they said: The typical high school graduate needs to be *better* than his predecessors because the knowledge and analytic demands of science and the economy are ever increasing. The claim that American education was being watered down was made up of four subclaims:

1. The content of public school curricula was not challenging.
2. Expectations for students were set too low.

3. Students spent too little time in school and wasted much of their time while in school.

4. Teachers lacked ability and preparation.

The recommendations in A *Nation at Risk* focused on remedying these four perceived problems.

Very Uneven Progress

Progress on the recommendations of A *Nation at Risk* has not been even. It can be summed up as follows:

- Apparently substantial progress has been made on recommendations that could be fulfilled by rule changes, without corresponding *real* changes. For example, the report recommended that students take a greater number of advanced classes. While we can see whether this recommendation is being followed in form, it is nearly impossible to know whether it is being followed in spirit.

- Progress has also been made on recommendations that required real change, *if* they were supported by powerful political interest groups in education, especially teachers' unions. Higher teacher salaries are one such recommendation.

- Virtually no progress has been made on recommendations that required real change if they were opposed by these same interest groups. For example, merit pay for teachers remains negligible, and the school year has not lengthened.

- A *Nation at Risk* made several recommendations that were not quantified (for example, recommending cooperation in textbook development). It is difficult to assess progress on these recommendations, but it appears that they were largely ignored, based on their low prevalence in policy debates.

- Last but not least, there has been substantial progress on several recommendations that were *not* made in A *Nation at Risk*. For example, per pupil spending has risen sharply and class size has fallen significantly. Such changes have occurred because they are popular with powerful interest groups in education. Although they were not recommended by A *Nation at Risk*, their proponents used the climate of urgency created by A *Nation at Risk* to get their own preferred policies enacted.

Progress on Content

A *Nation at Risk* argued that public schools' curricula were poor in content, not because advanced classes were not offered, but because it was too easy for students to avoid advanced academic work. For example, the authors claimed that too few students enrolled in the college-preparatory track and too many enrolled in the vocational track. Figure 1 shows that in 1982 about 42 percent of American high school students took an academic track and 23 percent took a vocational track. By 1998, substantial apparent progress had been made toward getting students into the academic track—71 percent of students were in the academic track and only 4 percent took a vocational track.

A *Nation at Risk* also argued that students were earning too few credits in core subjects such as English, math, science, and history. The authors suggested that nonacademic and frivolous courses were especially common among students from impoverished educational backgrounds.

In Figure 2, we can see that American high school students were taking about 3.7 years of English in 1982 (this was a substantial increase over the 1970 level). Nevertheless, in the wake of A *Nation at Risk*, English course–taking rose by more than one semester (about 0.7 of a year). We can see that students from different backgrounds did *not* have significantly different patterns of English course–taking in 1982. Nor do they have different patterns today.

Between 1982 and today, math course–taking has risen more than

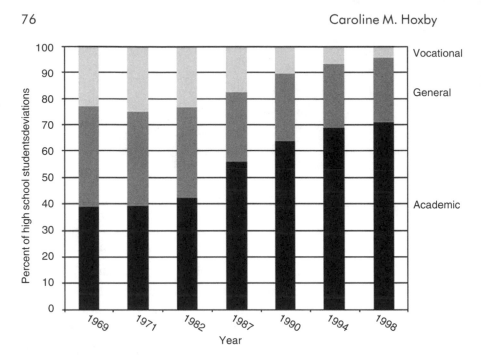

Fig. 1. American high school students taking academic, general, and vocational tracks

Notes: High school curriculum tracks are generally categorized into academic (college preparatory), vocational, and a series of other tracks. The academic and vocational tracks are consistently defined, and the general track absorbs all other tracks, including mixed tracks. The 1969 and 1971 numbers come from the High School Principals and Counselors portion of the *National Longitudinal Study of the High School Class of 1972* (United States Department of Education, 1994). The 1982 numbers come from the School Survey portion of the *High School and Beyond* study, Sophomore Cohort (United States Department of Education, 1995). The 1987, 1990, 1994, and 1998 numbers come from the relevant year's Transcript Study conducted as part of the relevant year's *National Assessment of Educational Progress* (United States Department of Education, 1990, 1993, 1998, 2001). In each case, the correct weights were used to generate nationally representative numbers.

English course–taking. For example, white students' math–taking has increased from 2.4 years to 3.4 years—an additional year of math. The gains were similar for Asians, and even larger for groups with the fewest math courses initially (Hispanics, Native Americans, African Americans). All racial/ethnic groups now take between 3.1 and 3.6 years of math in high school.

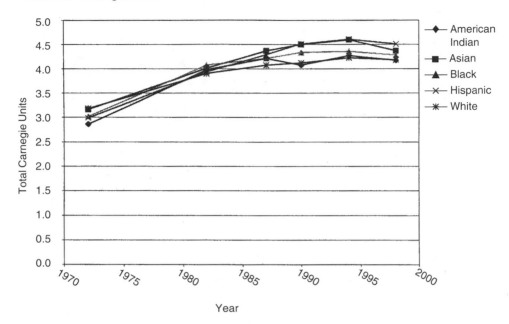

Fig. 2. English Units earned by U.S. high school graduates of various races/ethnicities

Notes: Courses are measured by Carnegie Units. A Carnegie Unit is one full school year of study in a course that meets at least 3 hours and 3 days per week during the school year. The 1972 numbers come from the Transcript portion of the *National Longitudinal Study of the High School Class of 1972* (United States Department of Education, 1994). The 1982 numbers come from the Transcript portion of the *High School and Beyond* study, Sophomore Cohort (United States Department of Education, 1995). The 1987, 1990, 1994, and 1998 numbers come from the relevant year's Transcript Study conducted as part of the relevant year's *National Assessment of Educational Progress* (United States Department of Education, 1990, 1993, 1998, 2001). In each case, the correct weights were used to generate nationally representative numbers.

Science course–taking rose by a little less than a year between 1982 and 1998. For example, in 1982, a typical white student took at 2.3 years of science in high school; by 1998, he was taking 3.2 years of science. Racial/ethnic groups that initially took fewer science courses did not catch up with other groups: All groups took about one more course.

A Nation at Risk recommended a specific high school curriculum,

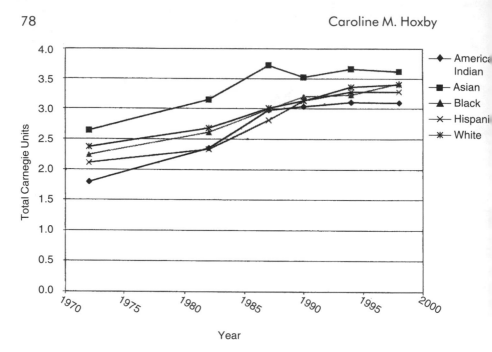

Fig. 3. Math Units earned by U.S. high school graduates of
various races/ethnicities

Notes: Courses are measured by Carnegie Units. A Carnegie Unit is one full school year of study in a course that meets at least 3 hours and 3 days per week during the school year. The 1972 numbers come from the Transcript portion of the *National Longitudinal Study of the High School Class of 1972* (United States Department of Education, 1994). The 1982 numbers come from the Transcript portion of the *High School and Beyond* study, Sophomore Cohort (United States Department of Education, 1995). The 1987, 1990, 1994, and 1998 numbers come from the relevant year's Transcript Study conducted as part of the relevant year's *National Assessment of Educational Progress* (United States Department of Educational Progress, 1990, 1993, 1998, 2001). In each case, the correct weights were used to generate nationally representative numbers.

termed the New Basics: at least 4 years of English, 3 years of math, 3 years of science, 3 years of history (and/or social studies), and half a year of computer science. The report also recommended, though less strongly, 2 years of foreign language.

Figure 5 shows that only 2 percent of 1982 American high school graduates were meeting these standards when the recommendations

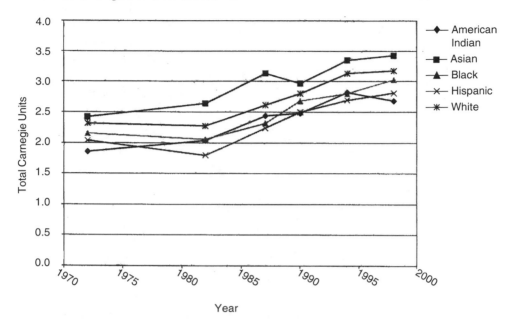

Fig. 4. Science Units earned by U.S. high school graduates of various races/ethnicities

Notes: Courses are measured by Carnegie Units. A Carnegie Unit is one full school year of study in a course that meets at least 3 hours and 3 days per week during the school year. The 1972 numbers come from the Transcript portion of the *National Longitudinal Study of the High School Class of 1972* (United States Department of Education, 1994). The 1982 numbers come from the Transcript portion of the *High School and Beyond* study, Sophomore Cohort (United States Department of Education, 1995). The 1987, 1990, 1994, and 1998 numbers come from the relevant year's Transcript Study conducted as part of the relevant year's *National Assessment of Educational Progress* (United States Department of Education, 1990, 1993, 1998, 2001). In each case, the correct weights were used to generate nationally representative numbers.

were made (the share rises to 10 percent if the computer science requirement is excluded). By 1998, many more students were taking the recommended set of courses, although American schools were far from achieving *universal* compliance with the recommendations: 29 percent of 1998 graduates met all of the requirements, 44 percent met

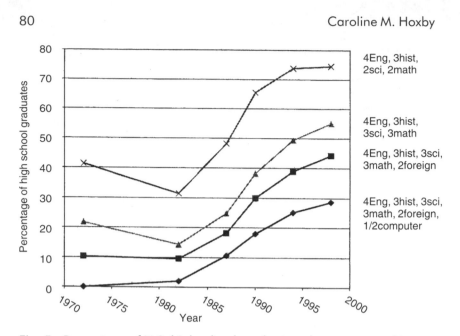

Fig. 5. Percentage of U.S. high school graduates whose course-taking meets various curricular standards

Notes: Courses are measured by Carnegie Units. A Carnegie Unit is one full school year of study in a course that meets at least 3 hours and 3 days per week during the school year. The 1972 numbers come from the Transcript portion of the *National Longitudinal Study of the High School Class of 1972* (United States Department of Education, 1994). The 1982 numbers come from the Transcript portion of the *High School and Beyond* study, Sophomore Cohort (United States Department of Education, 1995). The 1987, 1990, 1994, and 1998 numbers come from the relevant year's Transcript Study conducted as part of the relevant year's *National Assessment of Educational Progress* (United States Department of Education, 1990, 1993, 1998, 2001). In each case, the correct weights were used to generate nationally representative numbers.

all but the computer science requirement, and 55 percent met all but the computer science and foreign language requirements.

The authors of *A Nation at Risk* suggested that their course-taking recommendations be implemented through state-level standards for graduation. Most states considered adopting the recommendations, but only twenty-two had done so by 2001 (as shown in table 1). This is not primarily because states objected to the recommendations per

Table 1. States' graduation requirements

Meet ANAR recommendations in English, math, science, and history	Currently have a minimum competency test for graduating	Future minimum competency test for graduating is planned	No minimum competency test for graduating
22 of 45 "states"	15 of 51 "states"	16 of 51 "states"	20 of 51 "states"

Notes: The 51 "states" include the District of Columbia. In the first column, we consider graduation requirements in only 45 "states" because the other 6 rely exclusively on district-level requirements. The source for table 1 is the *Digest of Education Statistics: 2001* (United States Department of Education, 2002).

se, but because many states have a strong tradition of allowing local districts to set curriculum. In such "local control" states, the state government generally does not set curricular standards that are meant to be optimal; it sets only minimal curricular standards. This does not mean that districts in local control states have low curricular standards. In fact, students in local control states are *more* likely to satisfy the *Nation at Risk* recommendations. They do so in order to meet their local districts' graduation requirements.[1]

Progress on Raising Expectations

The authors of A *Nation at Risk* wanted students to master more advanced material. They argued that American schools sent students the wrong signals—signals that set expectations too low. For example, they argued, juniors and seniors were offered a wide range of elective courses, which encouraged them to think that variety was more important than mastering advanced material in core subjects. Also, they argued, American grades were excessively relative. Grades, rather than being indicators of mastery on an absolute scale, simply showed a student his relative standing in his own school. As a result, able students who obtained grades of A or B saw little room for greater achievement, even though many failed to master—or did not even attempt to master—material suitable for high school students.

Thus, A *Nation at Risk* recommended that students take *advanced* courses in core subjects rather than electives and repeated surveys of basic material (such as "general math for seniors"). The spirit of this recommendation was clearly mastery of material, but schools could comply with the *form* of the recommendation simply by specifying advanced material for courses taken by juniors and seniors. For example, a school could specify that senior math courses contain calculus and senior science courses contain physics without ensuring that students master the material.

American students have increasingly complied with at least the form of the recommendation: they are taking more courses said to cover advanced material. Figure 6 shows that the rate of calculus-taking almost tripled between 1982 and 1998 (from 6.6 percent to 17.7 percent) and the rate of trigonometry-taking doubled over the same period (from 14.2 percent to 32.0 percent).

Similarly, figure 7 shows that the rates at which students took physics and chemistry courses nearly doubled, and the taking of honors science courses also increased significantly.

The correlation between students' grades and their scores on standardized achievement tests has traditionally been low in the United States. Since both grades and standardized scores are meant to measure achievement, their correlation should differ from 100 percent only because grades measure performance on a wider variety of tasks than standardized tests do. When grades measure absolute (not relative) mastery of material, their correlation with standardized scores is 85 percent or higher.[2] Yet, in 1982, the correlation between grades and standardized test scores was only 49 percent. By 1998, the correlation had risen very slightly, to 56 percent. As long as the correlation between grades and achievement tests is in the 50 percent range, grading in American high schools remains largely relative and does not inform students about their absolute level of mastery. Recent survey

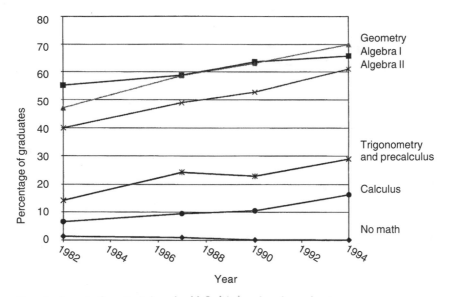

Fig. 6. Level of math taken by U.S. high school graduates

Notes: The sources for this figure are the same as the sources for figures 2, 3, 4, and 5. A student is recorded as having taken a mathematics or science course if a course with the relevant content appears on his transcript, regardless of the length of the course. The correct weights were used to generate nationally representative numbers.

data show that some A students from low-performing schools perform worse on standardized achievement tests than D and F students from high-performing schools.[3]

In order that students might know their absolute level of mastery, *A Nation at Risk* recommended that schools employ tests that indicated students' proficiency, rather than just their place in the national distribution. Today, such tests are known as "criterion-referenced" exams. In order that students form higher expectations, *A Nation at Risk* also recommended that tests be aligned to challenging curricula. Today's tests are frequently aligned to a state's curriculum, but these are not all equally challenging (see the chapter 10 essay by Herb Walberg, "Real Accountability"). Districts may also employ criterion-referenced tests aligned to a challenging curriculum designed by col-

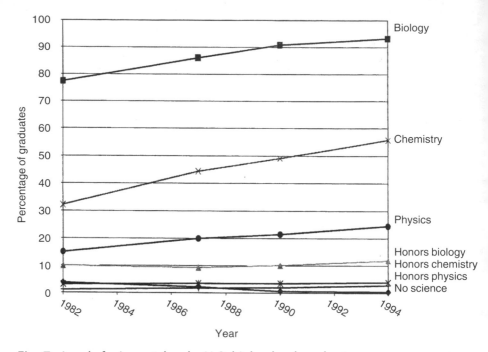

Fig. 7. Level of science taken by U.S. high school graduates
Notes: The sources for this figure are the same as the sources for figures 2, 3, 4, and 5. A student is recorded as having taken a mathematics or science course if a course with the relevant content appears on his transcript, regardless of the length of the course. The correct weights were used to generate nationally representative numbers.

leges (the College Board's Advanced Placement tests are an example) or written to an international standard (the International Baccalaureate exams). Very recently, schools have made a good deal of progress toward the recommendation that they employ criterion-referenced tests. This is primarily owing to state governments' initiatives in English and mathematics, as shown in table 2.

The authors of *A Nation at Risk* did not merely want students to know their level of mastery. They wanted student grouping, promotion, and graduation to be based on mastery. Schools have made very little progress in this direction. As shown in tables 1 and 3, only fifteen

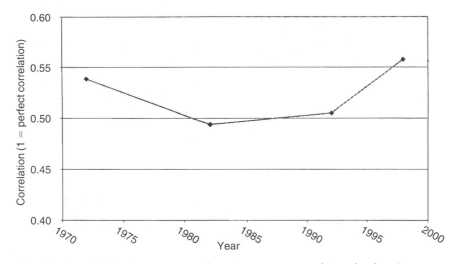

Fig. 8. Correlation between grade point average and standardized test scores, American high school students

Notes: The figure shows simple correlation coefficients between a student's grade point average and his average standardized score on a battery of achievement tests (in English, mathematics, science, and history). The grade point average variable is coded in categories: 8 for "mostly As," 7 for "As and Bs," 6 for "mostly Bs," 5 for "Bs and Cs," 4 for "mostly Cs," 3 for "Cs and Ds," 2 for "mostly Ds," and 1 for "mostly grades below D." The 1972 number uses the standardized tests administered by the National Center for Education Statistics to respondents of the *National Longitudinal Study of the High School Class of 1972* (United States Department of Education, 1994). The 1982 number uses the standardized tests administered by the National Center of Education Statistics to respondents of the *High School and Beyond* study, Sophomore Cohort (United States Department of Education, 1995). The 1992 number uses the standardized tests administered by the National Center of Education Statistics to respondents of the *National Education Longitudinal Study* (United States Department of Education, 1996). The 1998 number uses the 1998 *National Assessment of Educational Progress* tests (United States Department of Education, 2001). In each case, the correct weights were used to generate nationally representative numbers.

states require students to pass a minimum competency test in order to graduate from high school, and the minimum competency tests never come close to the challenging standards envisioned by *A Nation at Risk*. Sixteen more states plan to require tests for graduation, but it remains to be seen whether these politically unpopular requirements are enforced at more than a minimal level.

Table 2. Percentage of states with criterion-referenced tests aligned to a curriculum, 2001

	English/ lang. arts	Mathematics	Science	History/social studies
Elementary grades	92.2	82.4	37.3	29.4
Middle school grades	88.2	78.4	41.2	31.4
Secondary grades	88.2	82.4	47.1	39.2

Notes: Some schools use criterion-referenced tests that are not aligned to a state curriculum. These schools are not included in the table. The source for table 2 is the *Digest of Education Statistics: 2001* (United States Department of Education, 2002).

Progress on Time Use

Time was the subject of several key findings and recommendations in *A Nation at Risk*. The report argued that America's school day and school year were too short and should be lengthened to, respectively, seven hours and between 200 and 220 days. No progress has been made on either of these recommendations, perhaps because there is no way to comply with the form of the recommendations without complying with the spirit. The average school day in the United States was six hours in 1982 and remains six today. Between 1982 and today, the length of the average school year has actually fallen by a couple of days, from 180 days to 178 days, and even that understates the loss of instructional time because an increasing number of hours has been set aside for teacher training. Such days are included in the official school year, but students are sent home for at least part of the school day.[4]

On a more positive note, American students are spending more of their school day on academic coursework, as recommended by *A Nation at Risk*. This is not surprising, given the increase in academic course-taking that we have already recorded. The changes in time use are not great, however: The average high school student spends forty

Table 3. State requirements for high school graduation in Carnegie Units, 2001

State	English	Math	Science	History	First graduating class to which requirements apply	Minimum competency test required to graduate
Alabama	4	4	4	4	2000	Yes
Alaska	4	2	2	3	1978	Yes (class of 2004)
Arizona	4	2	2	2.5	1996	Yes (class of 2002)
Arkansas	4	3	3	3	2004	No
California	3	2	2	3	1989	Yes (class of 2004)
Colorado	Local	Local	Local	Local	N/A	No
Connecticut	4	3	2	3	2004	Yes
Delaware	4	3	3	3	2000	Yes
Dist. of Columbia	4	3	3	3.5	1995	No
Florida	4	3	3	3	2003	Yes (class of 2003)
Georgia	4	4	3	3	2001	Yes
Hawaii	4	3	3	4	1997	No
Idaho	4.5	2	2	2.5	2001	No
Illinois	3	2	1	2	1988	Yes
Indiana	4	2	2	2	2004	Yes
Iowa	Local	Local	Local	Local	N/A	No
Kansas	4	2	2	3	2001	No
Kentucky	4	3	3	3	2002	No
Louisiana	4	3	3	3	2003	Yes
Maine	4	2	2	2	1989	No
Maryland	4	3	3	3	1997	Yes (class of 2007)
Massachusetts	Local	Local	Local	Local	N/A	Yes (class of 2003)
Michigan	Local	Local	Local	Local	N/A	No
Minnesota	5	3	2	4		Yes
Mississippi	4	3	3	3	2002	Yes (class of 2002)
Missouri	3	2	2	2	1988	No
Montana	4	2	2	2	1993	No
Nebraska	Local	Local	Local	Local	1991	No
Nevada	4	3	2	2	2003	Yes
New Hampshire	4	2	2	2	1989	No

Table 3. (*continued*)

State	English	Math	Science	History	First graduating class to which re-quirements apply	Minimum compe-tency test required to graduate
New Jersey	4	3	3	3	2005	Yes (class of 2004)
New Mexico	4	3	2	3	1990	Yes
New York	4	3	3	4	2005	Yes
North Carolina	4	4	3	3	2004	Yes (class of 2005)
North Dakota	4	2	2	3	N/A	No
Ohio	4	3	3	3	2004	Yes (class of 2005)
Oklahoma	4	3	3	3	2003	Yes
Oregon	3	2	2	3	2001	No
Pennsylvania	Local	Local	Local	Local	N/A	Yes (class of 2003)
Rhode Island	4	3	2	2	1990	No
South Carolina	4	4	3	3	2001	Yes
South Dakota	4	2	2	3	2004	No
Tennessee	4	3	3	3	1998	Yes
Texas	4	3	2	3	2001	Yes
Utah	3	2	2	3	1997	Yes (class of 2005)
Vermont	4	3	3	3	2002	No
Virginia	4	3	3	3	2002	Yes (class of 2004)
Washington	3	2	2	2.5	2008	Yes (class of 2008)
West Virginia	4	3	3	3	2003	No
Wisconsin	4	2	2	3	2004	Yes (class of 2004)
Wyoming	4	3	3	3	2003	Yes (class of 2003)

Notes: The state requirements in English, mathematics, science, and history are measured in Carnegie Units. The word "Local" in the requirements columns indicates that the curricular requirements for a high school diploma are set by the Local district. Some of the "Local control" states do require districts to submit to the state their curricular requirements for a diploma. "N/A" indicates that the question of state curricular requirements is not applicable because districts set their requirements Locally. The tests required for graduation vary in difficulty. The source for table 3 is the *Digest of Education Statistics: 2001* (United States Department of Education, 2002).

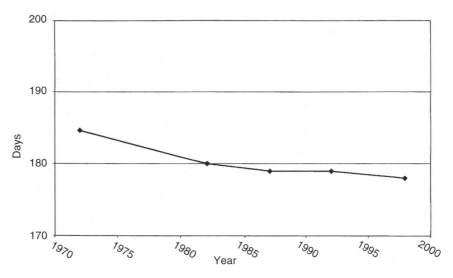

Fig. 9. Length of school year, in days

Notes: The 1972 number comes from the High School Principals and Counselors portion of the *National Longitudinal Study of the High School Class of 1972* (United States Department of Education, 1994). The 1982 number comes from the School Survey portion of the *High School and Beyond* study, Sophomore Cohort (United States Department of Education, 1995). The 1987, 1992, and 1998 numbers come from the relevant year's *Transcript Study* conducted as part of the relevant year's *National Assessment of Educational Progress* (United States Department of Education, 1990, 1993, 1998, 2001). In each case, the correct weights were used to generate nationally representative numbers.

more minutes per school day in academic classes, and nineteen of those extra minutes are devoted to math and science classes.

Homework is a crucial part of learning advanced material, and the authors of *A Nation at Risk* argued that American students were assigned too little homework and insufficiently challenging homework. It is difficult to assess how challenging homework is, but it is clear that no progress has been made toward the recommendation of more homework. In 1982, the average American tenth-grader was assigned just under one hour of homework per day (in all subjects combined). The amount is nearly the same today—indeed, a few minutes less.

Absenteeism was another time problem highlighted by *A Nation*

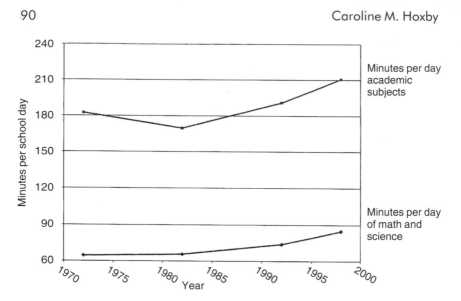

Fig. 10. Minutes per school day on math, science, and academic subjects, American public high school students

Notes: Minutes per day are calculated using the length of a class period and the number of days a class meets during a typical week. The 1972 numbers come from the Transcript portion of the *National Longitudinal Study of the High School Class of 1972* (United States Department of Education, 1994). The 1982 numbers come from the Transcript portion of the *High School and Beyond* study, Sophomore Cohort (United States Department of Education, 1995). The 1992 numbers come from the Transcript portion of the *National Education Longitudinal Study* (United States Department of Education, 1996). The 1998 numbers come from the *Transcript Study* conducted as part of the 1998 *National Assessment of Educational Progress* (United States Department of Education, 2001). In each case, the correct weights were used to generate nationally representative numbers.

at Risk. The authors argued that absent or tardy students forced teachers to waste much of the school day, delaying the presentation of material or requiring that material be repeated. In fact, American students were absent no more often in 1982 than they had been in 1972: On an average school day, 8 percent were absent. Today, a little progress has been made on this front: On an average school day, 7 percent are absent.

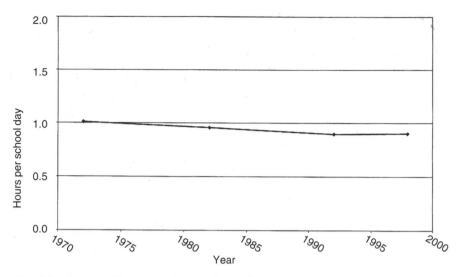

Fig. 11. Hours of homework per school day, average American high school student

Notes: Homework in all subjects is counted, including homework actually performed at school during a study period. The 1972 number comes from the student portion of the *National Longitudinal Study of the High School Class of 1972* (United States Department of Education, 1994). The 1982 number comes from the Transcript portion of the *High School and Beyond* study, Sophomore Cohort (United States Department of Education, 1995). The 1992 number comes from the Transcript portion of the *National Education Longitudinal Study* (United States Department of Education, 1996). The 1998 number comes from the *Transcript Study* conducted as part of the 1998 *National Assessment of Educational Progress* (United States Department of Education, 2001). In each case, the correct weights were used to generate nationally representative numbers.

Finally under the heading of time, *A Nation at Risk* argued that schools spent too little time teaching study skills and should arrange more hours of specialized instruction for students with special needs, including gifted students. It is difficult to assess how the teaching of study skills has changed, but specialized instruction has been on the decline, owing to schools' increasing tendency to mainstream disabled students and dismantle ability tracking.[5]

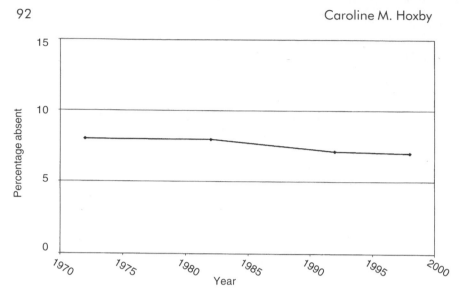

Fig. 12. Percentage of U.S. high school students absent on an average day

Notes: The percentage-absent numbers are reported by school administrators for high school students. The 1972 number comes from the High School Principals and Counselors portion of the *National Longitudinal Study of the High School Class of 1972* (United States Department of Education, 1994). The 1982 number comes from the School Survey portion of the *High School and Beyond* study, Sophomore Cohort (United States Department of Education, 1995). The 1992 number comes from School Survey portion of the *National Education Longitudinal Study* (United States Department of Education, 1996). The 1998 number comes from the survey conducted as part of the 1998 *National Assessment of Educational Progress* (United States Department of Education, 2001). In each case, the correct weights were used to generate nationally representative numbers.

Progress on Teaching

The authors of *A Nation at Risk* recognized the importance of teaching and argued that American schools had been watered down partly because teachers were not able or prepared enough to teach challenging material. Teachers, they argued, ought *not* to be drawn from the bottom third of American college graduates.

A superficial look would suggest that progress has been made toward this goal: Figure 13 shows that more teachers have master's

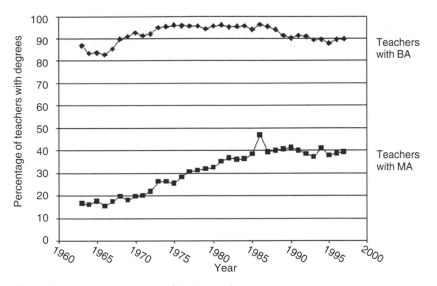

Fig. 13. College degrees of U.S. teachers

Notes: The numbers are based on public school teachers' self-reports of their educational attainment. Each year's number comes from the relevant year's *Current Population Survey of United States* (United States Bureau of Labor Statistics, 1964, 1966–2001), which is the 1-in-1,000 survey of the American population. It is the survey used to generate nearly all official labor market statistics for the United States. For each year, the March survey, which records the previous year's earnings, is used. For each year, the correct weights were used to generate nationally representative numbers.

degrees today (39 percent) than in 1982 (31 percent). However, the share of teachers with baccalaureate degrees has actually fallen slightly (from 94 to 90 percent); this reflects the granting of emergency certificates to teachers in areas with class-size reduction or rapidly growing student populations.

Moreover, today's new teachers are still drawn disproportionately from the bottom third of American college students. Figure 14 shows the distribution of college students by the decile of their score on high school achievement tests (English, math, science, and history combined). For example, students in decile 1 scored in the bottom 10 percent of college students, students in decile 10 scored in the top 10 percent of college-going students, and so on. Thus, the bottom third of college students is in deciles 1, 2, 3, and part of 4. The top third is in deciles 10, 9, 8, and part of 7.

Figure 14 shows that a college student's probability of majoring in education peaks in decile 2 and is generally high for students in deciles 1 through 4. Similarly, a college student's expected probability of becoming a teacher peaks in decile 3 and is generally high in deciles 1 through 4. The figure is based on recent longitudinal data (*National Education Longitudinal Study*, third follow-up, 2000), so it indicates that teachers are still being drawn disproportionately from the lowest third of college students.[6]

It is difficult to teach advanced material with little knowledge of the subject in question. Thus, it is not surprising that A *Nation at Risk* recommended that prospective teachers take more subject area courses and fewer courses in educational methods. Moreover, prospective teachers need to earn a degree in their subject area if we are to ensure that they master the material at a challenging level. For example, a mathematics major must master math at the level necessary for someone who wishes to use it. But there is no guarantee that one who majors in *mathematics education* attains such mastery.

No progress has been made toward the recommendation that American teachers take more subject area courses. The share of teachers with a baccalaureate degree in a subject area fell from 28 percent to 23 percent between 1982 and 1999. The share of teachers with a master's degree in a subject area fell even more sharply—from 17 percent to 5 percent between 1982 and 1999.

Because they foresaw today's demand for workers who can analyze information and handle technology, the authors of A *Nation at Risk* were particularly concerned about the paucity of math and science knowledge among American teachers. They recommended that prospective teachers take more college-level math and science courses. This is particularly important for the 10 percent of teachers whose

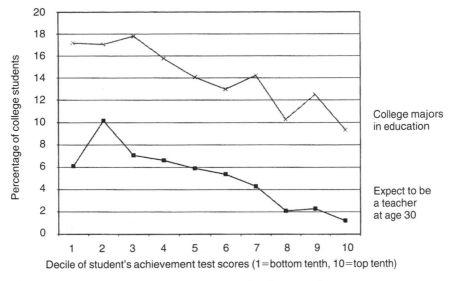

Fig. 14. **From where in the distribution of college students are teachers drawn?**

Notes: The numbers are based on all respondents of the *National Education Longitudinal Study* (United States Department of Education, 2002) who enrolled in college at some time before late spring 1994 (that is, within two years of their high school graduation). The college-going survey respondents reported their most recent (final) college major and their expected occupation at age 30. The respondents are categorized into achievement deciles based on the standardized achievement tests (English, mathematics, science, history) administered to them in the tenth and twelfth grades by the National Center for Education Statistics.

primary teaching assignment is secondary school mathematics or science.

We can see that U.S. teachers have moved away from, not toward, fulfilling this recommendation. The percentage of teachers who have a degree (either a baccalaureate or a master's) in math or science fell from about 7 percent to 5 percent between 1982 and 1999. In 1982, the average teacher had taken almost six semesters of math and science in college; by 1999, the average teacher had taken only four semesters.

In order to attract able people to the teaching profession, *A Nation at Risk* recommended that teachers be paid on the basis of their

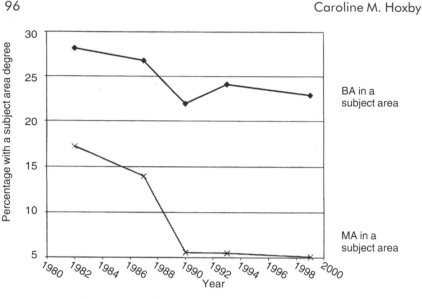

Fig. 15. Teachers with college degrees in a subject area (as opposed to educational methods)

Notes: Subject area degrees are all degrees that are not in educational methods. Although the vast majority of education degrees are in elementary education, degrees in secondary education, English education, and so on are also counted as education degrees. The 1982 numbers come from the Teacher Surveys conducted as part of the *High School and Beyond* study (United States Department of Education, 1995). The 1987, 1990, 1993, and 1999 numbers come from the teacher portions of the relevant year's *Schools and Staffing Survey* (United States Department of Education, 1998, 1998, 1998, 2001). For each year, the correct weights were used to generate nationally representative numbers.

performance and that teachers be paid more. The recommendation for performance pay has been much discussed but almost never practiced. In 1982, less than 1 percent of all teacher pay was associated with performance, as opposed to seniority and degree-based salary scales. Today, the percentage of teacher pay associated with performance is still less than 1 percent.

By contrast, the level of teacher pay has, however, risen since 1982, a year that was close to the nadir for teacher pay in recent U.S. history. In 1982, the average full-time teacher earned $33,884; in 2000, it was $37,865. These numbers (and all of figure 17) are in inflation-adjusted

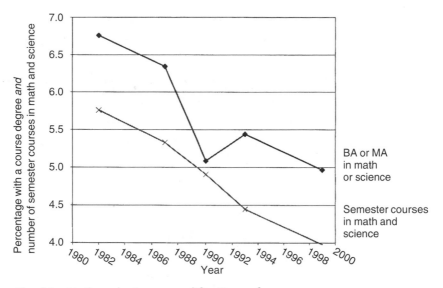

Fig. 16. Math and science qualifications of U.S. public school teachers

Notes: Math and science qualifications are based on the responses of middle and high school teachers only. Quarter courses in math and science are converted into semester courses on a three-to-two basis. The data sources are the same as the sources for figure 15.

dollars (2001 dollars). Thus, *real* teacher pay has risen 12 percent since 1982.

How does this compare with the earnings of other workers? Figure 18 shows that the average teacher salary kept pace with the average worker's earnings in wages and salaries from 1982 to 1994. After that, the average teacher salary lagged behind, not because teacher salaries rose at a rate that was low compared to history, but because the increase in *other college graduates'* earnings was unusually rapid between 1994 and 2000. Indeed, a large number of studies have demonstrated that the earnings of particularly able and well-educated workers have risen most quickly over the past two decades, presumably because such workers are best equipped to meet employers' demands for people who can analyze information and handle new technology.

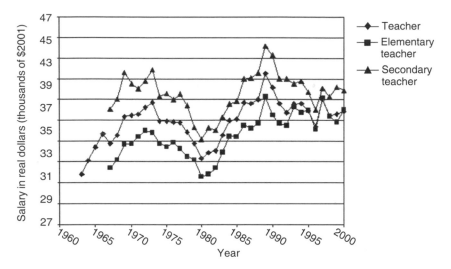

Fig. 17. Average teacher salary in the United States (in inflation-adjusted 2001 dollars)

Notes: The numbers are based on public school teachers' self-reports of all earnings from wages and salaries on their teaching jobs in the previous year. Part-time teachers, such as substitute teachers, are not included. Each year's number comes from the relevant year's *Current Population Survey of United States* (United States Bureau of Labor Statistics, 1964, 1966–2001), which is the 1-in-1,000 survey of the American population used to generate nearly all official labor market statistics for the United States. For each year, the March survey, which records the previous year's earnings, is used. For each year, the correct weights were used to generate nationally representative numbers. Dollars of the day are converted into inflation-adjusted 2001 dollars using the Consumer Price Index. The *Current Population Survey* records a teacher's occupation at a detailed level and also records whether a teacher works in the public or private sector. It is therefore an excellent source of national earnings data for teachers, especially because its sampling is accurate, highly scrutinized, and comparable with all other earnings data commonly used for U.S. labor statistics. We have decided not to rely on the often-publicized earnings reports from the National Education Association's *Status of the American Public School Teacher*. Details of the sampling and imputation methods used for the National Education Association survey are not published, and its statistics appear to substantially overstate actual teacher earnings. This may be because the National Education Association oversamples its own members, who are disproportionately likely to be urban, unionized teachers (whose earnings tend to be higher than those of nonurban, nonunionized teachers).

The slower rise in teacher salaries is related to the fact that they are drawn disproportionately from the bottom third of college graduates. Because they are the less able college graduates, they can get fewer alternative job offers that would put upward pressure on their teaching salaries; because teaching salaries are not based on performance and are lower than the average college graduate's, able college graduates tend not to join the teaching profession.

The authors of A Nation at Risk argued that too few math and science teachers were qualified to teach their subjects and that math and science salaries ought to be high enough to attract teachers into these fields, where vacancies are a chronic problem. We have seen that, compared with teachers in 1982, today's teachers are less likely to have a degree in math or science and have taken fewer courses in math and science. This may be because the salary premium for math and science teachers remains small. It was 3.4 percent in 1982 and 3.9 percent in 1999. In the private sector, the earnings premium associated with math and science skills is significantly larger.

Nevertheless, the percentage of math and science teachers who claim to be certified in their subject area declined only slightly, from 89.4 percent in 1982 to 86.3 percent in 1999. These certification rates are similar to those for other teachers. Taken in conjunction with the numbers on college training in math and science, the certification rates suggest that a teacher can be certified to teach secondary math or science with relatively little mastery of college-level material in her subject.

Along with its recommendation that students have a longer school year, A Nation at Risk recommended that teachers be employed for 11 months of the year, rather than 9. Both recommendations have been unpopular with the teachers' unions, and teacher salaries are still based on 9 months of work.[7]

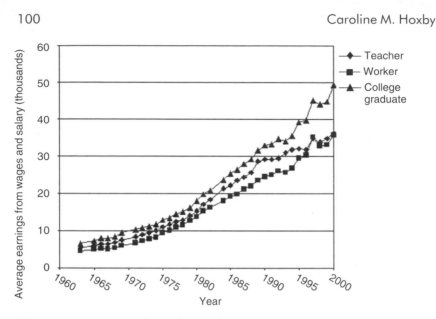

Fig. 18. Average teacher salary in the United States (in dollars of the day)

Notes: The sources for this figure are same as those for figure 17. For the average worker numbers, the wage and salary earnings of all full-time wage and salary workers are included. For the average college graduate numbers, the wage and salary earnings of all full-time wage and salary workers with at least 16 years of education (a baccalaureate degree) are included. The numbers shown in the figure are in dollars of the day.

Recommendations That
A Nation at Risk Did *Not* Make

Although *A Nation at Risk* exhorted Americans to rise to the challenge of improving their public schools, its authors did not recommend higher spending. On the whole, *A Nation at Risk* was an argument for *refocusing* American schools on academics and *reallocating* resources toward teachers and away from other staff and activities. With the exception of the longer school year and school day (which would have required more resources), its authors did not argue for *more of the same resources*, but argued that American schools must concentrate their existing resources on an academic mission.

Table 4. Incentives and certification for teachers in math and science
(main areas of shortage)

	1982	1987	1990	1993	1999
Percent by which math and science teachers' salaries exceed other teachers'	3.40	3.53	5.92	4.27	3.88
Percent of math and science teachers certified in their teaching area	89.4	88.8	90.5	87.9	86.3
Percent of all other teachers certified in their main teaching area	89.5	89.3	91.4	90.3	89.5

Notes: The first row records the percentage by which the average American math or science teacher's salary exceeds that of the average teacher who is not a math or science teacher. Nearly all math and science teachers are secondary school teachers, and secondary school teachers typically earn slightly more than elementary school teachers. Thus, some of the salary "premium" for math and science teachers is shared by other secondary school teachers. Teacher certification is based on teachers' self-reports of whether they have normal state certification (not emergency or provisional certification) in the main area in which they teach. The 1982 numbers come from the Teacher Surveys conducted as part of the High School and Beyond study (United States Department of Education, 1995). The 1987, 1990, 1993, and 1999 numbers come from the teacher portions of the relevant year's Schools and Staffing Survey (United States Department of Education, 1998, 1998, 1998, 2002). For each year, the correct weights were used to generate nationally representative numbers.

Nevertheless, because A Nation at Risk created an atmosphere of urgency and did not explicitly recommend against spending increases, it was used by advocates of higher spending to trigger the decade of fastest per-pupil spending growth in recent American history. Between 1982 and 1992, real (inflation-adjusted) per-pupil spending grew from $5,930 to $8,008. This is an increase of 35 percent in 10 years, in excess of inflation. Although spending did not rise as quickly in the next 8 years, it reached $9,230 in 2000. In short, from A Nation at Risk until today, per-pupil spending has risen by 60 percent.

The increase in spending has occurred disproportionately in schools that were initially low-spending, so that the distribution of U.S. per-pupil spending has narrowed. In 1982, spending at the 10th percentile was only 0.67 of median per-pupil spending. By 1999, spend-

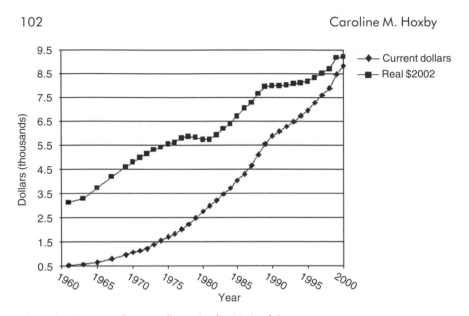

Fig. 19. Per-pupil expenditure in the United States, current dollars and real 2002 dollars

Notes: Per-pupil spending is calculated by dividing the total expenditure of public elementary and secondary schools by average daily attendance. (Dividing by enrollment is an inferior method because enrollment numbers systematically overstate the actual school population of the United States, owing to double-counting of students who are switching schools.) The sources of the data are several publications of the National Center for Education Statistics: *Statistics of State School Systems, Statistics of Public Elementary and Secondary School Systems,* and the *Common Core of Data* (all United States Department of Education, 2002). Dollars of the day are converted into inflation-adjusted 2002 dollars using the Consumer Price Index.

ing at the 10th percentile had risen to 0.80 of median per-pupil spending. The spending distribution also narrowed because schools that were initially high-spending raised their spending more slowly than other schools. In 1982, spending at the 90th percentile was 1.6 times the median per-pupil spending. By 1999, it had fallen to 1.47 times the median per-pupil spending.

In short, the major increase in per-pupil spending between *A Nation at Risk* and today occurred disproportionately at the schools most likely to need extra resources to meet the report's recommendations.

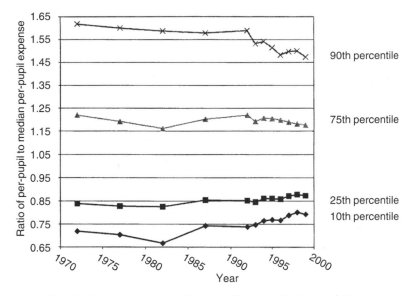

Fig. 20. Variation in per-pupil expenditure in the United States

Notes: Per-pupil spending is calculated in the same manner as for figure 19. However, the numbers were computed using administrative, district-level data. For each year, the national percentiles of per-pupil spending are computed in a manner that treats all pupils equally. In other words, the percentile computations account for the enrollment differences among public school districts. The sources of data are several publications of the United States Bureau of the Census: the 1972, 1977, 1982, and 1987 *Censuses of Governments* (United States Bureau of the Census, 1975, 1980, 1985, and 1992) and the 1992 through 1999 *School Finance* censuses (United States Department of Education, 2001).

Where did all of the additional spending go? We have already seen that real teacher salaries rose by 12 percent between 1982 and today, so they account for only part (about a fifth) of the 60 percent increase in real per-pupil spending. The policy that accounts for the single largest share of the spending increase is a substantial decrease in the pupil-teacher ratio, which fell from 18.6 in 1982 to 15.0 in 1999. Reducing the pupil-teacher ratio is expensive: A 10 percent reduction in the pupil-teacher ratio raises per-pupil costs by about 10 percent. Yet a 10 percent reduction in the pupil-teacher ratio represents only 2 fewer students per teacher, which does not sound like a major change. The reduction in the pupil-teacher ratio from 1982 to 1999 accounts for about a third of the 60 percent increase in real per-pupil spending.

Given the decrease in the student-teacher ratio, it is not surprising that the size of regular U.S. classrooms also fell from 1982 to 1999. The size of the average self-contained class fell from 23 to 21; the size of the average departmentalized class fell from 23 to 19. Middle schools and high schools tend to use departmentalized classes (For example, English class); elementary schools tend to use self-contained classes where children learn most subjects from the same teacher.

Parents often puzzle over the fact that the pupil-teacher ratio and class size are not identical. If every teacher were to teach the entirety of every school day, the pupil-teacher ratio and class size *would* be identical. But most teachers do not teach the entire school day. This is particularly true of teachers who teach departmentalized classes. However, even elementary school teachers who have self-contained classrooms typically turn over their students to other teachers (gym teachers, music teachers, art teachers) for some part of each week. They also turn over particular students to specialized teachers. For example, many disabled students receive pull-out instruction, one on one or in a very small group.

When parents think about class size, they rarely account for the fact that some reductions in the teacher-student ratio are absorbed by reductions in teachers' hours of teaching or by the tiny classes used for pull-out instruction. It is difficult to measure teaching hours of teachers who have self-contained classrooms, but the teaching hours of departmentalized teachers can be measured exactly because their classes meet in periods, on well-defined schedules. In 1982, the average departmentalized teacher taught 4.5 hours per school day; by 1999, she taught only 3.8 hours per school day. For this reason, the pupil-teacher ratio fell faster than the size of regular classrooms.

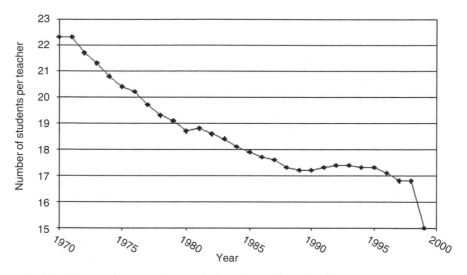

Fig. 21. The student-teacher ratio in U.S. public schools
Notes: The student-teacher ratio is calculated by dividing average daily attendance in the United States by the number of full-time-equivalent teachers in the United States. (Using enrollment is an inferior method because enrollment numbers systematically overstate the actual school population of the United States, owing to double-counting of students who are switching schools.) The sources of the data are same as those for figure 19. The 1999 number is based on preliminary estimates.

Why Such Uneven Progress?

A *Nation at Risk* was something of a shock to Americans, awakening them to the mediocrity of their schools. Nonetheless, the nation sensed the essential truth of the report's central claims and were energized by it to change public schools. The report enjoyed very widespread support among parents and employers. Why, then, do we see the uneven progress described above? Indeed, as we suspected and as Paul Peterson demonstrates in chapter 2, even the uneven progress was largely superficial: Achievement could have risen unevenly; in fact, it has not risen at all.

The reason that progress has been so uneven and superficial is that

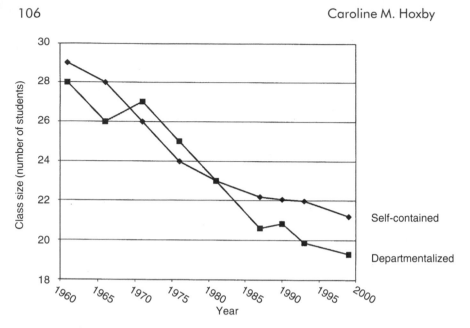

Fig. 22. Class size in regular U.S. public elementary and secondary classrooms
Notes: Class size numbers are based on teachers' reports. The 1961 through 1981 numbers are based on the National Education Association's *Status of the American Public School Teacher.* It appears that this source is not representative of the United States, but it is the only large-scale source of teacher self-reported class size before 1987. See the notes to figure 17 for comments on the problems associated with this source. The 1987, 1990, 1993, and 1999 numbers are based on the relevant year's *Schools and Staffing Survey* (United States Department of Education, 1990, 1993, 1998, 2002), which is representative of the United States when the correct weights are applied, as they are here.

the authors of *A Nation at Risk* were good at recognizing the symptoms of mediocrity in American schools, but bad at identifying the underlying reasons for the mediocrity. They assumed, naively, that schools had *accidentally* fallen into mediocrity, which could be eliminated by a commission that showed schools where the pitfalls lay. In fact, as upcoming chapters in this volume show, the same interest-group politics that made American schools mediocre in the first place would control the implementation of the report's recommendations.

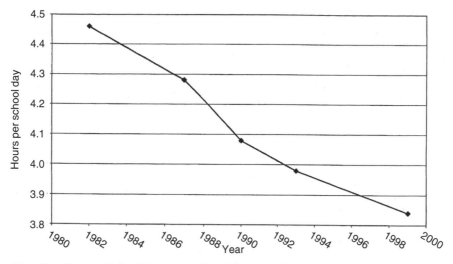

Fig. 23. Hours of teaching per school day, teachers in departmentalized settings

Notes: Teaching hours per day for departmentalized teachers are based on the following information: Each teacher reports all of the classes that she teaches and the number of periods that each class meets each week. The length of the teacher's class periods is reported by her principal. The 1982 numbers come from the Teacher Surveys conducted as part of the *High School and Beyond* study (United States Department of Education, 1995). The 1987, 1990, 1993, and 1999 numbers come from the teacher portions of the relevant year's *Schools and Staffing Survey* (United States Department of Education, 1990, 1993, 1998, 2002). For each year, the correct weights were used to generate nationally representative numbers.

Notes

1. The claim regarding students in local control states being more likely to satisfy the curricular recommendations of *A Nation At Risk* is based on two recent sources: the Transcript survey that was part of the National Education Longitudinal Study (United States Department of Education, 1996) and the Transcript Study that was part of the 1998 National Assessment of Education Progress (United States Department of Education, 2001).

2. The claim regarding the correlation between standardized test scores and grades that measure absolute performance can be substantiated using any of several longitudinal surveys, converting grades to an absolute scale

by controlling for schools' systematic differences in the level of grades (eliminating a school-fixed effect). The most suitable longitudinal surveys are the *National Longitudinal Study of the High School Class of 1972* (United States Department of Education, 1994), the study *High School and Beyond* (United States Department of Education, 1995), and the *National Education Longitudinal Study* (United States Department of Education, 1996).

3. The claim regarding A and D and F students is based on the *National Education Longitudinal Study* (United States Department of Education, 1996). The participants' grades are recorded, as are their scores on four subject tests (English, mathematics, science, history) administered by the National Center for Education Statistics.

4. The key sources for information on teacher training days are the 1987–88, 1990–91, 1993–94, and 1999–2000 versions of *The Schools and Staffing Survey* (United States Department of Education, 1998, 1998, 1998, and 2002).

5. Information on placement of special education students (more precisely, students with individual education programs) and ability tracking may be garnered from the following federal sources: the *National Longitudinal Study of the High School Class of 1972* (United States Department of Education, 1994), the *High School and Beyond* study (United States Department of Education, 1995), and the *National Education Longitudinal Study* (United States Department of Education, 1996). In addition, the administrative data of individual states often include detailed placement statistics. Maintaining consistent definitions of special education and ability tracking is challenging when comparing data from different periods of time.

6. The figure is based on the *National Education Longitudinal Study* (United States Department of Education, 2002). See also the notes associated with the figure.

7. Contract length is described by 1987–88, 1990–91, 1993–94, and 1999–2000 versions of *The Schools and Staffing Survey* (United States Department of Education, 1998, 1998, 1998, and 2002).

Chapter Bibliography

United States Department of Commerce, Bureau of the Census. *Census of Governments*. 1972, 1977, 1982, and 1987 censuses. Electronic data originally released in various years. Washington, D.C.: Bureau of the Census, 2002.

United States Department of Labor, Bureau of Labor Statistics. *Current Population Survey.* March 1964 and March 1966 through March 2001 surveys. Electronic data originally released in various years. Washington, D.C.: Bureau of Labor Statistics, 2002.

United States Department of Education, National Center for Education Statistics. *Statistics of Public Elementary and Secondary School Systems.* Washington, D.C.: National Center for Education Statistics, 2002.

United States Department of Education, National Center for Education Statistics. *Statistics of State School Systems.* Washington, D.C.: National Center for Education Statistics, 2002.

United States Department of Education, National Center for Education Statistics. *School Finance* censuses. Washington, D.C.: National Center for Education Statistics, 2002.

United States Department of Education, National Center for Education Statistics. *Common Core of Data: School Years 1987–88 through 1999–2000.* Electronic data originally released in various years. Washington, D.C.: National Center for Education Statistics, 2002.

United States Department of Education, National Center for Education Statistics. *National Longitudinal Study of the High School Class of 1972.* Public-use electronic data. Washington, D.C.: National Center for Education Statistics, 1994.

United States Department of Education, National Center for Education Statistics. *High School and Beyond: 1992.* Restricted-use electronic data. Washington, D.C.: National Center for Education Statistics, 1995.

United States Department of Education, National Center for Education Statistics. *National Education Longitudinal Study: 88/94.* Restricted-use electronic data. Washington, D.C.: National Center for Education Statistics, 1996.

United States Department of Education, National Center for Education Statistics. *The Schools and Staffing Survey: 1987–88.* Restricted-use electronic data originally released in 1992. Washington, D.C.: National Center for Education Statistics, 1998.

United States Department of Education, National Center for Education Statistics. *The Schools and Staffing Survey: 1990–91.* Restricted-use electronic data originally released in 1994. Washington, D.C.: National Center for Education Statistics, 1998.

United States Department of Education, National Center for Education Statistics. *The Schools and Staffing Survey: 1993–94.* Restricted-use electronic data originally released in 1996. Washington, D.C.: National Center for Education Statistics, 1998.

United States Department of Education, National Center for Education Statistics. *The Schools and Staffing Survey: 1999–2000.* Restricted-use electronic data (preliminary version). Washington, D.C.: National Center for Education Statistics, 2002.

United States Department of Education, National Center for Education Statistics. *Digest of Education Statistics: 2001.* Washington, D.C.: National Center for Education Statistics, 2002.

United States Department of Education, National Center for Education Statistics. *National Education Longitudinal Study: 88/2000.* Public-use electronic data. Washington, D.C.: National Center for Education Statistics, 2002.

United States Department of Education, National Center for Education Statistics. *The 1998 High School Transcript Study*, part of the *1998 National Assessment of Educational Progress.* Washington, D.C.: United States Government, 2001.

United States Department of Education, National Center for Education Statistics. *The 1994 High School Transcript Study*, part of the *1994 National Assessment of Educational Progress.* Washington, D.C.: United States Government, 1998.

United States Department of Education, National Center for Education Statistics. *The 1990 High School Transcript Study*, part of the *1990 National Assessment of Educational Progress.* Washington, D.C.: United States Government, 1993.

United States Department of Education, National Center for Education Statistics. *The 1987 High School Transcript Study*, part of the *1987 National Assessment of Educational Progress.* Washington, D.C.: United States Government, 1990.

4

Minority Children at Risk

Paul T. Hill
Kacey Guin
Mary Beth Celio

A *Nation at Risk* played the national security card. Just as a nuclear exchange with the Soviet Union would devastate all Americans, so, it argued, would ignorance. Just as no American could be safe against nuclear war unless all Americans were safe, so could no American be protected from the consequences of a bad school system. Bomb shelters and privileged educational enclaves were shortsighted solutions, from which the privileged would emerge only to face the tribulations of a devastated society.

The national security analogy worked, in that K–12 education became a national issue, and Americans became convinced that general improvements, not just islands of excellence, were necessary. But like all metaphors this one was imperfect. When it came to solutions, *A Nation at Risk* drew uniform prescriptions analogous to national security strategies. Like strategic missile defenses that protect everyone, *A Nation at Risk* prescribed educational standards and investments that would lift up everyone.

The benefits of A *Nation at Risk*'s prescriptions were not uniform, however, or indivisible because they overlooked the distinctive problems of poor and minority students, especially in the big cities. The remedies the report suggested, more exacting course requirements and higher graduation standards, though not always bad for these groups, were nonetheless grossly insufficient for them. Subsequent sections of this chapter will show that

- A *Nation at Risk*'s prescriptions for reform ignored the special problems of poor and minority children in big cities.
- These children have benefited little if at all from the reform initiatives stimulated by A *Nation at Risk* and are still desperately behind national averages.
- To transform the educational opportunities of poor and minority children, very different reforms are necessary.

A *Nation at Risk* Ignored the Special Problems of Urban Poor Children

A *Nation at Risk* prescribed remedies that made sense for students whose basic preparation for school was sound and for school systems that had the capacity to respond to pressure by offering more rigorous courses. But raised expectations alone are not good remedies for the problems of children who enter any level of schooling unprepared to do the work normally expected. Similarly, requirements that schools teach more challenging materials and move students to higher levels of mastery are not sufficient remedies for schools that cannot provide competent instruction. Nor is the prescription to increase entry requirements for teaching necessarily helpful to schools and districts that are the least attractive employers and generally recruit from the very bottom of the labor pool.

Here we abandon the national security metaphor for a nautical one. A rising tide might lift all boats, but if the tide rises only slightly, those boats that are thoroughly stuck on sandbars might still not float. As this essay will show, though poor and minority students might have gained slightly since the days of A *Nation at Risk*, their educational performance remains low, low enough to keep millions out of good jobs and higher education.

Although these disadvantaged and minority students were numerous when A *Nation at Risk* was written, their numbers have only continued to grow. Hispanic students are the fastest-growing population among K–12 school-age children. In 1983, Hispanics made up 9 percent of K–12 public school students, compared with 16 percent in 1999.[1] For black students, the population increase was minor, going from 16 percent in 1983 to 17 percent in 1999. But these minority students are becoming increasingly concentrated in urban school districts. During the 1990–1991 school year, of the fifty-seven districts that are members of the Council of the Great City Schools, forty reported majority-minority student populations. By the 1997–1998 school year, that number had risen to forty-six districts.

Being a member of a minority group nearly doubles the probability that a student will be educated in urban schools. Black and Hispanic students are more than twice as likely as white students to attend central city schools. White students are disproportionately educated in suburbs and rural areas. Another way to understand the concentration of minority students in big cities is this: Though there are 15,000 school districts in the United States, ten big districts educate 19 percent of all black children, and six educate 21 percent of all Hispanic students.[2]

Not only are minority students disproportionately concentrated in urban school districts, students in these urban districts are likely to be poor and to attend school with others who are poor. According to *Education Week*, 53 percent of students in urban districts attend high poverty schools, compared with 22 percent of students in nonurban districts.[3]

The remainder of this chapter provides the best evidence available on post–A *Nation at Risk* trends in performance of urban minority students. Because the best sources—nationwide and state tests—are not always designed to track results by both student ethnicity and locality, some of the data presented represent minority students nationwide, and some represent students from urban areas. Taken together, these diverse sources of information illustrate the point that students who are both minority *and* in big cities are the ones who have benefited least from A *Nation at Risk* reforms.

Minority Students Are Less Ready for School

Preschool preparation is a class phenomenon in America. Middle-class children, disproportionately white, come to school knowing letters and colors, understand that people record ideas on paper and learn by reading, and expect to learn via a combination of listening and doing. Poor and lower-working-class children, of whatever race, are far less likely to know these things.[4] Studies of learning in kindergarten show that black and Hispanic children are able to close the gap in basic reading and math skills, but they acquire advanced communication and reasoning skills more slowly than their white counterparts.[5]

A longitudinal study of early childhood found that white children were likely to enter kindergarten with higher proficiency in reading, mathematics, and general knowledge than black or Hispanic children.[6] Table 1, taken from this work, illustrates the difference in kindergarten reading performance. Scores in mathematics and general knowledge followed similar patterns.

Poor Minority Students Learn at a Slower Rate

Schools are engineered for students who are motivated and who can concentrate on learning. The correlates of poverty, including family turbulence and lack of consistent support for study, put poor and minority students at a disadvantage throughout their school careers.[7]

Table 1. Distribution of first-time kindergarteners' reading scores

	Lowest Quartile (0–25)	2nd Quartile (26–50)	3rd Quartile (51–75)	Highest Quartile (76–100)
Black	34%	30%	21%	15%
Hispanic	42%	24%	19%	15%
White	18%	24%	28%	30%

Note: Estimates based on first-time kindergarteners who were assessed in English (approximately 30% of Hispanic children were not assessed because testers assumed they could not understand English).

In a 1998 study, it was found that for children entering school with similar test scores and socioeconomic backgrounds, black children learn less than white children by the time they graduate from high school.[8] Important to note is that children in this comparison were attending the same schools.

Most of *A Nation at Risk*'s prescriptions concerning standards of instruction and graduation requirements focused on the secondary level, by which time many students are already too far behind to catch up. Many minority and low-income students are not able to benefit from more demanding high school courses because they lack skills normally taught in the upper-elementary grades—such as reasoning by analogy and converting fractions, decimals, percentages, and rates—that allow them to take normal secondary school courses. In the 1999–2000 National Assessment of Educational Progress (NAEP), 5 percent of black, 10 percent of Hispanic, and 34 percent of white fourth-graders scored at the *proficient* level or above in mathematics.[9] Forty percent of white fourth-graders scored at *proficient* or above in reading, compared with 12 percent of black and 16 percent of Hispanic fourth-graders.

A 2001 study shows that passing normal secondary school courses matters.[10] Minority students who graduate from high school with high academic skills are equally as likely as white students with high academic skills to attend college. In addition, the college graduation rate of black, Hispanic, and white students with the same tenth-grade academic skills are very similar. Unfortunately, black and Hispanic students, on average, have significantly lower tenth-grade academic skills.

Poor and Minority Children
Remain Desperately Behind

Though some poor and minority students are doing better than at the time of *A Nation at Risk*, most are still as far behind as ever on criteria such as tested skills, high school graduation rate, college enrollment and completion rates, and readiness for the labor market. In this section, we will show that minority students' test scores have increased marginally, if at all, since *A Nation at Risk*. The gaps between minority and white achievement are as great now as then. Moreover, gaps in "authentic" indicators such as high school completion and college entry rates continue to be very large.

Persistent Gaps in National Test Scores

In a preceding chapter, Paul Peterson showed that national average scores on the NAEP had risen only slightly. Here, we compare the scores of white, black, and Hispanic children on the same test. Trends in NAEP reading and math scores show no consistent change in the achievement gap between black and Hispanic students and their white peers. For example, as figure 1 shows, the reading gap between white and black students was 0.73 standard deviation units in 1984: Twenty-four years later, in 1998, the gap was the same. The gap has both narrowed and widened over time, attesting to the reality of measurement error and differences among age cohorts, but currently it remains right where it was in 1984. Close reading of figure 1 will show that the achievement gap did narrow in the years immediately pre-

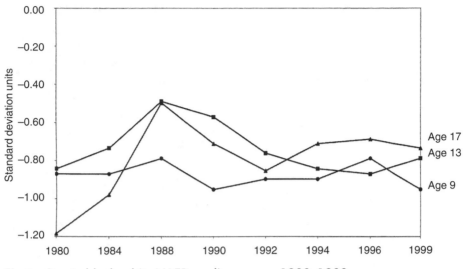

Fig 1. Gap in black-white NAEP reading scores, 1980–1999

ceding publication of *A Nation at Risk*, but that it has not narrowed since.

Figures 1 through 4 show that these generalizations hold for the gaps between white and black and white and Hispanic students, for most age groups and in both reading and mathematics. As of 1999, some relative gains are evident, notably for black and Hispanic seventeen-year-olds in reading. Whether these small gains will be sustained is difficult to predict. One might hope to predict gains by following particular age cohorts, reasoning that if scores for nine-year-olds in one testing rose, scores for thirteen-year-olds would rise four years later. However, scores on successive tests of particular cohorts appear to vary at random.

Similar patterns—small and and inconsistent gains, with no significant narrowing of the gap between poor and minority students—are also evident in norm-referenced tests administered by states and city school systems. Disadvantaged students in California are much less likely than well-off students to score at national norms (24 percent

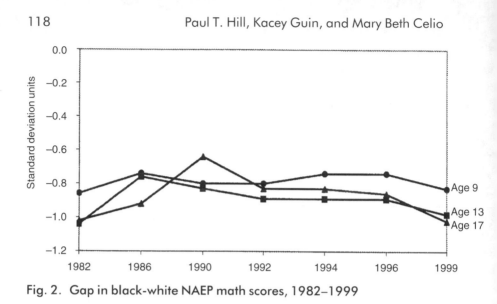

Fig. 2. Gap in black-white NAEP math scores, 1982–1999

versus 70 percent in fourth-grade reading). And a comparison of minority and majority students, not controlling for socioeconomic status, yielded similar results, 23 percent versus 63 percent.[11]

Gaps in State Standards-Based Tests

Critics of conventional norm-referenced tests hoped that state-specific standards-based tests would be more closely tied to school curriculum and therefore be less biased against children who have fewer opportunities for out-of-school learning. However, state standards-based testing reveals the same large gaps as do NAEP and other more conventional tests.

Statewide standards-based testing programs did not exist when *A Nation at Risk* was published, so there are no trend data from 1983. But current results show huge gaps between poor minority children and others. We focus on results from two states, Massachusetts and Washington, the first because detailed results are available in published form and the second because we have access to data that sup-

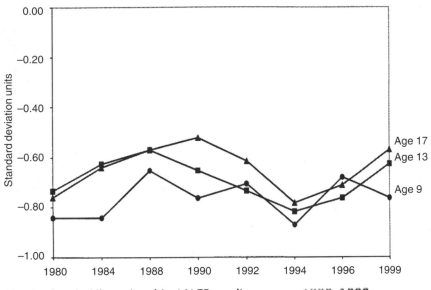

Fig. 3. Gap in Hispanic-white NAEP reading scores, 1980–1999

ports a unique form of analysis (reported below). Results from other states are likely to be similar.

Though each state designs its own tests, differences in composition do not lead to diverse results. White scores are uniformly higher; on most subjects and at most grade levels white and Asian students are roughly twice as likely as black and Hispanic students to meet standards. The pattern evident in national tests such as the SAT is evident in most states' standards-based tests: Average scores for white and minority students are between half and three-quarters of a standard deviation apart.

Massachusetts Results

As is typically the case in state standards-based tests, black fourth-graders taking the Massachusetts Comprehensive Assessment System (MCAS) are twice as likely as white students to have a failing score in reading and three times as likely to have a failing score in mathematics.

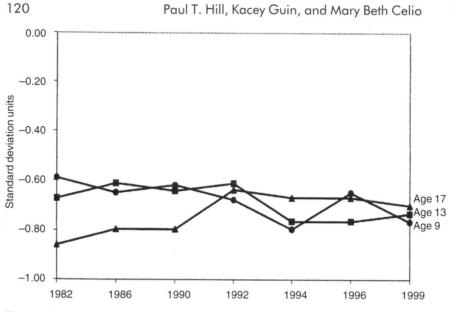

Fig. 4. Gap in Hispanic-white NAEP mathematics scores, 1982–1999

Tables 2 and 3 show the distribution of fourth-grade scores by students' race or ethnicity.[12]

Whether these score differences are important depends on the quality of the test and the true performance gap between categories such as those in tables 2 and 3—advanced, proficient, needs improvement, and failing. Tests like the MCAS have been given for only a few years, so it is impossible to say for sure whether assignment to different score categories leads to differences in outcomes such as high school completion, college attendance, or access to gainful employment. Moreover, every state creates its own categories, and some might be more predictive than others.

Washington Results

We conducted our own analysis of results from the Washington Assessment of Student Learning (WASL). These results suggest that gaps between white and minority performance on state tests might be even more significant than the bland category names might suggest.

Table 2. 2001 MCAS fourth-grade reading test:
Percentage of students at each performance level

	Advanced	Proficient	Needs improvement	Warning/failing
Black	1%	23%	52%	24%
Hispanic	1%	18%	50%	31%
White	5%	38%	45%	12%

As in other states, WASL results show that white students are twice as likely as black students to meet state standards in reading and slightly more than twice as likely to meet standards in mathematics.

As table 4 shows, the black-white test score gap ranges from one-half to a full standard deviation across grade levels in both math and reading. However, the gap is largest for students in urban schools.

Close analysis using relative distribution methods shows that even these clear disparities mask even more severe differences. For all grade levels and in both reading and math, black and Hispanic scores fall into the lowest ranges of white scores, and the concentration of minority scores in the lowest ranges of the distribution is significantly worse for minority students in urban schools.

Figure 5 shows the distribution of seventh-grade black, Hispanic, and white math and reading scores in urban schools in Washington. The straight line at 10 percent indicates that 10 percent of the white scores fall into each of the reference deciles. In contrast, more than 30 percent of black and Hispanic students in urban schools receive scores earned by only 10 percent of white students. Another 20 percent or more of minority students fall into the second-lowest 10 percent of white scores, so that half or more of minority students in urban schools in Washington receive math and reading scores that the lowest 20 percent of white students receive. Another way of saying all of this is that although the proportion of black and Hispanic students who fail to meet standards is only twice that of whites, the proportion of black

Table 3. 2001 MCAS fourth-grade math test:
Percentage of students at each performance level

	Advanced	Proficient	Needs improvement	Warning/failing
Black	1%	9%	50%	40%
Hispanic	2%	9%	45%	44%
White	13%	29%	46%	12%

and Hispanic students whose scores are in the lowest 10 percent is more than three times as great as for whites.

These results are especially significant because the bottom decile can include many extremely low scores: Students who answered many questions correctly (albeit far fewer than most children of their age) can fall into the bottom decile, along with students who could answer few or no items correctly. Thus, the gap in performance between a student who scored in the 1st percentile and one who scores in the 11th percentile can be far larger than the gap between students at the 11th and 21st percentiles. Based on the Washington analysis, there is reason to fear that simple comparisons of average scores for whites and minorities mask a troubling fact—that a third or more of minority students in urban schools perform at extremely low levels.

Among black students, those attending school in city districts are far more likely to cluster at the bottom of the distribution. This is true at all grade levels and for both math and reading. Figure 6 illustrates this pattern for seventh-graders taking the WASL. Although one-third of black seventh-graders in urban schools fall into the bottom 10 percent of white math scores, only 26 percent of black seventh-graders in nonurban schools do the same. More than 54 percent of black urban students fall into the bottom two deciles of the white scores, while the percentage of black nonurban students in these lowest deciles is 46 percent.

Another way of looking at the deficits in achievement that face minority students, particularly in urban schools, is displayed in figure

Table 4. The black-white achievement gap in Washington

	4TH-GRADERS		7TH-GRADERS		10TH-GRADERS	
	Math	*Reading*	*Math*	*Reading*	*Math*	*Reading*
Urban schools	0.75	0.63	0.86	0.73	0.95	0.85
All nonurban schools	0.62	0.53	0.66	0.55	0.74	0.59
Urban fringe	0.70	0.59	0.72	0.59	0.80	0.63
Town	0.40	0.29	0.56	0.55	0.84	0.65
Rural	0.42	0.36	0.46	0.31	0.60	0.48

Note: These figures represent the gap measured in standard deviations.

7. Here the changes in scale scores for seventh-graders from the first year of testing are compared for white, black, and Hispanic students. In general, improvements in math were proportionally greater than improvements in reading for all racial groups, but the rate of improvement needed to close the gap over the four-year period is at least three times greater than what was experienced.

Minority students in Washington have improved their average performance, but not at rates that would close the gap in the foreseeable future under present practices.

Real Outcomes

Aside from test scores, we tried to assess three other indicators that have profound implications for children's futures: the school dropout rate, the high school graduation rate, and the college enrollment rate. Compared with test scores obtained in a particular school year, each of these indicators is affected by many factors not controlled by school officials and more closely linked to a young person's ultimate ability to find productive and well-paid work.[13]

Dropout Rates

Students are less likely to abandon school definitively now than in 1983. Nationwide, dropout rates for white students have decreased

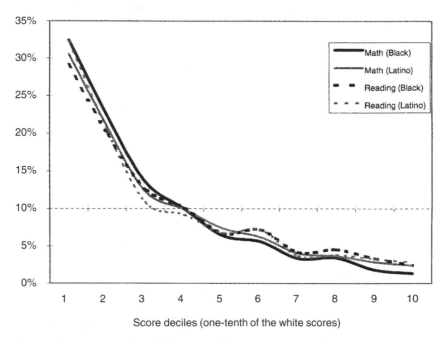

Fig. 5. Relative density of black and Hispanic versus white math and reading scores, urban schools (combined 7th-grade WASL, 1998–2001)

Note: In Washington, black and Hispanic students cluster in the bottom deciles of white scores.

from 11 percent to 7 percent, and for blacks, from 18 percent to 13 percent.[14] In 2000, the dropout rates for first- and second-generation Hispanic youth were only slightly higher than for blacks (15 percent and 16 percent respectively), but foreign-born Hispanic students dropped out at rate of 44 percent.[15]

The national averages, however, do not reflect the reality in large, predominately minority, urban school districts. In seventy-four urban districts studies by *Education Week*, less than 50 percent of the freshmen entering high school in 1990 graduated four years later.[16] A 2001 study found that more than 40 percent of all students in the Chicago public schools drop out by age 19.[17]

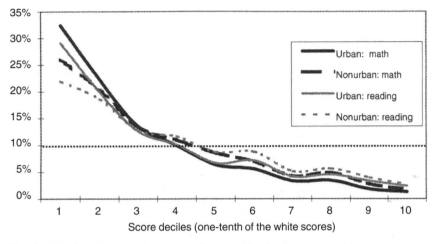

Fig. 6. **Black urban students are clustered in the lowest deciles**

Reforms arising out of *A Nation at Risk* were intended to decrease student academic failure, but in situations where standards are raised but instruction is not improved, they might, in fact, increase the dropout rate. Russell Rumberger suggests that some high schools might "push out" students expected to get low test scores.[18] Melissa Roderick and Eric Cambron have also shown that students drop out owing to fear of being unable to complete all required credits.[19] They suggest that large, impersonal high schools and poor elementary and middle school preparation lead to early failure in key courses and hence to dropping out.[20]

High School Graduation

According to the National Center for Educational Statistics (NCES), 77 percent of blacks aged eighteen to twenty-four completed high school in 1983. By 2000, that number had risen to 84 percent. For whites, the numbers were 87 percent and 92 percent respectively. For Hispanics, the number rose from 59 percent in 1983 to 64 percent in 2000.[21] (See chapter 2 by Paul Peterson for a more detailed discussion of overall graduation rates and how they are calculated.)

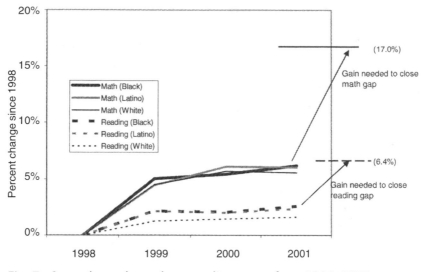

Fig. 7. Seventh-grade math vs. reading scores from 1998–2001

These figures are positive, but there is reason to question whether they represent educational progress or favorable methods of calculation. Many school districts calculate graduation rates based on a denominator that includes only students with whom they maintained contact through all four years of high school. The NCES counts as a high school graduate anyone eighteen to twenty-four years old who obtained a high school diploma or a General Educational Development certificate (GED).

In a recent study, J. P. Greene found that the national graduation rate for the class of 1998 was only 71 percent.[22] White students graduated at a rate of 78 percent, while the rates for black and Hispanic students were 56 percent and 54 percent, respectively.

Greene compared the number of eighth-grade students enrolled in the fall of 1993 with the number of high school diplomas awarded in the spring of 1998. Adjustments were made for varying enrollment numbers and student population increases during that period. GEDs were not included because of the overwhelming evidence that a GED is inferior to a high school diploma as a ticket to later earnings and higher education.[23]

According to Greene, seven states graduated less than 50 percent of their black students, while eight states graduated less than 50 percent of their Hispanic students. Among the nation's fifty largest school districts, sixteen districts have a graduation rate for their black students at or below 50 percent, with three districts graduating less than 40 percent (Cleveland, Milwaukee, and Memphis). Milwaukee graduates 34 percent of black students and 42 percent of Hispanic students, compared with 73 percent of its white students. For Hispanic students, only fifteen of the fifty largest school districts have a graduation rate above 50 percent, with six districts having a rate below 40 percent. Conversely, only five of the fifty largest school districts fail to graduate more than 50 percent of their white students.

College Enrollment and Completion

Minority students who successfully navigate their way through high school face additional challenges in entering and completing higher education. From 1983 to the present, the college attendance rate for blacks has remained constant, about 84 percent of the rate for whites. Between 1975 and 1998, the black-white gap in the four-year-college completion rate of twenty-five- to twenty-nine-year-olds with a high school diploma increased slightly, from about 13 percent to about 17 percent.[24] Similar to the increase in the dropout rate, this decline in the educational fortunes of poor and minority students could well be linked to initiatives inspired by A Nation at Risk—in this case, changes in university admission requirements that provide an edge to students who take advanced placement courses, which are offered less frequently in high schools serving minority students.[25]

In addition, those minority students who reach college often lack the academic preparation necessary to succeed in university-level courses. For first- or second-year undergraduate students in 1999–2000, 46 percent of blacks and 45 percent of Hispanics reported having taken at least one remedial course, compared with 32 percent of their white counterparts.[26] The quality of black students' high school preparation matters: For black students whose prior educational achievement was similar to whites, their college attendance rate equaled or exceeded that of white students across all years.

Well-prepared minority students are sought by colleges, and they do well, both in college and later. In their study on high school math curriculum, Heather Rose and Julian Betts found that minority students who take advanced math courses in high school obtain higher levels of education and earn significantly higher incomes than students who completed lower-level high school courses.[27] However, on average, black and Hispanic students are less likely than their white and Asian counterparts to take advanced math courses. This is owing in part to the low availability of such courses in the high schools minority students attend—and, in turn, to the low level of mathematics instruction in elementary and middle schools serving minority students.[28]

Why A *Nation at Risk* Reforms Missed the Point for Urban Poor Children

It is plausible to expect that tougher standards, more time for instruction, better teachers, and more accountability for leaders are all good for students and schools. But, in education at least, plausibility is a weak guide to action. Courses of action that sound reasonable can be ineffective because they ignore confounding factors. Thus, as the newspapers constantly document, outcome measurement and consequences for performance, plausible in themselves, can lead some schools to cheat on testing and some students to give up.

These facts do not argue against higher standards. Students need to know what the broader society expects, and they need to learn this while in school, not later when they try to get advanced training or find a good job. However, in places where schools lack capacity or are held firmly in place by arrangements made to protect adults, raised expectations alone do not lead to improved student performance.

The most important questions lie between the poles in the dispute about raised expectations: What is required to make higher standards influential in schools that have never met the lower standards, and what will it take to significantly improve academic performance for the most disadvantaged children?

The initiatives derived from A Nation at Risk did not answer these questions. They assumed that pressure would stimulate educators to work harder and to focus on skills instruction, leading to achievement gains. These assumptions ignored some critical facts about big-city public school districts, such as the following:

- Local school boards are political bodies pursuing many agendas, of which educational effectiveness is only one, and they are insulated from the performance pressures targeted at schools.

- School districts allow money and other resources to follow political influence, so that poor students end up receiving the least and worst of what is available.

- Teachers with experience, superior preparation, or other attributes that make them attractive to the "nicer" schools within a district can avoid working in schools that teach the most disadvantaged children.

Faced with the ineffectiveness of raised expectations in these cases, some disciples of A Nation at Risk have proposed additional measures, including sanctions against school districts in which the same schools fail year after year. The Bush administration's No Child Left Behind program, enacted in early 2002, threatens the withdrawal of federal funds unless districts improve failing schools or offer children in those schools choices, including the option to attend privately run schools. Opposition to No Child Left Behind is driven in part by fear that school districts cannot comply: They are frozen by local politics, state regulations, and union contracts.

Clearly, in our existing public education system, raised expectations are not sufficient to drive universal improvement. High expectations are necessary, as long as they reflect what children really need to know, not a utopian vision of what every child in a perfect world would know.[29] But the expectations need to be coupled with fundamental changes in the education system such as those described below.

An Open Entrepreneurial System

A common observation among social service workers and foundation heads is that big-city public school systems are the toughest and least malleable bureaucracies they deal with. Moreover, public education has little capacity to invest in new ideas. The vast preponderance of money in K–12 schools goes for salaries, and certification rules and union contract provisions control employment. Even when government increases education spending, unions make sure that most of it is used for salary increases. Though there are substantial amounts of funds for teacher in-service training, the money is separated into small pots controlled by different federal and state programs. When there are new investments—for example, California's recent major spending increase to reduce elementary school class size—they are targeted via political entrepreneurship and bargaining, not via competition over what works.

These facts make it difficult for new ideas and new people to penetrate public education. Public schools allow small-scale innovation by individual teachers, but these are usually limited to one classroom or school, leading to complaints among educators concerning the futility of random acts of innovation and the impossibility of scaling up good ideas. There is no mechanism for a promising idea to capture a wider market, and no incentive for other teachers or schools to adopt a promising idea.

Being an unfriendly environment for entrepreneurship hurts public education in two ways: First, it is not oriented to a continual search for better ways of serving students; second, it can seldom take full advantage of ideas and resources available in the broader society.

With respect to a search for better ways of providing instruction, big-city school systems are constrained by rules and individual ownership of jobs. Districts can do anything that their funders and regulators (including courts with which they have consent decrees) will permit. Unfortunately, in practice, the aggregate effect of these constraints is to make any action outside the status quo risky. Almost any reallocation of time, money, teachers, or students is likely to generate objections.[30] Teacher union contracts in most cities also prevent schools from choosing teachers and assume that a good "fit" does not matter: teachers are interchangeable and schools are created only by assembling standard parts. This attitude ignores the reality that schools with inferior or mismatched parts, such as less capable teachers, will likely produce inferior products (that is, low-achieving students).

With respect to use of ideas available in the broader society, public school systems limit the use of civic resources in the schools. Our cities are treasure houses filled with human talent and great institutions—museums, universities, orchestras, religious institutions, and foundations, all of them dedicated to learning. Unfortunately, the way we now run public education has kept these institutions on the sidelines. They can give money and moral support, but they cannot create or operate public schools, nor can their musicians, scientists, writers, and artists teach students, except before and after school hours or as volunteers.

This combination of inflexibility and distance from the rest of society gives many cities a much weaker and less effective public education system than they could have. Often, even school superintendents, generally cast as defenders of the systems they run, are candid about their school systems' inability to meet the needs of the most disadvantaged children. In interviews conducted by Paul Hill, big-city superintendents consistently say that making schools effective for poor minority children will require reallocating money and personnel.[31] They dreamed of creating all-literacy primary schools, reading-focused preschools for poor children only, ungraded primary schools to eliminate the stigma of children being held back, back-to-basics and charter schools, longer school years for disadvantaged students, and even boarding schools for children in abusive or dangerous homes. Rather than relying on learning goals or professional development—stock solutions that do not perturb the current system—these superintendents talked tough about reading, longer school days, and giving the most at-risk kids extra time. For them, control of money is the core issue: "You need to be able to change how every dollar is spent," said one. "You have to try to get hold of the central office. This requires getting hold of the money it now controls."

Making Sure Poor Children Get the Benefit of Public Expenditures

The high negative correlation between poverty and student achievement is well-known. Less well-known is that the schools serving the poor get less money, even within districts. In a pathbreaking analysis of real-dollar funding levels in a sample of big-city districts, Marguerite Roza and Karen Hawley Miles found that per-pupil funding in schools can vary by as much as a factor of three and that elementary schools in low-income areas receive between 10 percent and 30 percent fewer dollars per pupil than higher-income schools in the same districts.[32] These differences are offset slightly by funds from state and federal programs targeted to the poor, but at best these funds equalize spending rather than, as advertised, support higher per-pupil spending for children considered the most difficult to educate.

Quality Teachers in Low-Income Schools

In cities, the schools serving low-income black and Hispanic children also employ the least experienced teachers and experience the highest rate of teacher turnover.[33] Under union contracts, teachers with even one or two years' experience have some say over where they teach, and the vast majority of teachers with any choice avoid the most challenging schools. As Marguerite Roza has found in several large school districts in the West, schools in wealthier neighborhoods may receive more than a hundred applications for a teacher vacancy while schools in poor neighborhoods might receive only two or three. For schools serving the poorest children, this means three things: They have almost no choice of whom they employ; they always employ green teachers and those who have no alternative; and they open every fall with a group of teachers who have never worked together.

Union leaders argue that teacher performance is not correlated with pay, and they are right, at least in big cities. Because teachers are tenured and promoted automatically, raises come to anyone whose performance is not grossly deficient. Schools are prevented from paying more for the best teachers and less for poorly prepared teachers and individuals who have not proven themselves. Schools pay the same high salaries for experienced teachers who are "stars" as for those who have burned out, and cannot pay more for brilliant young teachers than for marginal ones. Thus, the consistent finding of no correlation between teacher salaries and productivity could be an artifact of the rules under which teachers are now paid and assigned to schools.

If there were a true teacher labor market, in which teachers were paid on the basis of their reputations for productivity, would there be a correlation between pay and performance? One way to explore this question is to take advantage of one marketlike feature of the teacher allocation process, the fact that teachers with even a little seniority can choose which school vacancies to apply for. Because highly paid senior teachers claim vacancies in the schools that are considered to have the best working environments, other schools are forced to hire mainly younger and lower-paid teachers. As a result, there is significant within-district variation in schools' average teacher salaries.

As Marguerite Roza has argued, schoolwide average teacher salaries might be correlated with performance even if individual teacher salaries are not. In preparation for this essay, Robin Lake and Kacey Guin made a preliminary test of this hypothesis on data from Seattle. Even controlling for students' socioeconomic status, they found a positive correlation between schoolwide average salary and student test scores. For every dollar increase in average teacher salary, the percentage of students reaching "standard" increased by 0.0014 percent.[34] This means that for every $5,000 increase in schoolwide average teacher salary, the percentage of students reaching standard would increase by 7 percent.

Though A Nation at Risk prescribed more rigorous teacher training and licensing, it said nothing about changing the distribution of teachers, to reverse the pattern of more demanding schools' having the weakest teaching forces. In fact, as states have raised their teacher certification standards, the concentration of poorly prepared teachers in high-poverty schools has grown. This is not because there is an absolute shortage of teachers: the numbers of experienced, certified teachers of working age who are not teaching far exceeds the number of unqualified teachers high-poverty schools employ. It is because qualified teachers have other alternatives—nicer schools, central offices, lines of work other than teaching, and early retirement.

The consequences for the education of the poorest children are dire. Their schools experience the highest rate of teacher turnover, ensuring that whatever teachers learn on the job will move elsewhere with them. Schools that consistently lose in the market for experienced teachers often have annual teacher turnover rates above 50 percent. Such schools are turbulent and difficult to lead. They are also impenetrable for parents, who cannot build stable and mutually confident working relationships with teachers and principals. A *Nation at Risk*'s preoccupation with credentialing and licensing of teachers does not touch this problem. In the absence of financial incentives to attract teachers and without freedom from regulation to allow improvements in working conditions, the poorest schools will always get the teachers with the fewest options and lose those teachers as soon as they gain seniority.

Conclusion

Raised expectations have their place, but they are not enough for the poorest children in the poorest schools. A *Nation at Risk* did not perturb the system of constraints and incentives that lead big-city school districts to tolerate disastrously low-performing schools. Schools that are well staffed and enjoy the support of parents and local school officials can adapt to performance pressure. But schools that get the worst of everything and are frozen in place by rules and contract provisions cannot transform themselves. State and local superintendents and board members know this: that is why they think it is unfair to demand more of the schools serving the most disadvantaged children.

There might be some slackers in public education, but lack of effort is not the greatest barrier to improvement of urban schools. False certainty—the belief that a school board or the educational bureaucracy can mandate the best methods of instruction and the most effective uses of time and money—is the greatest barrier.

Schools and school districts need to become problem-solving organizations whose job is to find the best possible way to educate the children entrusted to them. Schools need to have the entrepreneurial freedom to find the best combination of people and technologies for the children they serve. Parents and taxpayers need to know exactly how individual schools and districts are performing, and they need to have the power to move children from stagnant schools to better ones.

Low-performing schools need investments in order to attract excellent people and to replace ineffective methods with effective ones. Finally, teachers and administrators need to join other Americans, gaining benefits—pay and job security—from good performance and putting those benefits at risk when performance is lacking.

High expectations are necessary, and fine as far as they go. But in the absence of accountability, choice, and transparency, high expectations have largely become unfulfilled hopes.

As the members of the Koret Task Force have argued, progress requires accountability, choice, and transparency. Together these features add up to honest engagement of difficult problems and open acknowledgment of uncertainty. Improvement in big city schools requires imagination, talent, money, and time, all disciplined by a system that rewards success and creates alternatives to failure.

Notes

1. U.S. Department of Commerce, Bureau of the Census, *Current Population Surveys, October Supplement* (Washington, D.C., 1972–99). http://nces.ed.gov/programs/coe/2001/section1/tables/t03_1.html.
2. Council of Great City Schools.
3. "Quality Counts 1998: The Urban Challenge," *Education Week* 17, January 8, 1998, 15.
4. R. J. Coley, *An Uneven Start: Indicators of Inequality in School Readiness*, Policy Information Center (Princeton, N.J.: Educational Testing Service, 2002).
5. J. West, K. Denton, and L. M. Reaney, *The Kindergarten Year: Findings from the Early Childhood Longitudinal Study, Kindergarten Class of 1998–99* (Washington, D.C.: U.S. Department of Education, National Center for Education Statistics, 2001).
6. Denton West and E. Germino Hausken, *America's Kindergarteners: Early Childhood Longitudinal Study, Kindergarten Class of 1998–99, Fall 1998* (Washington, D.C.: U.S. Department of Education, National Center for Education Statistics, 2000).
7. For a thorough review of the forces at work creating the race- and class-

achievement gaps, see Christopher Jencks and Meredith Phillips's final chapter in *The Black-White Test Score Gap*, ed. C. Jencks and M. Phillips (Washington D.C.: Brookings Institution Press, 1998).

8. M. Phillips, J. Crouse, and J. Ralph, "Does the Black-White Test Score Gap Widen after Children Enter School?" in Jencks and Phillips, eds., *The Black-White Test Score Gap*.

9. National Assessment of Educational Progress (NAEP), *Mathematics Assessment* (Washington, D.C.: U.S. Department of Education, National Center for Education Statistics, 1999–2000).

10. Emiliana Vegas, Richard J. Murnane, and John B. Willett, "From High School to Teaching: Many Steps, Who Makes It?" *Teachers College-Record* 103, no. 3 (June 2001): 427–49.

11. Julian R. Betts, Kim S. Rueben, and Anne Danenberg, *Equal Resources, Equal Outcomes? The Distribution of School Resources and Student Achievement in California* (San Francisco: Public Policy Institute of California, 2000), chap. 7.

12. "State Results by Race/Ethnicity and Student Status," *Spring 2001 MCAS Tests: Summary of State Results*, Massachusetts Department of Education, October 2001. http://www.doe.mass.edu/mcas/results.html.

13. Lawrence Steinberg, Bradford Brown, and Sanford M. Dornbusch, *Beyond the Classroom: Why School Reform Has Failed and What Parents Need to Do* (New York: Simon & Schuster, 1996).

14. Phillip Kaufman, Martha N. Alt, and Christopher D. Chapman, *Dropout Rates in the United States: 2000* (Washington, D.C.: U.S. Department of Education, National Center for Education Statistics, 2001).

15. Kaufman, Alt, and Chapman, *Dropout Rates*, 15.

16. "Quality Counts 1998: The Urban Challenge," *Education Week* 17, January 8, 1998, 13.

17. Elaine Allensworth and John Q. Easton, *Calculating a Cohort Dropout Rate for the Chicago Public Schools* (Chicago: Consortium on Chicago School Research, 2001).

18. Russell W. Rumberger, "Why Students Drop Out of School and What Can Be Done," paper prepared for the conference "Dropouts in America: How Severe Is the Problem? What Do We Know about Intervention and Prevention," Harvard University, January 13, 2001.

19. M. Roderick and E. Camburn, E., "Risk and Recovery from Course

Failure in the Early Years of High School," *American Educational Research Journal* 36, no. 2 (1999): 303–43.

20. See also D. Lillard and P. DeCicca, "Higher Standards, More Dropouts? Evidence Within and Across Time," *Economics of Education Review* 20, no. 5 (2001), who estimate that increasing state course graduation requirements by one standard deviation could result in 3 to 7 percent increase in dropout rates.

21. Kaufman, Alt, and Chapman, *Dropout Rates*, 39.

22. J. P. Greene, *High School Graduation Rates in the United States*, revised April 2002 (New York: Manhattan Institute, 2001).

23. See R. J. Murnane, J. B. Willett, and J. H. Tyler, *Who Benefits from Obtaining a GED? Evidence from High School and Beyond*, Working Paper No. w7172 (Cambridge, Mass.: National Bureau of Economic Research, 1999). They find that dropouts who leave school with weak cognitive skills ultimately earn more if they complete a GED than if they do not; but these gains are small relative to the value of a high school diploma.

24. Jonathan Jacobson, Cara Olsen, Jennifer King Rice, Stephen Sweetland, and John Ralph, *Education Achievement and Black-White Inequality* (Washington, D.C.: U.S. Department of Education, National Center for Education Statistics, 2001), 5.

25. S. Hebel, "A.P. Courses Are New Target in Struggle over Access to College in California," *Chronicle of Higher Education*, November 26, 1999; J. Oakes, J. Rogers, P. McDonough, D. Solorzano, H. Mehan, and P. Noguera, "Remedying Unequal Opportunities for Successful Participation in Advanced Placement Courses in California High Schools: A Proposed Action Plan," an expert report submitted on behalf of the defendants and the American Civil Liberties Union in the case of Daniel v. the State of California, January 2000.

26. National Center for Education Statistics. http://nces.ed.gov/surveys/npsas/table_library/tables/npsas50.asp.

27. See, for example, Heather Rose and Julian R. Betts, *Math Matters: The Links Between High School Curriculum, College Graduation and Earnings* (San Francisco: Public Policy Institute of California, 2001).

28. Betts, Rueben, and Danenberg, *Equal Resources, Equal Outcomes?*

29. For an analysis of the critical difference between aspirational and empirically grounded standards, see Paul T. Hill and Robin J. Lake, "Standards and Accountability in Washington State," in *Brookings Papers on Edu-*

cation Policy 2002, ed. Diane Ravitch (Washington, D.C.: Brookings Institution Press, 2002).

30. On how state regulations rule out most plausible approaches to reform of big school districts, see David Menefee-Libey and Charles Taylor Kerchner, "Making Sense of School Reform Politics: An Updated Framework Applied to the Los Angeles Case," prepared for the 2002 annual meeting of the American Educational Research Association, New Orleans, April 2002.

31. See Paul T. Hill and James Harvey, "Superintendents' 'Coach Speak' Is Misleading," *Education Week*, April 2002.

32. See Marguerite Roza and Karen Hawley Miles, *A New Look at Inequities in School Funding: A Presentation on the Resource Variations within Districts* (Seattle: University of Washington, Center on Reinventing Public Education, 2002).

33. See, for example, Betts, Rueben, and Danenberg, *Equal Resources, Equal Outcomes?* chap. 4. By their estimate, low-SES elementary teachers have 29 percent more inexperienced teachers than high-SES schools. See also Stephen J. Carroll, *The Distribution of Teachers among California's School Districts and Schools* (MR-1298.0-JIF) (Santa Monica, Calif.: RAND Corp., 2000).

34. Robin Lake and Kacey Guin, *Do School-Level Characteristics Influence Student Performance? A Study of Seattle Public Schools* (Seattle: University of Washington, Center on Reinventing Public Education, 2002).

5

The Importance
of School
Quality

Eric A. Hanushek

The ideas ventured by *A Nation at Risk*, though prescient in many respects, have distorted the nation's understanding of the relationship between education and the economy for two decades now. Written during a recession, *A Nation at Risk* implied that the general state of the economy could be directly traced to the current performance of a nation's education system. The economic trends of the eighties and early nineties reinforced this interpretation. When the economies of Japan, Korea, Thailand, and other East Asian countries were growing at rates so fast that they were predicted to surpass the U.S. economy within short periods of time, the education system was often blamed for the nation's seeming loss of competitive advantage. Once the tide turned, with the United States experiencing a long burst of growth

Helpful comments were provided by Caroline Hoxby, Lance Lochner, Paul Peterson, and Macke Raymond. This work was supported by funding from the Packard Humanities Institute.

and innovation for most of the nineties while the East Asian "miracle" evaporated, the rhetorical environment was ripe for a turning of the tables. Observers who never bought *A Nation at Risk*'s thesis of mediocrity and stagnation in the nation's schools were quick to cite the nation's economic performance as evidence of a high-performing education system.

Consider Alfie Kohn, a prominent critic of academic standards and testing, who wrote in 2000:

> As proof of the inadequacy of U.S. schools, many writers and public officials pointed to the sputtering condition of the U.S. economy. As far as I know, none of them subsequently apologized for offering a mistaken and unfair attack on our educational system once the economy recovered, nor did anyone credit teachers for the turn-around.[1]

Another prominent defender of the school system, Gerald Bracey, took the argument one step further. Noting that a variety of people from before and after *A Nation at Risk* had argued for improving schools in order to maintain U.S. economic strength, he wrote, "None of these fine gentlemen provided any data on the relationship between the economy's health and the performance of schools. Our long economic boom suggests there isn't one—or that our schools are better than the critics claim."[2]

The fact is that the supporters and the critics of *A Nation at Risk* have woefully misinterpreted the economic trends. They have been all too eager to jump on almost any economic news and to link it to today's schools. Any pattern of bad economic results demonstrates to some that the education system is broken, while to others any good news confirms the superiority of U.S. schools. What this perspective fails to do is to distinguish between short-term swings in the business cycle and long-term trends in economic growth. It also ignores other factors that might affect both current economic conditions and overall patterns of economic growth and development. That the Japanese economy is in recession while the U.S. economy booms in any particular year says virtually nothing about the relative quality of schools in the different countries. It might instead say something about the quality of their governments' current fiscal and monetary policies. It might even bear some relationship to the skills workers learned in past decades—when the full spectrum of the labor force was attending school. But it can't tell us anything about the quality of the instruction that this year's tenth-grade class is receiving.

By contrast, an economy's ability to grow over time—its ability to innovate and to raise both productivity and real incomes—is at least in part a function of the quality of its education system. Research shows that the skills possessed by workers, while not the only input, are an increasingly important factor in economic growth. The increased importance of skills appears in its effects on the earnings of individuals and on the subsequent distribution of income in the economy. Moreover, the education system is central to the development of skills, a fact long recognized by parents, policy makers, and educators. In the past century, the United States led the world in the expansion of its education system. This expansion has contributed to the pre-eminent position of the U.S. economy in the world. Nonetheless, concerns exist about the future. There is little evidence that the K–12 education system in the United States is in fact competitive in the world economy or that it can be counted on to fuel future U.S. economic growth. These are matters that should be taken very seriously.

The fact that other aspects of the U.S. economy are sufficient to compensate for the mediocre quality of its schools should not be taken as justification for allowing the current state to continue. The quality of schooling has a clear impact on both individual earnings and the growth of the overall economy, and the available evidence suggests that improvements in the schools would translate into substantial long-run gains.

Had we undertaken policies after A *Nation at Risk* that truly reformed our schools, we could today be enjoying substantially higher national income. Indeed, direct estimates of the lost opportunities suggest that we could today pay for the entire budget for K-12 education from the dividends of effective reform.

Education and Human Capital

Economists have devoted considerable attention to understanding how "human capital" affects a variety of economic outcomes. The underlying notion is that individuals make investment decisions in themselves through schooling and other routes. The accumulated skills that are relevant for the labor market from these investments over time represent the human capital of an individual. The investments made to improve skills then return future economic benefits in much the same way that a firm's investing in a set of machines (physical capital) returns future production and income. In the case of public education, parents and public officials act as trustees for their children in setting many aspects of the investment paths.

In looking at human capital and its implications for future outcomes, economists are frequently agnostic about where these skills come from or how they are produced. Although we return to that below, it is commonly presumed that formal schooling is one of several important contributors to the skills of an individual and to human capital. It is not the only factor. Parents, individual abilities, and friends undoubtedly contribute. Schools nonetheless have a special place because they are most directly affected by public policies. For this reason, we frequently emphasize the role of schools.

The human capital perspective immediately makes it evident that the real issues are ones of long-run outcomes. Future incomes of individuals are related to their past investments. It is not their income while in school or their income in their first job. Instead, it is their income over the course of their working life.

The distribution of income in the economy similarly involves both the mixture of people in the economy and the pattern of their incomes over their lifetime. Specifically, most measures of how income and well-being vary in the population do not take into account the fact that some of the low-income people have low incomes only because they are just beginning a career. Their lifetime income is likely to be much larger as they age, gain experience, and move up in their firms and career. What is important is that any noticeable effects of the current quality of schooling on the distribution of skills and income will only be realized years in the future, when those currently in school become a significant part of the labor force. In other words, most workers in the economy were educated years and even decades in the past—and they are the ones that have the most impact on current levels of productivity and growth, if for no reason other than that they represent the larger share of active workers.

Much of the early development of empirical work on human capital rightfully concentrated on the role of school attainment, that is, the quantity of schooling. This focus was natural. The revolution in the United States during the twentieth century was universal schooling. Moreover, quantity of schooling is easily measured, and data on years attained, both over time and across individuals, are readily available. Today, however, policy concerns revolve much more around issues of quality than issues of quantity. The completion rates for high school and college have been roughly constant for a quarter of a century. Meanwhile, the standards movement has focused on what students know as they progress through schools and the knowledge and skills of graduates. It is these attributes that matter in discussions of economic growth.

Individual Productivity and Incomes

It is useful to establish some facts about the value of "quality." One of the challenges in understanding the impact of quality differences in human capital has been simply knowing how to measure quality.

Much of the discussion of quality—in part related to new efforts to provide better accountability—has identified cognitive skills as the important dimension. And, while there is ongoing debate about the testing and measurement of these skills, most parents and policy makers alike accept the notion that cognitive skills are a key dimension of schooling outcomes. The question is whether this proxy for school quality—students' performance on standardized tests—is correlated with individuals' performance in the labor market and the economy's ability to grow. Until recently, little comprehensive data have been available to show any relationship between differences in cognitive skills and any related economic outcomes. Such data are now becoming available, so that some of the fundamental questions about quality measurement can be addressed.

There is mounting evidence that quality—generally measured by test scores—is positively related to individual earnings, productivity, and economic growth. While focusing on the estimated returns to years of schooling, early studies of wage determination tended to indicate relatively modest impacts of variations in cognitive ability after holding constant quantity of schooling. More recent direct investigations of cognitive achievement, however, have suggested generally larger labor market returns to measured individual differences in cognitive achievement. A variety of researchers document that the earnings advantages to higher achievement on standardized tests are quite substantial.[3] While these analyses emphasize different aspects of individual earnings, they typically find that measured achievement has a direct impact on earnings after allowing for differences in the quantity of schooling, the experiences of workers, and other factors that might also influence earnings. In other words, higher quality as measured by tests similar to those currently being used in accountability systems around the country is closely related to individual productivity and earnings.

Much of the work by economists on differences in worker skills has actually been directed at the issue of determining the average labor market returns to additional schooling. The argument has been that higher-ability students are more likely to continue in schooling. Therefore, part of the higher earnings observed for those with additional schooling really reflects pay for added ability and not for the additional schooling. Economists have pursued a variety of analytical approaches for dealing with this, including adjusting for measured cognitive test scores, but this work generally ignores issues of variation in school quality.[4]

An additional part of the return to school quality does come through continuation in school. There is substantial U.S. evidence that students who do better in school, either through grades or scores on standardized achievement tests, tend to go farther in school.[5] Each of the available investigations highlights the independent role of achievement in affecting the schooling choices and investment decisions of individuals.

This work has not, however, investigated how achievement affects the ultimate outcomes of higher education. For example, if over time lower-achieving students tend increasingly to attend college, colleges may be forced to offer more remedial courses, and the variation of what students know and can do at the end of college may expand commensurately. This possibility, suggested in A Nation at Risk, has not been investigated, but may fit into considerations of the widening of the distribution of income.

The role of schooling and human capital in altering the distribution of incomes in society has received considerable separate attention. The idea of relating distributional outcomes to school quality was a key element of the War on Poverty. It was hoped that through schooling family poverty would not be transferred to the next generation— specifically, that high-quality school investments could overcome deficits originating in the home. Researchers have focused on skill differences as being important in, for example, explaining the patterns of black-white earnings differences or the expansion of earnings differences among people with the same levels of schooling.[6] These analyses have emphasized the growing rewards to skills and have developed the implications of this for wage inequality. Owing to lack of sufficient data over time, they have mostly not looked directly at measured cognitive skills.[7] Nonetheless, building on the findings about individual earnings, it is reasonable to conclude that variations in cognitive skills have a direct impact on variations in the distribution of incomes. As suggested above, variations in the skills of those with similar amounts of schooling—say, completing four years of college—may actually be growing over time and may reinforce income differences that come from increased rewards to skills.

This discussion has concentrated on the importance of skill differences, particularly those measured by tests of cognitive knowledge. As such data have become available, research has underscored the importance of skills in determining economic outcomes for individuals. Thus, for the individual, research offers a clear answer to a fundamental question that has recently been voiced: Do differences in observed and measured achievement matter? Yes!

Economic Growth

The relationship between measured labor force quality and economic growth is perhaps even more important than the impact of human capital and school quality on individual productivity and incomes. Economic growth determines how much improvement will occur in the overall standard of living of society. Moreover, the education of each individual has the possibility of making others better off (in addition to the individual benefits just discussed). Specifically, a more educated society may lead to higher rates of invention; may make everybody more productive through the ability of firms to introduce new and better production methods; and may lead to more rapid introduction of new technologies. These "externalities"—influences on others of individual education outcomes—provide extra reason for being concerned about the quality of schooling. Because this is so important and because it has received little attention, we give this feature of the economy the most attention here.

The current economic position of the United States is largely the result of its strong and steady growth over the twentieth century. Strangely, over much of the period after World War II, economists did not pay as much attention to economic growth as they did to macroeconomic fluctuations. In the past fifteen years, economists have returned to questions of economic growth. While a variety of models and ideas have been developed to explain differences in growth rates across countries, they invariably include (but are not limited to) the importance of human capital.[8]

The empirical work supporting growth analyses has emphasized school attainment differences across countries. Again, this is natural because, while compiling comparable data on many things for different countries is difficult, assessing quantity of schooling is more straightforward.

The typical study finds that quantity of schooling is highly related to economic growth rates. But, again, quantity of schooling is a very crude measure of the knowledge and cognitive skills of people. Few people would be willing to assume the amount learned during the sixth grade in a rural hut in a developing country equals that learned in an American sixth grade. Yet that is what is implicitly assumed when empirical analyses focus exclusively on differences in average years of schooling across countries.

Recent work by Dennis Kimko and me goes beyond that and delves into quality of schooling.[9] We incorporate the information about international differences in mathematics and science knowledge that has been developed through testing over the past four decades. And we find a remarkable impact of differences in school quality on economic growth.

In 1963 and 1964, the International Association for the Evaluation of Educational Achievement (IEA) administered the first of a series of mathematics tests to a voluntary group of countries. These assessments were subject to a variety of problems, including: issues of developing an equivalent test across countries with different school structure, curricula, and language; issues of selectivity of the tested populations; and issues of selectivity of the nations that participated. The first tests did not document or even address these issues in any depth. These tests did, however, prove the feasibility of such testing and set in motion a process to expand and improve on the undertaking.

Subsequent testing, sponsored by the IEA and others, has included both math and science and has expanded on the group of countries that have been tested. In each, the general model has been to develop a common assessment instrument for different age groups of students and to work at obtaining a representative group of students taking the tests. An easy summary of the participating countries and their test performance is found in figure 1. This figure tracks performance aggregated across the age groups and subject area of the various tests and scaled to a common test mean of 50.[10] The United States and the United Kingdom are the only countries to participate in all of the testing. There is some movement across time of country performance on the tests, but for the one country that can be checked—the United States—the pattern is consistent with other data. The National Assessment of Educational Progress (NAEP) in the United States is designed to follow performance of U.S. students for different subjects and ages. NAEP performance over this period shows a sizable dip in the seventies, a period of growth in the eighties, and a leveling off in the nineties. This pattern on the NAEP (see figure 3 in chapter 2 by Paul Peterson) closely matches the international results and provides support for the validity of the international tests.[11]

Our analysis is very straightforward. We combine all of the available earlier test scores into a single composite measure of quality and consider statistical models that explain differences in growth rates across nations during the period 1960 to 1990.[12] The basic statistical models, which include the initial level of income, the quantity of

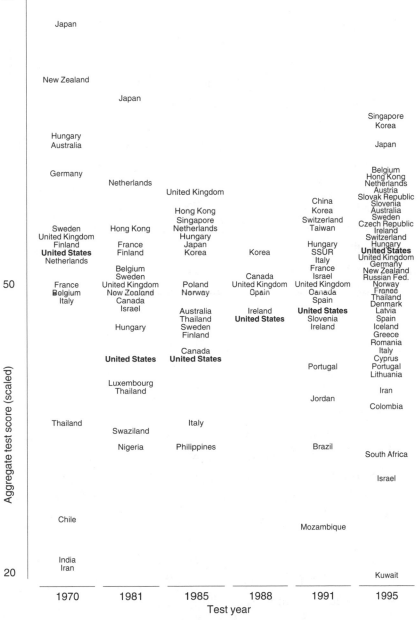

Fig. 1. Normalized test scores on mathematics and science examinations, 1970–1995

Note: Country positions are relative and approximate.

schooling, and population growth rates, explain a substantial portion of the variation in economic growth across countries.

Most important, the quality of the labor force as measured by math and science scores is extremely important. One standard deviation difference on test performance is related to 1 percent difference in annual growth rates of gross domestic product (GDP) per capita. Moreover, adding other factors potentially related to growth, including aspects of international trade, private and public investment, and political instability, leaves the effects of labor force quality unchanged.

As shown in figure 2, the implications of such a difference in growth rates are very large. The figure begins with the value of per capita GDP for the United States in 2000 and projects its value in 2050 under different growth rates. If the economy grows at 1 percent each year, this measure of U.S. income would increase from $34,950 to $57,480—or more than a 50 percent increase over the period. If it were to grow at 2 percent per year, it would reach $94,000 in 2050. Small differences in growth rates have huge implications for the income and wealth of society. One percent per year higher growth—say, 2 percent versus 1 percent—over a 50-year period yields incomes that are 64 percent higher!

One common concern in analysis such as this is that schooling might not be the actual cause of growth but, in fact, may just reflect other attributes of the economy that are beneficial to growth. For example, as seen in figure 1, the East Asian countries consistently score very highly on the international tests, and they also had extraordinarily high growth over the 1960–1990 period. It may be that other aspects of these East Asian economies have driven their growth and that the statistical analysis of labor force quality simply is picking out these countries. But in fact, even if the East Asian countries are excluded from the analysis, a strong—albeit slightly smaller—relationship is still observed with test performance. This test of sensitivity of the results seems to reflect a basic importance of school quality, a

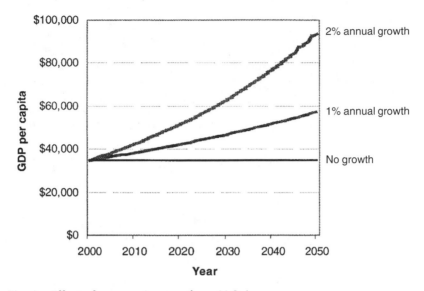

Fig. 2. Effect of economic growth on U.S. income

factor that contributes also to the observed growth of East Asian countries.

Another concern might be that other factors that affect growth, such as efficient market organizations, are also associated with efficient and productive schools—so that, again, the test measures are really a proxy for other attributes of the country. In order to investigate this, we concentrate on immigrants to the United States who received their education in their home countries. We find that immigrants who were schooled in countries that have higher scores on the international math and science examinations earn more in the United States. This analysis makes allowance for any differences in school attainment, labor market experience, or being native English-language speakers. In other words, skill differences as measured by the international tests are clearly rewarded in the United States labor market, reinforcing the validity of the tests as a measure of individual skills and productivity.

Finally, the observed relationships could simply reflect reverse causality, that is, that countries that are growing rapidly have the resources necessary to improve their schools and that better student performance is the result of growth, not the cause of growth. As a simple test of this, we investigated whether the international math and science test scores were systematically related to the resources devoted to the schools in the years prior to the tests. They were not. If anything, we found relatively better performance in those countries spending less on their schools.

In sum, the relationship between math and science skills on the one hand and productivity and growth on the other comes through clearly when investigated in a systematic manner across countries. This finding underscores the importance of high-quality schooling and leads to a more detailed consideration of the growth of the U.S. economy.

Why Has U.S. Growth Been So Strong?

We started this discussion by recounting America's successful economic growth during the twentieth century. Yet, looking at figure 1, we see that the United States has been at best mediocre in mathematics and science ability. Regardless of the set of countries taking the test, the United States has performed in the middle of the pack or below. Some people find this anomalous. How could math and science ability be important in light of the strong U.S. growth over a long period of time?

The answer is that quality of the labor force is just one aspect of the economy that enters into the determination of growth. A variety of factors clearly contribute, and these factors work to overcome any deficits in quality. These other factors may also be necessary for growth. In other words, simply providing more or higher-quality schooling may yield little in the way of economic growth in the absence of other elements, such as the appropriate market, legal, and governmental institutions to support a functioning modern economy. Past experiences investing in less developed countries that lack these institutional features demonstrates that schooling is not itself a sufficient engine of growth.

Nonetheless, the fact that economic growth has been strong in America is no reason to ignore issues of school quality. Better schools would, by the available evidence, reinforce and amplify the other advantages that have supported the strong and consistent growth of the U.S. economy.

This section describes some of the other contributing factors. It does this in part to understand more fully the character of economic growth, but, more important, to highlight some issues that are central to thinking about future policies.

Economic Structure

Almost certainly the most important factor sustaining the growth of the U.S. economy is the openness and fluidity of its markets. The United States maintains generally freer labor and product markets than most countries in the world. The government generally has less regulation on firms (both in terms of labor regulations and in terms of overall production), and trade unions are less extensive than those in many other countries. Even broader, the United States has less intrusion of government in the operation of the economy—not only less regulation but also lower tax rates and minimal government production through nationalized industries. These factors encourage investment, permit the rapid development of new products and activities by firms, and allow U.S. workers to adjust to new opportunities. While identifying the precise importance of these factors is difficult, a variety of analyses suggests that such market differences could be very important explanations for differences in growth rates.[13]

Because of the generally favorable institutional conditions, U.S. growth has been strong, even if some of the underlying factors are not as competitive. In other words, the economic structure can mask problems within the economy. But this does not negate the fact that improving our schools and the quality of our labor force would enhance growth and incomes.

Substitution of Quantity for Quality

Over the twentieth century, the expansion of the education system in the United States outpaced that around the world. The United States pushed to open secondary schools to all citizens. With this also came a move to expand higher education with the development of land grant universities, the G.I. bill, and direct grants and loans to students. In comparison with other nations of the world, the U.S. labor force has been better educated, even after allowing for the lesser achievement of its graduates. In other words, more schooling with less learning each year has yielded more human capital than found in other nations that have less schooling but learn more in each of those years.

This historical approach, however, appears on the verge of reaching its limits. Other nations of the world, both developed and developing, have rapidly expanded their schooling systems, and many now surpass the United States. Figure 3 shows secondary school completion rates for both Organization for Economic Cooperation and Development (OECD) countries and a selection of others in 1999.[14] Remarkably, the United States trailed a large number of other countries in 1999 and falls just slightly below the OECD average completion rate. The United States gains some by having rates of college attendance above the typical OECD country. Nonetheless, as summarized in figure 4, U.S. students are not likely to complete more schooling than those in a significant number of other developed and developing countries.

The past advantage of the United States in amount of school completed has gone away as other nations have discovered the importance of schooling. Thus, going into the future, the United States appears unlikely to continue dominating others in human capital unless it can improve on the quality dimension.

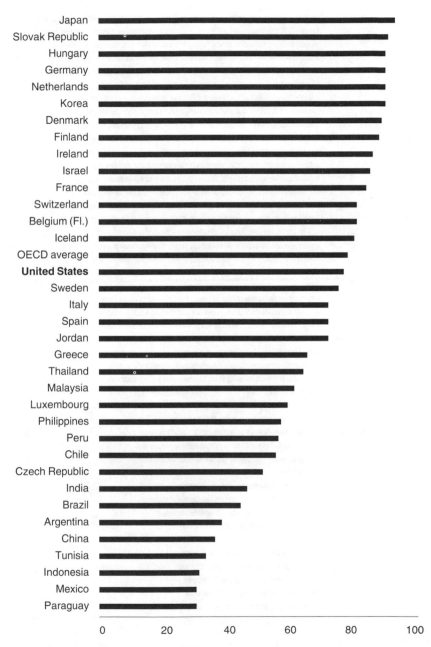

Fig. 3. Secondary school completion rates, 1999

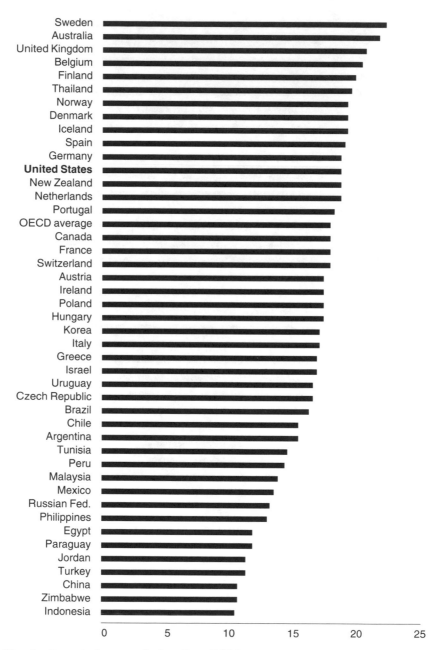

Fig. 4. Expected years of schooling, 1999

Quality of U.S. Colleges

The analysis of growth rates across countries emphasizes quality of the elementary and secondary schools of the United States. It did not include any measures of the quality of U.S. colleges. By most evaluations, U.S. colleges and universities rank at the very top in the world. No direct measurements of quality of colleges across countries exist. However, there is indirect evidence. Foreign students by all accounts are not tempted to emigrate to the United States to attend elementary and secondary schools—except perhaps if they see this as a way of gaining entry into the country. They do emigrate in large numbers to attend U.S. colleges and universities. They even tend to pay full, unsubsidized tuitions at U.S. colleges, something that many fewer American citizens do.

A number of the economic models of economic growth in fact emphasize the importance of scientists and engineers as a key ingredient to growth. By these views, the technically trained college students who contribute to invention and to development of new products provide a special element to the growth equation. Here, again, the United States appears to have the best programs. If this view is correct, U.S. higher education may continue to provide a noticeable advantage over other countries.

But the raw material for U.S. colleges is the graduates of our elementary and secondary schools. As has been frequently noted, the lack of preparation of our students leads to extensive remedial education at the postsecondary level, detracting from the ability of colleges and universities to be most effective. And precollege preparation is likely an important factor in driving the increased proportions of foreign-born graduates from the science and engineering programs of U.S. colleges and universities.

Interpreting the Evidence on Quality

The measurement of student outcomes has been pulled in two differ-ent directions. On the one hand, the movement toward standards and testing has emphasized the need to test student performance and to use information from those tests in judging the accomplishments of both students and schools. On the other hand, a segment of the school policy community has argued against the current testing—either be-cause it does not measure attributes they think are important or be-cause the test outcomes are irrelevant.

One aspect of this discussion is to demonstrate that differences in performance on existing tests have significant implications for both individual and aggregate success. Performance on standardized tests of math and science is directly related to individual productivity and earnings and to national economic growth.

None of this says that the existing tests are the best possible. It just indicates that the existing tests identify something real, some-thing that has important ramifications for individuals and the econ-omy.[15]

Further, just because this dimension is important does not mean that other dimensions could not also be important. In fact, some research suggests that there are other important quality dimensions for individuals.[16] Similarly, to the extent that aggregate growth is fueled by invention, creativity is likely to be important, and this may differ from measured cognitive skills. To be useful, however, these other dimensions must be identified and measured, and thought and analysis must go into determining how these dimensions might be improved. Currently, a variety of people argue that schools do more than produce reading, math, and science skills—which schools un-doubtedly do. But such arguments do not deny that cognitive skills are also important. And they do not say what should be done if one wants to enhance these other, currently unmeasured areas.[17]

Finally, this discussion has not pursued the issue of where the measured skills come from. We have learned through extensive research that families, schools, and others contribute to the knowledge of students. The foregoing analysis has simply considered the skills of individuals and how those skills translate into economic outcomes. The issue facing the United States is how to align policies that will enhance those outcomes.

It is interesting in this light that international evidence, like that for the United States, does not show test scores being strongly related to school resources.[18] As mentioned previously, the international math and science scores used in the analysis of growth rates are not related to spending or other measures of school resources, such as pupil-teacher ratios.[19] These statistical results simply reinforce well-known differences, such as the very large class sizes in East Asian countries. Similarly, looking within countries that participated in the 1995 TIMSS, there is no systematic pattern to resource usage within these countries and student performance.[20]

In contrast, a large body of evidence suggests that schools do have a large influence on student outcomes.[21] It is just that high-quality schools are not only those that spend the most or have the smallest class sizes.

One final aspect of U.S. performance is important. U.S. students start out doing well in elementary grades, then fade by the end of high school. Figure 5 shows the slip that occurs over time in comparison with other countries participating in the TIMSS math and science testing. To the extent that performance at the end of secondary schooling is the most important—because it represents the input of college, because it sets the stage for science and engineering skills, or because it is important in its own right for workers in the labor force—schools in the United States are not keeping up in the preparation of students.

The Cost of Not Improving Quality

A *Nation at Risk* issued a call for improved schooling, but this call went unheeded. To be sure, schools introduced new programs, pur-

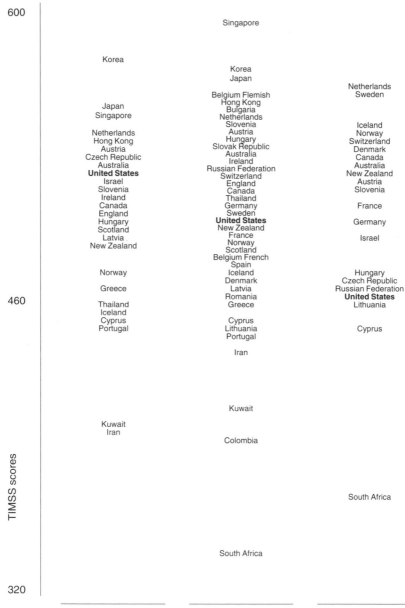

Fig. 5. Performance on TIMSS by age groups

Note: Country positions are relative and approximate.

sued different visions of improvement, and spent considerably more on schools. But student performance remained essentially flat.

What might have been the effect if schools had improved? Consider a hypothetical scenario where schools instituted truly effective reform in math and science instruction at the time of the A *Nation at Risk* report. Had the reform translated into achievement growth of 0.12 standard deviations per year for the remainder of the decade, scores of graduates would be one standard deviation higher going into the nineties and the future. This would have been Herculean effort but within the bounds of expectations. An improvement of that magnitude would put U.S. student performance in line with that of students in the United Kingdom and a variety of other European countries, but they still would not be at the top of the world rankings.

Such a path of improvement of course would not have had an immediately discernible effect on the economy, because new graduates are always a small portion of the labor force, but the impact would mount over time. If past relationships between quality and growth held, GDP in the United States would end up more than 4 percent higher than realized in 2002.[22] With close to a $10.5 trillion economy, the unrealized gain for 2002 alone would amount to $450 billion, or more than the total annual expenditure on K–12 education.

Unfortunately, we have increased spending on schools for the two decades since A *Nation at Risk*, but we have failed to get the desired improvement in outcomes, and our economy—while strong—has not met its potential.

Conclusions

In February 1990, in an unprecedented meeting of the nation's governors with President George H. Bush, an ambitious set of goals was set for America's schools. Goal Number 4 was that by 2000, "U.S. students will be first in the world in mathematics and science achievement." By 1997, as it was evident that this goal was not going to be met, President Clinton, in his State of the Union speech, returned to the old model of substituting quantity for quality: "We must make the thirteenth and fourteenth years of education—at least two years of college—just as universal in America by the twenty-first century as a high school education is today."[23] The quality goal, while perhaps more difficult to meet, appears to be a better approach than reverting to our past practice of emphasizing just quantity of schooling.

A variety of commentators, dead set against any fundamental changes in the nation's schools, rely on a combination of simplistic arguments: The poor performance of U.S. students does not matter because the tests are not valid; we could improve our scores if only we devote more resources to our public schools; schools cannot be expected to deal with the problems of learning that emanate from the home. Gerald Bracey goes one step further.[24] He ends his discussion of how competitiveness of economies is uncorrelated with student performance by warning that innovation may be inversely related to student achievement: "We should think more than twice before we tinker too much with an educational system that encourages questioning. We won't benefit from one that idolizes high test scores. It could put our very competitiveness as a nation at risk." No evidence is presented, however, to demonstrate that creativity is lessened by improving the mathematics and scientific skills of students. Nor does he speak to the costs placed on those individuals who neither reap rewards for exceptional creativity nor have the skills necessary to perform in the modern economy.

Research underscores the long-run importance of high achievement of our students and our future labor force. Higher achievement is associated both with greater individual productivity and earnings and with faster growth of the nation's economy. It no longer appears wise or even feasible to rely on more years of low-quality schooling.

Notes

1. Alfie Kohn, *The Case against Standardized Testing: Raising the Scores, Ruining the Schools* (Heinemann, 2000).

2. Gerald W. Bracey, "Why Do We Scapegoat the Schools?" *Washington Post*, May 5, 2002.

3. These results are derived from quite different approaches. The clearest analyses are found in the following references (which are analyzed in Eric A. Hanushek, "Publicly Provided Education," in *Handbook of Public Economics*, ed. Alan J. Auerbach and Martin Feldstein (Amsterdam: Elsevier, 2002). See John Bishop, "Achievement, Test Scores, and Relative Wages," in *Workers and Their Wages*, ed. Marvin H. Kosters (Washington, D.C.: AEI Press, 1991); John Bishop, "Is the Test Score Decline Responsible for the Productivity Growth Decline?" *American Economic Review* 79, no. 1 (1989); June O'Neill, "The Role of Human Capital in Earnings Differences Between Black and White Men," *Journal of Economic Perspectives* 4, no. 4 (1990); Jeffrey T. Grogger and Eric Eide, "Changes in College Skills and the Rise in the College Wage Premium," *Journal of Human Resources* 30, no. 2 (1993); McKinley L. Blackburn and David Neumark, "Are OLS Estimates of the Return to Schooling Biased Downward? Another Look," *Review of Economics and Statistics* 77, no. 2 (1995); McKinley L. Blackburn and David Neumark, "Omitted-Ability Bias and the Increase in the Return to Schooling," *Journal of Labor Economics* 11, no. 3 (1993); Richard J. Murnane, John B. Willett, and Frank Levy, "The Growing Importance of Cognitive Skills in Wage Determination," *Review of Economics and Statistics* 77, no. 2 (1995); Derek A. Neal and William R. Johnson, "The Role of Premarket Factors in Black-White Differences," *Journal of Political Economy* 104, no. 5 (1996); Richard J. Murnane et al., "How Important Are the Cognitive Skills of Teenagers in Predicting Subsequent Earnings?" *Journal of Policy Analysis and Management* 19, no. 4 (2000); Joseph G. Altonji and Charles R. Pierret, "Employer Learning and Statistical Discrimination," *Quarterly Journal of Economics* 116, no. 1 (2001); and Richard J. Murnane et al., "Do Different Dimensions of Male High School Students' Skills Predict Labor Market Success a Decade Later? Evidence from the NLSY," *Economics of Education Review* 20, no. 4 (2001).

4. The approaches have included looking for circumstances where the

amount of schooling is affected by things other than the student's valu-
ation of continuing and considering the income differences among twins
(see David Card, "Causal Effect of Education on Earnings," in *Handbook
of Labor Economics*, ed. Orley Ashenfelter and David Card (Amsterdam:
North-Holland, 1999). The various adjustments for ability differences
typically make small differences on the estimates of the value of schooling, and James J. Heckman and Edward Vytlacil, "Identifying the Role
of Cognitive Ability in Explaining the Level of and Change in the Return
to Schooling," *Review of Economics and Statistics* 83, no. 1 (2001), argue
that it is not possible to separate the effects of ability and schooling. The
only explicit consideration of school quality typically investigates expenditure and resource differences across schools, but these are known to be
poor measures of school quality differences (Hanushek, "Publicly Provided Education").

5. See, for example, Dennis J. Dugan, "Scholastic Achievement: Its Determinants and Effects in the Education Industry," in *Education As an
Industry*, ed. Joseph T. Froomkin, Dean T. Jamison, and Roy Radner
(Cambridge, Mass.: Ballinger, 1976); Charles F. Manski and David A.
Wise, *College Choice in America* (Cambridge: Harvard University Press,
1983). Steven G. Rivkin, "Black/White Differences in Schooling and
Employment," *Journal of Human Resources* 30, no. 4 (1995), finds that
variations in test scores capture a considerable proportion of the systematic variation in high school completion and in college continuation, so
that test score differences can fully explain black-white differences in
schooling. Bishop, "Achievement, Test Scores, and Relative Wages," and
Eric A. Hanushek, Steven G. Rivkin, and Lori L. Taylor, "Aggregation
and the Estimated Effects of School Resources," *Review of Economics
and Statistics* 78, no. 4 (1996), in considering the factors that influence
school attainment, find that individual achievement scores are highly
correlated with continued school attendance. Neal and Johnson, "The
Role of Pre-Market Factors in Black-White Differences," in part use the
impact of achievement differences of blacks and whites on school attainment to explain racial differences in incomes. Jere R. Behrman et al.,
"The Microeconomics of College Choice, Careers, and Wages: Measuring the Impact of Higher Education," *Annals of the American Academy
of Political and Social Science* 559 (1998), find strong achievement effects
on both continuation into college and quality of college; moreover, the
effects are larger when proper account is taken of the various determi-

nants of achievement. Eric A. Hanushek and Richard R. Pace, "Who Chooses to Teach (and Why)?" *Economics of Education Review* 14, no. 2 (1995), find that college completion is significantly related to higher test scores at the end of high school.

6. See, for example, O'Neill, "The Role of Human Capital in Earnings Differences Between Black and White Men"; Chinhui Juhn, Kevin M. Murphy, and Brooks Pierce, "Accounting for the Slowdown in Black-White Wage Convergence," in *Workers and Their Wages*, ed. Marvin H. Kosters (Washington, D.C.: AEI Press, 1991); Chinhui Juhn, Kevin M. Murphy, and Brooks Pierce, "Wage Inequality and the Rise in Returns to Skill," *Journal of Political Economy* 101, no. 3 (1993); Kevin M. Murphy and Finis Welch, "The Structure of Wages," *Quarterly Journal of Economics* 107, no. 1 (1992); Brooks Pierce and Finis Welch, "Changes in the Structure of Wages," in *Improving America's Schools: The Role of Incentives*, ed. Eric A. Hanushek and Dale W. Jorgenson (Washington, D.C.: National Academy Press, 1996).

7. Identifying the changing impact of measured ability on the distribution of outcomes over time is also a very difficult problem, particularly given the structure of available data (see James Cawley et al., "Understanding the Role of Cognitive Ability in Accounting for the Recent Rise in the Economic Return to Education," in *Meritocracy and Economic Inequality*, ed. Kenneth Arrow, Samuel Bowles, and Steven Durlauf (Princeton, N.J.: Princeton University Press, 2000); Heckman and Vytlacil, "Identifying the Role of Cognitive Ability in Explaining the Level of and Change in the Return to Schooling."

8. Robert J. Barro and Xavier Sala-I-Martin, *Economic Growth* (New York: McGraw-Hill, 1995), review recent analyses. Some have questioned the precise role of schooling in growth. William Easterly, *The Elusive Quest for Growth: An Economists' Adventures and Misadventures in the Tropics* (Cambridge, Mass.: MIT Press, 2002), for example, notes that education without other facilitating factors such as functioning institutions for markets and legal systems may not have much impact. He argues that World Bank investments in schooling for less developed countries that do not ensure that the other attributes of modern economies are in place have been quite unproductive. As discussed, schooling clearly interacts with other factors, and these other factors have been important in supporting U.S. growth.

9. Eric A. Hanushek and Dennis D. Kimko, "Schooling, Labor Force Quality, and the Growth of Nations," *American Economic Review* 90, no. 5 (2000).

10. The details of the tests and aggregation can be found in Hanushek and Kimko and Eric A. Hanushek and Dongwook Kim, "Schooling, Labor Force Quality, and Economic Growth," National Bureau of Economic Research (1995). This figure excludes the earliest administration and runs through the Third International Mathematics and Science Study (TIMSS) (1995). Other international tests have been given and are not included in the figure. First, reading and literacy tests have been given in 1991 and very recently. The difficulty of unbiased testing of reading across languages plus the much greater attention attached to math and science both in the literature on individual earnings and in the theoretical growth literature led to the decision not to include these test results in the empirical analysis. Second, the more recent follow-up to the 1995 TIMSS in math and science is excluded from the figure simply for presentational reasons.

11. The NAEP tests, like the international tests, consist of a series of separate examinations for different age groups. The NAEP patterns do differ some by age group with younger students showing more improvement than older ones (see figures 4 and 5 in chapter 2 by Paul Peterson). The same age differences hold in the international examinations, as shown in figure 5, and the averaging across age groups buoys up the U.S. position in the aggregations of figure 2.

12. We exclude the two TIMSS tests from 1995 and 1999 because they were taken outside of the analytical period on economic growth. We combine the test measures over the 1965–1991 period into a single measure for each country. The underlying objective is to obtain a measure of quality for the labor force in the period during which growth is measured.

13. See, for example, Anne O. Krueger, "The Political Economy of the Rent Seeking Society," *American Economic Review* 64, no. 3 (1974); World Bank, *The East Asian Miracle: Economic Growth and Public Policy* (New York: Oxford University Press, 1993); Stephen L. Parente and Edward C. Prescott, "Barriers to Technology Adoption and Development," *Journal of Political Economy* 102, no. 2 (1994); Stephen L. Parente and Edward C. Prescott, "Monopoly Rights: A Barrier to Riches," *American Economic Review* 89, no. 5 (1999).

14. Data come from the Organization for Economic Cooperation and Development (2001), which has made an effort to use standardized definitions. The non-OECD countries are included in the World Education Indicators project.

15. Note, however, that most of the existing analysis has relied on test results in which the scores might be regarded as a reflection of the student's true ability. It goes without saying that if tests were artificially inflated, say, by cheating or emphasizing just the mechanics of test-taking, they would not reflect skill differences. In such a case, the relationship between measured scores and economic outcomes might disappear.

16. For example, Murnane et al., "Do Different Dimensions of Male High School Students' Skills Predict Labor Market Success a Decade Later? Evidence from the NLSY."

17. Bracey, "Why Do We Scapegoat the Schools?" phrases his discussion in terms of "competitiveness," measured by the Current Competitiveness Index developed by the World Economic Forum. He correlates this index with current scores on the TIMSS. The most telling points, he believes, are that TIMSS scores are not perfectly correlated with this index and that the United States ranks high on the index. He goes on to explain why the United States ranks well on the competitiveness index by essentially the factors discussed for growth rate differences: higher quantity of education, greater college attendance, retaining our scientists and engineers (while attracting foreign immigrants), securing favorable rankings of its economy by international businessmen, and having greater innovative capacity.

18. For the U.S. evidence on resources, see Eric A. Hanushek, "Assessing the Effects of School Resources on Student Performance: An Update," *Educational Evaluation and Policy Analysis* 19, no. 2 (1997); Eric A. Hanushek, "The Evidence on Class Size," in *Earning and Learning: How Schools Matter*, ed. Susan E. Mayer and Paul E. Peterson (Washington, D.C.: Brookings Institution Press, 1999). International evidence can be found in Eric A. Hanushek, "The Failure of Input-Based Schooling Policies," *Economic Journal* 113 (2003).

19. Hanushek and Kimko, "Schooling, Labor Force Quality, and the Growth of Nations."

20. Eric A. Hanushek and Javier A. Luque, "Efficiency and Equity in Schools

around the World," *Economics of Education Review* 22, no. 4 (2003); Hanushek, "The Failure of Input-Based Schooling Policies."

21. See the review in Hanushek, "Publicly Provided Education."

22. These calculations assume that math and science performance of graduates improves steadily through the eighties until it is one standard deviation higher in 1990 than in 1982. After 1990, performance stays at this higher level. These changes then affect the labor force quality according to the proportion of the total labor force with higher achievement (that is, high achievers steadily become an increasing portion of the labor force over time). The growth rates implied from Hanushek and Kimko, "Schooling, Labor Force Quality, and the Growth of Nations" are then compounded over the entire period, based on the average performance of the labor force during each of the intervening years.

23. William J. Clinton, *State of the Union Address* (Washington, D.C.: 1997).

24. Bracey, "Why Do We Scapegoat the Schools?"

Chapter Bibliography

Altonji, Joseph G., and Charles R. Pierret. "Employer Learning and Statistical Discrimination." *Quarterly Journal of Economics* 116, no. 1 (2001): 313–50.

Barro, Robert J., and Xavier Sala-I-Martin. *Economic Growth*. New York: McGraw-Hill, 1995.

Behrman, Jere R., Lori G. Kletzer, Michael S. McPherson, and Morton Owen Schapiro. "The Microeconomics of College Choice, Careers, and Wages: Measuring the Impact of Higher Education." *Annals of the American Academy of Political and Social Science* 559 (1998): 12–23.

Bishop, John. "Achievement, Test Scores, and Relative Wages." In *Workers and Their Wages*, edited by Marvin H. Kosters, 146–86. Washington, D.C.: AEI Press, 1991.

———. "Is the Test Score Decline Responsible for the Productivity Growth Decline?" *American Economic Review* 79, no. 1 (1989): 178–97.

Blackburn, McKinley L., and David Neumark. "Are OLS Estimates of the Return to Schooling Biased Downward? Another Look." *Review of Economics and Statistics* 77, no. 2 (1995): 217–30.

————. "Omitted-Ability Bias and the Increase in the Return to Schooling." *Journal of Labor Economics* 11, no. 3 (1993): 521–44.

Bracey, Gerald W. "Why Do We Scapegoat the Schools?" *Washington Post*, May 5, 2002, B01.

Card, David. "Causal Effect of Education on Earnings." In *Handbook of Labor Economics*, edited by Orley Ashenfelter and David Card, 1801–63. Amsterdam: North-Holland, 1999.

Cawley, James, James J. Heckman, Lance Lochner, and Edward Vytlacil. "Understanding the Role of Cognitive Ability in Accounting for the Recent Rise in the Economic Return to Education." In *Meritocracy and Economic Inequality*, edited by Kenneth Arrow, Samuel Bowles, and Steven Durlauf, 230–65. Princeton, N.J.: Princeton University Press, 2000.

Clinton, William J. "State of the Union Address." Washington, D.C., 1997.

Dugan, Dennis J. "Scholastic Achievement: Its Determinants and Effects in the Education Industry." In *Education As an Industry*, edited by Joseph T. Froomkin, Dean T. Jamison, and Roy Radner, 53–83. Cambridge, Mass.: Ballinger, 1976.

Easterly, William. *The Elusive Quest for Growth: An Economists' Adventures and Misadventures in the Tropics*. Cambridge, Mass.: MIT Press, 2002.

Grogger, Jeffrey T., and Eric Eide. "Changes in College Skills and the Rise in the College Wage Premium." *Journal of Human Resources* 30, no. 2 (1993): 280–310.

Hanushek, Eric A. "Assessing the Effects of School Resources on Student Performance: An Update." *Educational Evaluation and Policy Analysis* 19, no. 2 (1997): 141–64.

————. "The Evidence on Class Size." In *Earning and Learning: How Schools Matter*, edited by Susan E. Mayer and Paul E. Peterson, 131–68. Washington, D.C.: Brookings Institution Press, 1999.

————. "The Failure of Input-Based Schooling Policies." *Economic Journal* 113 (2003): F64–F98.

————. "Publicly Provided Education." In *Handbook of Public Economics*, edited by Alan J. Auerbach and Martin Feldstein. Amsterdam: Elsevier, 2002.

Hanushek, Eric A., and Dongwook Kim. "Schooling, Labor Force Quality, and Economic Growth." Working Paper 5399, National Bureau of Economic Research, December 1995.

Hanushek, Eric A., and Dennis D. Kimko. "Schooling, Labor Force Quality, and the Growth of Nations." *American Economic Review* 90, no. 5 (2000): 1184–208.

Hanushek, Eric A., and Javier A. Luque. "Efficiency and Equity in Schools Around the World." *Economics of Education Review* 22, no. 4 (2003).

Hanushek, Eric A., and Richard R. Pace. "Who Chooses to Teach (and Why)?" *Economics of Education Review* 14, no. 2 (1995): 101–17.

Hanushek, Eric A., Steven G. Rivkin, and Lori L. Taylor. "Aggregation and the Estimated Effects of School Resources." *Review of Economics and Statistics* 78, no. 4 (1996): 611–27.

Heckman, James J., and Edward Vytlacil. "Identifying the Role of Cognitive Ability in Explaining the Level of and Change in the Return to Schooling." *Review of Economics and Statistics* 83, no. 1 (2001): 1–12.

Juhn, Chinhui, Kevin M. Murphy, and Brooks Pierce. "Accounting for the Slowdown in Black-White Wage Convergence." In *Workers and Their Wages*, edited by Marvin H. Kosters, 107–43. Washington, D.C.: AEI Press, 1991.

———. "Wage Inequality and the Rise in Returns to Skill." *Journal of Political Economy* 101, no. 3 (1993): 410–42.

Kohn, Alfie. *The Case against Standardized Testing: Raising the Scores, Ruining the Schools.* Portsmouth, N.H.: Heinemann, 2000.

Krueger, Anne O. "The Political Economy of the Rent Seeking Society." *American Economic Review* 64, no. 3 (1974): 291–303.

Manski, Charles F., and David A. Wise. *College Choice in America.* Cambridge: Harvard University Press, 1983.

Murnane, Richard J., John B. Willett, M. Jay Braatz, and Yves Duhaldeborde. "Do Different Dimensions of Male High School Students' Skills Predict Labor Market Success a Decade Later? Evidence from the NLSY." *Economics of Education Review* 20, no. 4 (2001): 311–20.

Murnane, Richard J., John B. Willett, Yves Duhaldeborde, and John H. Tyler. "How Important Are the Cognitive Skills of Teenagers in Predicting Subsequent Earnings?" *Journal of Policy Analysis and Management* 19, no. 4 (2000): 547–68.

Murnane, Richard J., John B. Willett, and Frank Levy. "The Growing Importance of Cognitive Skills in Wage Determination." *Review of Economics and Statistics* 77, no. 2 (1995): 251–66.

Murphy, Kevin M., and Finis Welch. "The Structure of Wages." *Quarterly Journal of Economics* 107, no. 1 (1992): 285–326.

Neal, Derek A., and William R. Johnson. "The Role of Premarket Factors in Black-White Differences." *Journal of Political Economy* 104, no. 5 (1996): 869–95.

O'Neill, June. "The Role of Human Capital in Earnings Differences Between Black and White Men." *Journal of Economic Perspectives* 4, no. 4 (1990): 25–46.

Parente, Stephen L., and Edward C. Prescott. "Barriers to Technology Adoption and Development." *Journal of Political Economy* 102, no. 2 (1994): 298–321.

———. "Monopoly Rights: A Barrier to Riches." *American Economic Review* 89, no. 5 (1999): 1216–33.

Pierce, Brooks, and Finis Welch. "Changes in the Structure of Wages." In *Improving America's Schools: The Role of Incentives*, edited by Eric A. Hanushek and Dale W. Jorgenson, 53–73. Washington, D.C.: National Academy Press, 1996.

Rivkin, Steven G. "Black/White Differences in Schooling and Employment." *Journal of Human Resources* 30, no. 4 (1995): 826–52.

World Bank. *The East Asian Miracle: Economic Growth and Public Policy.* New York: Oxford University Press, 1993.

PART TWO

WHY SO LITTLE WAS REFORMED

6

The Politics of the Status Quo

Terry M. Moe

Twenty years ago, *A Nation at Risk* set off alarms about the quality of America's schools. Since then our country has been caught up in a frenzy of education reform that has left no state untouched, bringing change upon change to the laws, programs, and curricula that govern public education, more money to see these changes carried out, and greater involvement by the federal government. Every governor now wants to be the education governor, every president the education president.

In some sense, this frenzy of reform is a positive statement about our national resolve. America is tackling a difficult challenge and staying the course. But there is something else going on as well, and it is hardly cause for celebration: namely, that the nation continues to be embroiled in education reform because, after untold billions of dollars and lofty reform packages too numerous to list, very little has actually been achieved—and more reforms are always called for. The frenzy continues because the reforms themselves are consistently ineffective.

Why have two decades of reform been so disappointing? No doubt many factors are responsible. But an important part of the answer rests with the political process by which our society makes its decisions about reform. The problem is that the politics of education is inherently biased toward the status quo. With rare exceptions, the only reforms that make it through the political process are those that are acceptable to the established interests and that leave the fundamentals—and the problems—of the current system intact. Most of what passes for reform, as a result, is really just more of the same and can't possibly provide the significant improvement people are looking for.

My aim in this essay is to shed light on the politics of education and its consequences for reform. A lot has happened since *A Nation at Risk*, and it is tempting to seek insight in blow-by-blow accounts of all the political actors, events, and conflicts that have brought us to where we are today. But this wouldn't tell us very much. To understand these developments, we need to get beyond most of the details to recognize that the politics of education has a deeper structure that explains much of what has happened—and not happened—over the last twenty years. That is what this analysis is about. It is about the structure of our nation's politics of education, and about how this structure has sabotaged the quest for true reform.

The Structure of Education Politics

There have been two transformations of American education during the last century. The first began during the early 1900s as part of the broader Progressive reform of American government and politics. The Progressives acted to rid the schools of political patronage, organize them into a rational bureaucratic system, and put them in the hands of professionals. The education system that emerged from this era eventually became institutionalized, and in basic structure is much the same as the one we have today: a bureaucratic system of top-down governance.

No one gives up power easily, and the political transition that accompanied reform was fractious, uneven, and took decades to be realized. Early on, business leaders, reform politicians, and educational administrators struggled to wrest power from political machines. And they ultimately did. But throughout all this, as well as after the defeat of the political machines, educational administrators were battling on a second front: they fought to take power from their erstwhile allies, the business and political leaders, and to achieve autonomous professional control over "their" education system. By mid-century, they had largely succeeded. The Progressive transformation of American education, then, probably took a good fifty years to unfold.[1]

Once this transformation was under way, the key defenders of the new education system were the administrative professionals charged with running it. The basis of their power was their expertise. The administrators were highly organized—the National Education Association, for example, was one of their major vehicles—and they did everything they could to make education a complex, technical business that only experts could possibly understand. They were the ones (to hear them tell it) who knew how to design, organize, and operate complex systems of schools; they were the ones who understood the mysteries of curriculum, testing, and teacher training; and they were the ones, as a result, that public officials and citizens should rely upon in all matters of public education.

This strategy worked well, yet the administrators also had an Achilles' heel: their political power was rooted solely in their expertise and not in any ability to deliver the votes that so motivated their elected superiors. As long as there was no political movement to reform the education system against their will, however—and until recently there wasn't—their expertise was enough to give them leverage over their elected bosses, to counter any political disruptions, and to keep their institution stable.

The second transformation occurred during the sixties and seventies. Until this point, teachers had been powerless within the hierarchy of education. But when states began changing their laws to permit (and promote) collective bargaining for public employees, and when the American Federation of Teachers began an aggressive campaign to organize teachers for that purpose, the NEA quickly morphed from a professional association into a labor union to meet the competition—and the system transformation was on. When the dust had cleared by 1980 or so, virtually all school districts of any size (outside the right-to-work states) had been organized, and collective bargaining and unionization had become the norm. In the process, the administrators lost control of the NEA as well as their leadership of the education establishment. The teacher unions reigned supreme.[2]

The result was essentially a new kind of education system: very similar in structure to the older one handed down by the Progressives, but different in its leadership and distribution of power. Today, this system defines the status quo of modern American education. Born of teacher revolution, it has been in equilibrium now for more than twenty years and is eminently stable, well entrenched and well protected.

Within it, the teacher unions are more powerful than the administrators ever were, because the sources of their power are perfectly suited to the hardball world of electoral politics. By gaining exclusive bargaining rights within school districts, the unions have been able to amass huge memberships—the NEA currently has more than two million members, the AFT more than one million—and tremendous financial resources, mostly from member dues. The money allows them to contribute generously to campaigns at all levels of government. More important, their members are located in virtually every political district in the country (wherever there are kids, there are teachers), and they regularly turn out armies of activists to ring doorbells, make telephone calls, distribute literature, and in countless other ways campaign for union-endorsed candidates. No other group can claim such an awesome capacity for in-the-trenches political action.

Over the last several decades, this capacity has been developed to a fine organizational art and employed almost entirely to the benefit of Democrats, whose constituencies already incline them in the "right" directions and who, with union pressure, can be counted on to support most union demands on education policy. With so many friends in high places and so much clout to ensure that friends follow through, the teacher unions have made it to the top of the political hill. Indeed, a recent study of interest group systems in each of the fifty states concludes that the teacher unions are the single most powerful interest group in the entire country.[3]

Although the teacher unions stand out as unusually powerful, they are otherwise just like other interest groups: they use their power to promote their own interests. In the unions' case, these interests arise from the primordial fact that, in order to survive and prosper as organizations, they need members and resources. This being so, their fundamental interests have to do with protecting and extending their collective bargaining arrangements, protecting member jobs, promoting member pay and working conditions, promoting member rights in the workplace, and increasing the demand for teachers. Note that these interests, and the behaviors they ultimately cause the unions to engage in, need have nothing to do with what is best for children, schools, or the public interest.

The teacher unions exercise political power in two basic ways: to pressure for the policies that they want and to block the policies they don't want. In the first role, they take the lead in pushing policy makers to support the existing system of public education—through higher spending, for example, or new programs and teacher protections. These sorts of policies bolster a system that works to the unions' great advantage; they also tend to result in more teachers (and union members), better pay and benefits, more secure jobs, and the like and thus dovetail nicely with specific union interests. The unions' second leadership role involves a different kind of system support: they use their power to oppose any reforms that are at all threatening to the established system. Here too, they are acting to bolster a system that works to their great advantage. But their opposition also arises because almost any change of real consequence is likely to unsettle the jobs, security, autonomy, or working conditions of teachers.

In the practice of politics, these two applications of union power are not equally attractive as strategic options. The reason is that policy making takes place within a political system of checks and balances, the effect of which is to make new legislation very difficult to achieve. Typically, a bill must make it past subcommittees, committees, and floor votes in each house of the legislature; it must be approved in identical form by each; it is threatened along the way by various parliamentary roadblocks (such as filibusters, holds, and voting rules); and if it makes it past all these hurdles, it can still be vetoed by the executive. For a group to get a favored policy enacted into law, then, it must win political victories at each and every step along the way, which is quite difficult. For a group to block a policy it opposes, on the other hand, it needs to succeed at just *one* of the many veto points in order to win, a much easier challenge to meet. The American political system is literally designed, therefore, to make blocking—and thus preserving the status quo—far easier than taking positive action. The advantage always goes to interest groups that want to keep things the way they are.

And so it is in education. The teacher unions are extraordinarily powerful, but getting their own policy agendas enacted is difficult for them too. More often than not, especially when the policies they seek are consequential to opposing groups, the unions will either lose or find that much of what they want has to be compromised away. Their power is likely to be stunningly effective, on the other hand, when all they want to do is block the policy initiatives they dislike—because not only do all blockers have a decided advantage, but the unions' massive political power magnifies that advantage many times over, making it quite likely that they can stop or thoroughly water down any reform proposals that threaten their interests.

Taken together, these basic elements coalesce to give a distinctive structure to the modern politics of education. For the first time in its history, the American education system has a powerful protector capable of shielding it from the unsettling forces of democratic politics. The teacher unions, now the unchallenged leaders of the education establishment, have amassed formidable power rooted in collective bargaining and electoral politics. They have fundamental interests that drive them to oppose almost all consequential changes in the educational status quo. And they operate in a political system that, by advantaging groups that seek to block change, makes it relatively easy to ensure that genuine reform doesn't happen.

Mainstream Reforms

It is a fact of great importance—and great irony—that A *Nation at Risk* burst onto the scene at precisely the time that the teacher unions were consolidating their power over American education and its politics. What we always hear about this famous governmental report is that it set off a tidal wave of reform. Indeed, the first few years after its appearance have been called the "greatest and most concentrated surge of educational reform in the nation's history."[4] What we don't hear is that, despite all the excitement and conflict that inevitably characterize such a monumental period of flux, it all took place within a tightly structured political process that constrained the outcomes and protected the status quo.

Were it up to the unions, there would have been no reform at all, save for massive increases in spending and taxing. But business groups saw it very differently. Acutely concerned about an economy plagued by high unemployment, high inflation, and low productivity, they saw the United States falling behind its international competitors and believed that the education system was a big part of the problem. The nation's human capital was in a sorry state. Far too many workers were poor readers, unable to do simple arithmetic computations, and ill-equipped to think autonomously and creatively in a fast-changing economic world. Major education reforms were called for, they argued, and the need was urgent.[5]

They found allies in the nation's governors, who (along with presidents) became the key political leaders of the education reform movement. This was no accident. Governors, unlike legislators, have large, eclectic constituencies that drive them to think about the broader interests of their states, and they are held politically responsible—as legislators are not—for the well-being of their state economies. When the link between education and economic competitiveness was forged during the early eighties, then, governors were the ones who pushed aggressively for reform. Their incentives were all the greater because, in a federal system of free trade in which businesses can choose where to locate, the governors were unavoidably competing against each other: all wanted to create economic environments—and thus education reforms—that businesses would find attractive.

In the search for solutions, governors and business leaders set up literally hundreds of task forces to study the problem, and turned for advice to acknowledged experts within the education community: to the administrators who run the schools, but especially to the academics—almost all of them in schools of education—whose research gave them a (presumably scientific) basis for claiming to know which reforms would be effective. While the leaders themselves were looking for significant improvement, then, their ideas came from experts wedded to the existing system—whose advice, with some exceptions, was predictably mainstream.

The way to improve the schools, these experts argued, was to spend more money (lots of it), increase teacher salaries, toughen graduation requirements, improve academic coursework, and strengthen teacher certification and training, among other things: reforms that could easily be pursued without changing the basic structure of the system.

These were precisely the kinds of reforms, moreover, that had been recommended by the authors of A *Nation at Risk*, whose expert advice came from the same sorts of mainstream sources.

The tidal wave of reforms that swept across the American states, then, involved almost nothing that was threatening to the teacher unions. So there was no need for the unions to be aggressive opponents of these efforts. Indeed, they actually had much to cheer about, because the reform movement gave them golden opportunities to pressure hard for what they wanted anyway—more spending and taxing—and to claim that, far from opposing reform, they were actually dedicated reformers just like everyone else. Moreover, they could count on political support from a wide array of true reform proponents, including those—business groups and even staunch conservatives—who had long opposed higher taxes and spending (especially in the southern and border states), but who now agreed that more money was needed for education and were eager to throw their weight behind what amounted to the unions' old-line demands.

While mainstream reforms rarely worried the teacher unions, some proposals were troublesome. In A *Nation at Risk* and many other reports, for example, there was support for moving away from the traditional salary schedule toward some form of performance pay—via career ladders, for instance—as a means of giving teachers stronger incentives to promote student achievement. This idea resonated with business leaders and was included in reform proposals in a number of states and localities. But the teacher unions were opposed to performance pay, which, from their perspective, creates competition and jealousies among their members, undermines solidarity, and gives too much discretion to administrators. On occasion, the unions toyed with the idea of career ladders as a means of giving teachers more opportunities for advancement—and of pumping more money into teacher salaries—but the negatives outweighed the positives for union interests, and they typically used their power to snuff out any serious departures from the traditional salary schedule. As a result, this line of reform made little headway.

With mainstream reforms doing little to change the system and with more serious reforms like pay-for-performance unable to gain adoption, it is hardly surprising that, by the late eighties, reformers generally agreed that reform efforts were not having the desired effects. The notion spread that this first wave of reforms had failed because it had restricted itself to incremental changes within the existing system, and that what the nation needed was a second wave that sought to restructure the system itself.

This shift in perspective led to a surge of support for two major movements that actually do have the potential to change the fundamentals of American education: the choice movement and the accountability movement (discussed below). But aside from these two movements, the newfound concern for restructuring didn't amount to much. Intellectually it was almost entirely lacking in coherence and served as little more than a big tent under which a hodgepodge of ideas—from decentralization to professional development to the teaching of higher-order thinking—could be packaged as exciting new exercises in break-the-mold reform. Which they weren't. There was no grand vision of how the system should be changed, and indeed no real sense of what it might mean to restructure the system. The word "restructuring" became a linchpin of reform rhetoric, but there was not much substance to it.

There were, of course, a few exceptions. The most notable (aside from choice and accountability) were various types of school-based management, which created school-site councils—usually of parents, teachers, and administrators—and granted them substantial authority to govern their own affairs. This idea was threatening to administrators, as it sapped their own authority. But it was far less problematic for the teacher unions, which, although faced with uncertainties they sought to avoid, also had opportunities to control the local governance bodies and their policies. In an environment of growing hostility toward bureaucracy and growing demand for parental participation, then, there was in some states and communities a real interest in seeking reform through decentralized decision making—and with the unions often willing to go along, no powerful political force to stop it. As a result, such restructurings have been adopted in the years since by several big-city school systems, including Chicago, Miami, and Rochester. And a number of states—Colorado, Florida, Kentucky, North Carolina, and Texas—have mandated certain forms of shared decision making in all their schools. There is no evidence that these reforms have led to higher achievement. But they did, at least, make an attempt at fundamental change.[6]

For the most part, though, the second wave of reforms was just a continuation of the first, its content firmly embedded in the educational mainstream—indeed, often consisting of exactly the same reforms. This entrenched tradition of reform-as-tinkering, moreover, was maintained throughout the nineties and is alive and well today. The states are still seeking to improve their schools through more spending, stricter requirements, new course content, more teacher training, and the like—all with great fanfare, as though this time around these recycled efforts will pay off.

Some "new" reforms have gained support and attention along the way. Perhaps the most notable of these is class-size reduction, which was heavily promoted by President Clinton via his effort to fund 100,000 new teachers for the public schools, and aggressively pursued in a number of states as well—particularly in California, which since 1996 has been spending more than $1 billion per year to reduce class sizes in the early grades. Needless to say, this is a reform the teacher unions strongly support, because it directly increases their membership and power. But the fact is, class-size reduction, like the other reforms, does nothing to restructure the system, and there is no evidence—nor has there ever been—that it works to bring about substantial improvement in student learning. Worse, it is hugely expensive.[7]

So why are the states investing so heavily in mainstream reforms? Because, despite their ineffectiveness in improving the schools, these reforms are political winners. They are popular with the public and appeal to common sense. The education-school experts make scientific claims on their behalf. The business community tends to believe these claims. And the teacher unions, whose power is usually sufficient to block anything they oppose, either support them or find them innocuous. From a political standpoint, then, mainstream reforms are all pluses and no minuses. For governors under constant pressure to "do something" in pursuit of better schools, therefore, these mainstream reforms are extremely attractive. They are all, at any rate, that the prevailing structure of politics usually allows them to do.

The School Accountability Movement

The greatest achievement of A *Nation at Risk* is not that it gave rise to countless education reforms. Most of them have been a waste of time and money. Its greatest achievement is that it directed attention to the problems of public education, brought political power to bear on the side of reform, and gave impetus to two political movements— one for accountability, the other for choice—that do have the capacity to transform American education for the better. Both are fighting against long odds, challenging a status quo that is heavily protected. But both are making progress.

To most anyone who knows about organization and management, the ideas behind school accountability have obvious merit. If the school system is to be effective in promoting academic excellence, then it must be clear about what its standards of academic achievement are, it must devise and implement tests that measure how well the standards are being met, and it must hold students, teachers, and administrators accountable for results—and give them incentives to do their very best—by attaching consequences to outcomes.

For business leaders, the general guidelines for effective management—setting goals, measuring performance, attaching consequences and incentives to performance—are an integral part of their everyday lives. So once these leaders got involved in education reform, it was only a matter of time before they realized that America's educators had never in history been held accountable for their performance, and only a matter of time before they began demanding that something be done about it. Governors, moreover, were sympathetic. They were the executive leaders of their state school systems, they were held responsible for getting results, and an accountability system offered them an organizational means of gaining control and taking action.[8]

With governors and business leaders embracing its ideals and with polls showing stratospheric levels of public support for standards and testing, the requisites of a political movement were in place. And when it became clear that the first wave of reform was not having the desired effect, the movement began to take off. What made accountability so attractive was that, unlike the other reforms (aside from choice), it offered a coherent way of thinking about the problems plaguing the system and a coherent plan for righting them. Moreover, because it was a top-down approach that sought only to make the existing top-down system function more effectively, it came across as a natural extension of mainstream reform efforts—and not nearly as radical or threatening as contemporaneous proposals for school choice. It was a reform that everyone could agree was desirable.[9]

Well, almost everyone. The teacher unions and their education allies had a very different view. For the goal of the movement was to hold *them* accountable, and that was something they wanted to avoid. This may sound slanderous to say, but in fact it is a simple reflection of their own interests. Historically, teachers and administrators have been granted substantial autonomy, and their pay and jobs have been almost totally secure regardless of their performance. A very cushy arrangement. Indeed, it is quite likely that these properties were part of what attracted many of them to the education system in the first place, and that those who have chosen to stay for more than several years (rather than leaving for other careers) are people who have found these properties particularly to their liking. So in light of all this, why would they want to have specific goals thrust upon them that they are expected to meet, their performance evaluated in a truly serious manner, their pay linked to their performance, and their jobs made less secure? They wouldn't. In their view, the absence of accountability is a terrific deal—and they want to keep the deal they have.

With accountability so popular, however, the unions and their allies were in something of a political bind. They were opposed to true accountability, but full-fledged opposition would have pegged them as self-interested defenders of the status quo. This being so, they chose a more sophisticated course of action: to provide rhetorical support for accountability, participate in the design of actual accountability plans, and block any components that are truly threatening. In this way, the unions could appear dedicated to system change, while ensuring that teachers and administrators would not really be held accountable.

In following this strategy over the years, they have been aided by the accountability issue's fortuitous fit with union interests: most aspects of the typical accountability plan are rather harmless and can be "supported" at little cost, especially if the unions can shape their design. After all, there is nothing about curriculum standards that is inherently threatening to union interests. The same thing can be said for tests of student achievement. They only become threatening when they are backed by consequences, particularly if teachers are to be sanctioned for poor performance. Thus, it is the consequences the unions most want to prevent and to which their blocking power is mainly directed. If they can do this successfully—and they almost always can—they can be reasonably content with the reforms that result: benign systems of standards and tests that, while impressive to the voting public, are weak as mechanisms of top-down control.

It oversimplifies, of course, to suggest that the unions aren't threatened at all by standards and testing. For even if there are no real teeth in the legislation (which is the norm), the states have often required—in moves the unions could hardly afford to oppose—that test scores and pass rates be made public. This in itself is a consequence because it subjects teachers and administrators to public pressure if their students fail to meet the standards. The unions want to avoid this, naturally, and have been active in trying to shape the standards and the tests in ways that take the pressure off.[10]

While both the NEA and the AFT tout themselves as supporters of rigorous standards, their state affiliates regularly use their political clout to push for standards that are easily met and easily taught and that will give the impression (through high pass rates) that teachers are doing a great job. When test results are disappointing, moreover, the unions are quick to argue that the tests are flawed, need revision, and cannot provide valid measures of performance. They "favor" tests, but they have almost never seen a test they actually like. What they want instead is for student performance to be evaluated using broader criteria—course grades, portfolios of student work, assessments of effort—based on the subjective judgments of teachers. This way, teachers would be controlling pass rates and public perceptions. And indirectly, they would be in charge of evaluating their own performance.

The unions' prime goal, however, is to block any formal system of consequences that might facilitate true accountability. Their highest priority is to ensure that there are no sanctions for poor performance and, above all, that *no one ever loses a job* and there is *no weeding-out process* by which the school system rids itself of mediocre or incompetent teachers. Other kinds of economic sanctions—pay cuts, school closings—are verboten as well. And so are commonsense policies that might lead to some of these sanctions: for example, the testing of veteran teachers to ensure that they meet minimal standards.

Another union bugaboo, for reasons I outlined earlier, is pay for performance: which in a genuine system of accountability would typically be the key means by which productive behavior is rewarded, unproductive behavior discouraged, and proper incentives introduced. The unions employ their power to see that these crucial functions cannot possibly be carried out. They demand that pay be determined by formal criteria—seniority, education, advanced certification—that are not measures of how much students learn (and not causes of student learning either, the research literature suggests) and that any teacher can potentially satisfy. Bad teachers and good teachers get paid the same. No one has an economic incentive to perform.

When consequences are actually adopted (against their wishes), the unions do everything they can to ensure that consequences take the form of rewards, and rewards only. Under duress, for example, they might reluctantly go along with bonuses for high-performing teachers. Or preferably, because they induce less competition among members, the unions might support bonuses for high-performing schools as a whole, especially if the unions are able to decide how the rewards are distributed among the teachers within each school (because typically they would distribute them equally, eliminating competition and jealousy). The idea is that, if there must be consequences, accountability should be a system of positive inducements—and more money (for the rewards)—in which there would only be winners. No losers.

This same logic applies to the problem of low-performing schools, a focus of most accountability reforms. State intervention and reconstitution are common proposals for dealing with persistently inadequate performance, but both are sanction-like approaches that threaten union interests. The unions prefer that low-performing schools be given greater funding, more assistance with programs, and more training for teachers: consequences that are essentially rewards for school personnel, and indeed the kinds of things the unions are always lobbying for anyway. Having them labeled as "consequences" in an accountability system is really just a back-door way of directing more resources to these schools. And making sure that no one is really held accountable.

The teacher unions are not the only groups that have fought to weaken school accountability. They are joined by a whole range of groups representing members of the education community, none of them happy about the new requirements being imposed from above. They are also joined on occasion by civil rights groups, concerned that high-stakes testing will lead to high failure and dropout rates among minorities; sometimes by groups of disaffected parents, who think their kids are being overtested and that too much time is taken away from important schoolwork; and almost always by a small army of academic and think-tank experts, who claim tests are misleading and can't be used as the basis for accountability. Even so, the unions are the 800-pound gorillas of the antiaccountability coalition, and their power is the key to the coalition's success in undermining the efficacy of reform.[11]

The extent of their success varies state by state, depending on how conducive the circumstances are to union power. Obviously, these circumstances may be quite complicated. But other things being equal (and I emphasize that), the teacher unions tend to be most success-ful—and accountability systems weaker—in states where Democrats (their staunch allies) are in control of the machinery of government, where collective bargaining laws are strong, and where the perfor-mance of the public schools is considered acceptable by business or the public. It is no accident that two states often singled out as having (relatively) strong accountability systems—states that acted early and aggressively—are Texas and North Carolina, which are right-to-work states where the teacher unions are at a disadvantage and where up-grading the education system has been given top priority. And it is also no accident that the federal government's first aggressive, broadly based attempt to hold the public schools accountable—the No Child Left Behind act, passed in 2001—was conceived and relentlessly pro-moted by George W. Bush, a southern Republican.[12]

The norm, however, is that accountability systems are substan-tially weakened by union influence and crafted in such a way that the requirements of effective top-down management—all of them having to do with consequences—are thoroughly violated. In particular, the typical accountability system includes

- no serious attempt to pay teachers based on their performance.

- no mechanisms to weed out mediocre or incompetent teachers.

- no real sanctions for poor performance.

The truth is, today's widely touted accountability systems aren't really designed to hold teachers and other school employees accountable. They look like accountability systems. And they are called accountability systems. But they can't do their jobs very well, because they literally aren't designed to.

The future may be brighter. We can't forget that the teacher unions are forced to fight these battles because there *is* genuine power behind the accountability movement. The movement, moreover, has notched political victories over the past two decades and become a tidal wave of reform in its own right. Thus far, there is more symbol than substance to all this. But the unions are clearly on the defensive, and the incremental gains of reformers may yet give rise (over many years) to accountability systems that do a much better job than the ones currently in place.

How might this happen? Why won't the unions just continue to eviscerate whatever the reformers propose? It has a lot to do with the second political movement that followed on the heels of *A Nation at Risk:* the movement for school choice.

The School Choice Movement

School choice has provoked the most tempestuous political conflicts over education in the last twenty years. On the surface, the idea couldn't be simpler: that parents should be able to choose where their children go to school. But its simplicity is deceptive, because if choice were seriously enacted it could generate a far-reaching transformation of the American education system. That is why its adherents are so fervent in their support. And that is why the teacher unions and their allies are so vehemently opposed.

A true choice system would do three things. First, by allowing families to choose, it would enable them to leave schools that aren't serving them well, particularly schools that are flat-out bad. In this way, families could take immediate action to improve their situations, and their children needn't be trapped in bad schools for years waiting for the promises of mainstream reformers to come to fruition (which is unlikely to happen anyway). Second, precisely because families would be empowered to leave inadequate schools, all schools would be put on notice that unless they perform at high levels they will lose children and resources. This would give schools strong incentives that they don't have under the current system—incentives to perform and innovate—and these incentives would energize (and potentially re-shape) every aspect of educational behavior and organization. Third, all of this would generate a redistribution of power within the educa-tion system. Parents, of course, would gain power relative to admin-istrators and teachers. But much more would happen too. The regular public school system would become smaller as (some) kids and money go to private or to charter schools, leaving the establishment with fewer resources to control. The unions would lose members, as the number of public school teachers falls; and they would find the growing number of private and charter school teachers much harder to orga-nize. The pressures of competition would force the regular public schools to embrace performance-enhancing reforms—like the rejec-tion of cumbersome collective bargaining requirements—that under-mine union power. And more.

There is no mystery, then, why the teacher unions are so intensely opposed to school choice. For when choice is seriously pursued, it threatens their most fundamental interests, far more so than any other type of reform, including accountability. Accountability, at least, leaves the traditional top-down system intact. But choice unleashes new forces that work from the bottom up to redistribute power, children, and resources; to give schools and teachers strong incentives to perform; and to hold them accountable—through automatically invoked consequences (the loss of children and resources)—if they don't do a good job. In effect, choice is a bottom-up form of accountability that does *not* fit neatly within the Progressive top-down structure and, indeed, virtually ensures that the structure will change dramatically in response to performance-based pressures from below. Just what the unions and their allies don't want.

The teacher unions, moreover, are not alone in their opposition to choice. They are the ones who spend the big money and mobilize the troops, but they also have important allies in the broader liberal coalition that add force and legitimacy to their war effort. Much of this liberal opposition (unlike the unions') derives from a genuine concern for basic principles, values, and deserving constituencies. The NAACP, for example, fears that vouchers and most other forms of choice would promote segregation. The ACLU is concerned about the separation of church and state, as well as issues of equal access and discrimination. Liberals in general tend to be supportive of government and the public schools, suspicious of markets, and worried that a shift toward choice would hurt the poor. And then, of course, there are Democratic public officials, who have an abiding self-interest in reelection and are heavily dependent on the teacher unions for campaign support. They don't get it for nothing. They earn the unions' much-valued support by doing their bidding on important educational issues, and school choice is right at the top of the list.[13]

Choice was first proposed in the mid-fifties by economist Milton Friedman, who argued for a full-blown voucher system. While the idea attracted attention over the next few decades, and while more muted versions of choice—magnet schools, for example—made their appearance during the seventies, the movement didn't pick up steam until the eighties when *A Nation at Risk* highlighted the need for major improvements in the schools, the first wave of reforms proved a disappointment, and more far-reaching reforms were suddenly given serious consideration. Other factors were at work too. This was a time when top-down approaches to government were falling into disrepute worldwide for their heavy bureaucracy and inefficiency, and when policy makers everywhere—from the United States to Western and Eastern Europe to South America to China—began turning aggressively to markets in reforming their approaches to economic and social policy. Meanwhile, the Reagan administration held power in Washington, and its commitment to market-based reforms—along with its willingness to cross swords with the teacher unions—led it to promote tuition tax credits and other forms of school choice, and to nurture the development of a nationwide network of activists for the cause.

But conservatism alone is no match for the blocking power of the union-led coalition. Nor, stereotypes aside, can school choice count on the support and political clout of business to even the balance. For while a number of business leaders have played prominent roles in the movement over the years—among them John Walton, Theodore Forstmann, Peter Flanagan, and J. Patrick Rooney—the fact is that most business leaders tend to think about education reform in terms of management, because management is essentially what they do for a living and what they believe determines effective organization. They are naturally inclined to be ardent supporters of accountability, but not to be ardent supporters of choice, markets, and competition.

From the beginning, then, the choice movement has always lacked the kind of institutional power base that its opponents benefit from. While business was the driving force behind the post–*Nation at Risk* frenzy of reform, business leaders in general did not throw their political weight behind school choice. Throughout the eighties, as a result, the choice movement was largely made up of conservative activists, along with supporters among parents, (some) private schools, and (some) churches. But this was hardly a power base capable of challenging the opposition. To do that, it needed to broaden its constituency and its agenda.

Which is just what it did. The spark came in 1990, through an event that may someday be regarded as among the most significant developments in the history of American education. What happened was that parents in inner-city Milwaukee, organized and led by local advocates for the poor, rose up to demand vouchers as a means of escaping their failing public schools. And by entering into a coalition with conservatives, led by Republican governor Tommy Thompson, the urban poor won a surprising victory over the powerful defenders of the existing system. The concrete result was the nation's first public voucher program: a small pilot program reserved (at the time) for no more than 1,000 disadvantaged kids. But the victory did more than put vouchers on the map. It also set the movement on a far different and more promising path.[14]

Since 1990, most of the movement's efforts have focused on pro- viding vouchers to poor and minority families in the inner cities: families that are concentrated in low-performing schools, trapped by the searing inequities of the current system, and value vouchers as a means of escape. The new arguments for vouchers have less to do with free markets than with social equity. And they have less to do with theory than with the common-sense notions that disadvantaged kids should be given immediate opportunities to get out of bad schools, and that experiments, pilot programs, and novel approaches are good ideas in failing urban systems for which the downside risk is virtually nil.

This shift has put the opponents of vouchers in an extremely awkward position. As liberals, they claim to be (and usually are) cham- pions of the poor. But on the voucher issue, they refuse to represent their own constituents—and indeed, find themselves fighting *against* poor families, who are only trying to escape conditions that liberals agree are deplorable. In doing so, moreover, liberals have essentially pushed the urban poor into an educational alliance with conservatives. And this alliance, whose arguments for equity, practicality, and low risk have a much broader public appeal than the conservative mantra of free markets, is sometimes powerful enough to bring about political victory—even in contexts heavily stacked against it.

This is the alliance that won in Milwaukee. It won again in creating the nation's second voucher program in Cleveland (1995), in vastly expanding the Milwaukee program (1995), in creating the first state-level voucher program in Florida (1999), and in making vouchers available to all of Florida's more than 350,000 children who qualify for special education (2000).[15] It also came close—which is saying a lot under the circumstances—in many state legislatures, as well as in the federal government, where Congress passed a low-income voucher program for Washington, D.C., only to have it vetoed by President Clinton. Outside of politics, this same alliance has also been responsible for creating a vast system of privately funded voucher programs— programs that opponents are powerless to block, and have put vouchers in the hands of more than 100,000 disadvantaged children.[16]

Meanwhile, the choice movement has also been fighting hard for two other kinds of market-based reforms: charter schools and privatization. Charter schools are public schools of choice that are granted substantial autonomy to pursue their own missions in their own ways. The choice movement sees them as desirable because, if charter plans are designed right, they create an important measure of choice and competition (and all the associated consequences) within the public sector. In the eyes of many advocates, they probably can't provide *as much* of these good things as choice plans that include vouchers. But vouchers are likely to be politically unattainable in most situations, at least for now—while battles for charter reform can often be won.[17]

For the teacher unions and their education allies, charters are a threat. While kids and money remain within the public sector—a major plus from the unions' standpoint—the regular public schools would still lose enrollments, jobs, and resources to the new charter schools; the unions would lose members and collective bargaining strength (because charters are usually nonunion and difficult to organize); there would be performance pressures to reduce bureaucracy and union-imposed restrictions; and, in general, the foundation of establishment power would be weakened.

Nonetheless, while the unions have drawn a line in the sand over vouchers—a survival issue for them—they have found it wise to follow a more accommodating strategy with charters, much as they have done with accountability. They have chosen not to come out in full-force opposition, but instead to feign support. In this way, they have tried to forge a social compromise on choice—allowing a few new alternatives in the public sector, a little bit of competition—in hopes that modest steps in this direction will satisfy the demand for choice, stall the progress of their worst nightmare, and at the same time make them appear open to change and innovation. They also have an eye on their allies in the liberal coalition, Democrats and liberal interest groups, who have their own reasons for wanting to appear sympathetic to charters: there is a real demand among their urban constituents for new educational opportunities. By showing flexibility on charters, then, the teacher unions allow their allies to make politically beneficial moves of their own without fear of retribution, and the coalition is more likely to stay together.

But how to "support" charter schools without hurting union interests? As with accountability, the unions and their allies have essentially solved this problem through the politics of program design: they "support" charters in concept, but use their power to impose so many design restrictions that the programs cannot possibly generate much choice or competition. Among other things, they lobby to have low ceilings placed on the numbers of charter schools allowed by law, to require that charters be authorized by their local school districts (which have incentives to prevent new competitors from entering), to require that charters be unionized and part of the districtwide contract, and to require that charters be subject to as many rules and controls as possible. Their ideal is to design charter systems that don't work.

Because charters have become the consensus approach to school choice with few outright enemies, charter programs have spread like wildfire across the American states during the last decade. Since their humble beginning in 1991, when Minnesota adopted the nation's first charter program (allowing just eight charter schools in the entire state), well over half the states have adopted their own programs. Today, more than 500,000 children attend some 2,700 charter schools, and the numbers are climbing year by year. The choice movement has made a good deal of progress by pushing for this kind of choice-based reform—yet there is much less here than meets the eye. Most charter programs are burdened by designs that have been heavily influenced by the teacher unions and their allies, and that sharply restrict how much real choice and competition the new charter schools can bring. In California, for instance, there are currently about 450 charter schools in a state that has more than 1,000 school districts and 8,500 schools. The charters are a drop in a very large bucket and can't change things much. Yet California is regarded as having one of the stronger charter systems.

Aside from vouchers and charters, another reform actively pushed by the choice movement is privatization. The idea here is that school districts or chartering agencies can contract with private firms to operate public schools (or even entire districts), in order to take advantage of the greater flexibility, expertise, and potential for innovation that the marketplace might have to offer. The attraction to the choice movement is obvious. While privatization need not involve choice at all, it often does—many of the schools currently operated by private firms are charter schools of choice—and even if it doesn't, the commonality is that they both are attempts to improve education by bringing market forces into the structure and operation of the current system. Privatization is a natural adjunct to choice.[18]

And naturally, it is also a threat to union interests. One problem is that the unions have far less control over private firms than over school districts, and they may find that the firms' practices and procedures—longer hours, different teaching methods, different curricula—could outperform and disrupt those of the regular public schools. But more important still, they worry that even small experiments in contracting to private firms could lead to far greater privatization in the future and to a flow of jobs, money, and control from the public to the private sector. The last thing the unions want is a demonstration that private firms can do a better job of educating children than the regular, unionized schools can do. Their political clout guarantees that many Democrats will go along with them in opposing privatization. And they are aided by the long-standing skepticism among liberal groups about the role of profits in provision of public services.

With such union-led opposition, only a small percentage of school districts—no more than a few hundred out of a total of almost 15,000 districts nationwide—have been willing to experiment with privatization, usually when they have been at the end of their rope: faced with failing schools that they have been unable to turn around, under intense pressure to improve, and not knowing what else to do. In these proportionately few cases, the unions have often licked their wounds and kept on fighting—making loud public claims about the firms' poor performance, inciting parent opposition, accusing firms of doctoring test scores, pursuing court cases to challenge the firms' authority and operating decisions, and otherwise making privatization a miserable, costly, and politically tumultuous experience for all concerned.

This is what they did to the first major firm to venture into the education management business—Education Alternatives, Inc. (EAI)—whose initial, nationally watched contracts in Baltimore and then Hartford in the early nineties ended when school authorities, overwhelmed by union-inspired political pressures, reneged on prior agreements and sent EAI packing (and nearly into bankruptcy). In the years since, other private firms have learned from EAI's experience and, among other things, been much more careful in choosing their districts and finding those rare local unions that, given dire circumstances, seem willing to work with them. Of these firms, the largest and most prominent is Edison Schools, which now runs about 150 public schools—including twenty-one in Philadelphia, whose public school system is currently under state takeover. But Edison too is up to its neck in troubles and is constantly forced to devote precious resources to defending itself from political attack. For these firms, simply being able to focus on the education of children is a luxury—which obviously makes success a difficult proposition. This is the way the unions want it. They want Edison and all the others to fail. They want privatization to fail. And they are using their power to bring these failures about.

Of course, the unions' success at playing defense needs to be appreciated in perspective. There is no denying that, since the Milwaukee breakthrough in 1990, the school choice movement has made real progress. Before then, choice was little more than a glimmer in Milton Friedman's eye, and the idea that markets should play an integral role in public education was regarded as some kind of heresy. But this is no longer the case. Choice, competition, and privatization are taken seriously in today's policy arenas, and they have clearly established a beachhead in American education, especially in inner-city areas where the public schools are in desperate need of reform.

As with accountability, however, there is more symbol than substance here. When a choice or privatization plan is adopted, which is the exception rather than the rule, it typically happens only after a bitterly fought political battle in which the unions and their allies, while accepting the outcome (or unable to prevent it), have played an influential role in the design of the program. They impose all manner of restrictions and limitations to ensure that there is actually very little choice, very little competition, very little reliance on market dynamics—and very little threat to their interests. What appear at the outset to be revolutionary reforms, therefore, are mostly gutted by the time they make it through the political process.

Not even the most avid supporter should expect these reforms to perform very well or to bring about significant improvements in American education. At least not yet. The hope has to be that these early attempts, hobbled by their enemies, will ultimately lead to more comprehensive reforms that are actually designed to do the job. The question is: can we realistically believe that such a thing will happen?

The Future

The politics of education hardly gives us much reason for optimism. Despite the pluralism that many observers seem to associate with it— the multiplicity of interest groups, the various levels and types of government officials, the never-ending clash of values—there is a very simple structure to it that renders most of the apparent pluralism irrelevant and misleading, at least when it comes to explaining the most basic policy outcomes. The structure of education politics arises from the fact that the teacher unions have vested interests in the existing system, from which they benefit enormously regardless of how poorly it performs; they have tremendous political power at all governmental levels; and in a political system of myriad checks and balances, they are able to use their power to block most reforms they do not like, and to water down or eviscerate virtually all of the rest by purposely imposing designs that prevent them from working effectively.

This is the politics of the status quo. And because it is what it is, "major" reforms of American education aren't likely to amount to much. Anything that is truly major, that promises to initiate a fundamental transformation of the system, will simply be defeated. And anything that survives the political process will be so whittled down, twisted, and emaciated that it may bear little resemblance to the ideas that motivated it and will almost surely do little to bring about the significant improvements that were intended. It won't be major anymore.

So are the aspirations of A *Nation at Risk* doomed to go unmet? The answer depends on whether the teacher unions can be dislodged from their roles as the supreme gatekeepers of education reform—

which in turn depends on whether their blocking power can be drastically reduced, so that genuine changes in the status quo can go forward. Obviously, there can be nothing easy about this. In the first place, there is a catch-22 at work: the unions are already powerful, and they will use that power to defeat any attempt to take their power away. The only way to reduce their power, it seems, is to be more powerful than they are. And in the politics of education, no other group or coalition is even close. In addition, the power of the teacher unions is reinforced by the power of their allies, Democratic office holders and liberal interest groups, which makes them even more difficult to dislodge.

Nonetheless, there is a power transition under way even now. It is almost imperceptible, and it may take many years to come to fruition, but it is happening. The main sources of the transition are the very reforms that the teacher unions have been fighting against over the last two decades: accountability and school choice. For the most part, the unions have been successful at stalling or weakening these efforts to bring about real change in the system. But they haven't prevented them from gaining a foothold—and because each is backed by a movement with genuine power, there is every reason to believe that they will expand their turf in the years ahead. As this happens, however slow and frustrating the process may be, it will take a toll on the teacher unions by eating away at the very roots of their power.

This is especially true for school choice. In the first place, the unions cannot hold their liberal coalition together for very long on this issue. Their problem is that Democrats and civil rights groups do not have the same self-interest in the current education system that the unions do. Rather, they have constituents in the inner city who are trapped in inadequate schools and very supportive of vouchers and other forms of choice. Until now, the civil rights groups have opposed choice because their leaders, whose generation came up through the ranks during the Civil Rights Movement decades ago, have long seen choice as a subterfuge for segregation. But younger black leaders have had very different life experiences, and they don't see it that way: they see choice as a means of empowering the poor. Soon they will be moving into positions of power, and as they do the civil rights groups will begin to take a much more positive stance toward school choice. Indeed, it could easily happen earlier, for the current leadership is under pressure from many of its own members—and competition from other groups (notably, the Black Alliance for Educational Options)—to shift sides. As this movement begins to happen, it will be much easier for Democrats to do what many of them would like to do anyway: represent their own constituents without regard for union retribution. The liberal coalition's battle against the poor is inherently out of sync with the political incentives and ideals of the liberals themselves, and it won't last. As it breaks down, the unions will increasingly be fighting their battles alone.

In the second place, whatever the politics may be, the very expansion of school choice has a corrosive effect on union power. So far, the teacher unions have been able to develop their organizations within a safe, secure environment of government regulation, insulated from competition and knowing that, whatever costs and rigidities they impose on the public schools, the kids and the resources and the union members would always be there. The conditions have been ideal for amassing power and exercising it with a vengeance. But school choice undercuts all this. By allowing kids and resources to leave the regular public schools for other alternatives and by forcing unionized schools to compete with nonunion schools, it ensures that the unions will lose members and resources—and thus become smaller and less politically powerful. It also ensures that they will have very different incentives in the exercise of what power they have: because to the extent they resist reforms that would make unionized schools less productive than nonunion schools, they will be slitting their own throats.

Accountability does not go for the jugular the way choice does, but it does make life more difficult for the unions. By insisting that performance be measured and made public, accountability systems provide concrete information that puts the spotlight on people, schools, and districts that are not doing their jobs well. And inevitably, it puts the spotlight on unions as well—because unions are in the business of protecting mediocre and incompetent teachers, ensuring that pay cannot be linked to performance, and making the schools less flexible and more bureaucratic. Through evidence and publicity, then, accountability reforms help to generate political pressure on the unions to stop using their power as they do—and help to convince those who want better schools, including many of the unions' own allies, that the unions have to start behaving more "responsibly." Even now, many liberals are openly embarrassed by the teacher unions' blatantly self-interested approach to the schools, and it is common to see editorials and op-ed pieces bashing them in major newspapers (such as the *New York Times* and the *Washington Post*) that are known for their liberal politics.

So far, accountability and choice have not gone far enough to make a real dent in union power. The unions have seen to it that, as things now stand, both reforms are hollow shells of what they might be. But time isn't standing still, and neither are the choice and accountability movements—which continue to fight for their causes, and continue step by step to create programs that are incrementally better and stronger than the ones that went before. As they do, the unions will be faced with more effective competition and with mounting organizational and political problems—and their power will slowly ebb. As that happens, they will be less able to defend the status quo from the relentless challenges of reformers, and there will be more and increasingly stronger reforms—which will undermine their power still further, leading to accelerating reforms. And so it will go.

This process may take decades, just as the Progressive transformation did during the early to mid-1900s. But the result is likely to be an education system that is far better than the one we have now. No system emerging from the pulling and hauling of the political process is likely to meet our highest expectations. But it will nonetheless embody changes that strike to the heart of some of the current system's most fundamental problems, combining top-down account-ability with the energizing, bottom-up forces of choice and competi-tion to put a premium on performance and drive out much of the stagnation and complacency that for so long has been the norm in American education. This, I think, will be the true legacy of A *Nation at Risk*. Not the tidal wave of mainstream reforms usually associated with it, but the far more significant achievements of choice and ac-countability—in changing our education system for the better, and in moving us beyond the politics of the status quo.

Notes

1. On the political history of Progressive education reform, see, for example, Paul E. Peterson, *The Politics of School Reform, 1870–1940* (Chicago: University of Chicago Press, 1985); also David B. Tyack, *The One Best System* (Cambridge: Harvard University Press, 1974).
2. On the rise of the teacher unions, the sources of the political power, and their exercise of it, see Myron Lieberman, *The Teacher Unions* (New York: Free Press, 1997).
3. Clive S. Thomas and Ronald J. Hrebnar, "Interest Groups in the Amer-ican States," in *Politics in the American States*, ed. Virginia Gray and Herbert Jacobs, 7th ed. (Washington, D.C.: CQ Press, 1999).
4. Denis P. Doyle and Terry W. Hartle, *Excellence in Education: The States Take Charge* (Washington, D.C.: American Enterprise Institute, 1985), 1.
5. Perhaps the most comprehensive account of the post–*Nation at Risk* reforms can be found in Thomas Toch, *In the Name of Excellence* (New York: Oxford University Press, 1991). See also Marshall S. Smith and Jennifer O'Day, "Systemic School Reform," in *The Politics of Curriculum and Testing*, ed. Susan H. Fuhrman and Betty Malen (New York: Falmer Press, 1991); and William A. Firestone, Susan H. Fuhrman, and Michael Kirst, "State Educational Reform Since 1983: Appraisal and the Future," *Educational Policy* 5, no. 3 (September 1991): 233–50.
6. For an empirical study, see Anthony Bryk, "No Child Left Behind, Chi-cago Style: What Has Really Been Accomplished?" (paper presented at

the conference on Taking Account of Accountability, John F. Kennedy School of Government, Harvard University, June 2002).

7. See, for example, Eric Hanushek, "The Evidence on Class Size," in *Earning and Learning: How Schools Matter*, ed. Susan E. Mayer and Paul E. Peterson (Washington, D.C.: Brookings Institution Press, 1999).

8. The following discussion of the politics of accountability relies upon Terry M. Moe, "Politics, Control, and the Future of Accountability," in *No Child Left Behind? The Politics and Practice of Accountability*, ed. Paul E. Peterson and Martin West (forthcoming).

9. For a perspective on the how the politics of accountability has unfolded across states, see Lance T. Izumi and Williamson M. Evers, "State Accountability Systems," in *School Accountability*, ed. Williamson M. Evers and Herbert J. Walberg (Stanford, Calif.: Hoover Press, 2002).

10. For empirical accounts that document how unions have acted to block or weaken serious accountability efforts in specific states, see Paul Hill and Robin J. Lake, "Standards and Accountability in Washington State," in *Brookings Papers on Education Policy*, ed. Diane Ravitch (Washington, D.C.: Brookings Institution Press, 2002); Frederick M. Hess, "Reform, Resistance . . . Retreat? The Predictable Politics of Accountability in Virginia," in *Brookings Papers on Education Policy*, ed. Ravitch; and Michele Kurtz, "Testing, Testing: School Accountability in Massachusetts" (working paper 1, Rappaport Institute for Greater Boston, John F. Kennedy School of Government, Harvard University, 2001).

11. On the role of groups other than unions in the politics of accountability, see especially Hess, "Reform, Resistance . . . Retreat," in *Brookings Papers on Education Policy*, ed. Ravitch.

12. For a description of accountability systems across states, see Education Week, *Quality Counts 2002* (Bethesda, Md.: Education Week, 2002).

13. For an overview of the politics and history of school choice, see Terry M. Moe, *Schools, Vouchers, and the American Public* (Washington, D.C.: Brookings Institution Press, 2001). See also Hubert Morken and Jo Renee Formicola, *The Politics of School Choice* (London: Rowman and Littlefield, 1999).

14. For an overview of the politics, content, and history of the Milwaukee voucher plan, see Moe, *Schools, Vouchers, and the American Public*; and John F. Witte, *The Market Approach to Education* (Princeton: Princeton University Press, 2000).

15. See Robert E. Moffit, Jennifer J. Garrett, and Janice A. Smith, *School Choice 2001* (Washington, D.C.: Heritage Foundation, 2001).

16. For figures on private voucher programs, see Matthew Ladner, *Just Do It 5* (Bentonville, Ark.: Children First America, 2001). On the private voucher movement, see Terry M. Moe, ed., *Private Vouchers* (Stanford, Calif.: Hoover Press, 1995); and William G. Howell and Paul E. Peterson, *The Education Gap* (Washington, D.C.: Brookings Institution Press, 2002).

17. On the charter movement generally, see Chester E. Finn, Bruno V. Manno, and Gregg Vanourek, *Charter Schools in Action* (Princeton: Princeton University Press, 2000).

18. On "contracting out" generally, see Paul T. Hill, Lawrence C. Pierce, and James W. Guthrie, *Reinventing Public Education: How Contracting Can Transform America's Schools* (Chicago: University of Chicago Press, 1997). For a discussion of its politics, see Terry M. Moe, "Democracy and the Challenge of Education Reform," in *Advances in the Study of Entrepreneurship, Innovation, and Economic Growth*, ed. Gary D. Libecap (Greenwich, Conn.: JAI Press, 1997).

7

Teacher Reform Gone Astray

Chester E. Finn Jr.

Introduction and Background

Teaching was one of the National Commission on Excellence in Education's (Excellence Commission) four urgent domains of diagnosis and prescription. Its central failings, as the commissioners analyzed the K–12 world in 1983, were that "not enough of the academically able students are being attracted to teaching; that teacher preparation programs need substantial improvement; that the professional working life of teachers is on the whole unacceptable; and that a serious shortage of teachers exists in key fields." This critique was then itemized and extended into the following six particulars:

- Too many teachers are drawn from the bottom of their high school and college classes.

- The teacher-preparation curriculum is heavy on methods and light on subject matter.

- The pay is too low *and* teachers have too little influence over "critical professional decisions," such as textbook selection.

- Teacher shortages exist in selected fields.

- The shortage is acute in math and science (a situation especially disturbing to the two world-class scientists who served on the Excellence Commission, Harvard physicist Gerald Holton and U.C. Berkeley Nobel laureate chemist Glenn Seaborg).

- Half the newly employed teachers of core subjects are "not qualified" to teach them.

To solve these problems, the Excellence Commission made seven recommendations.

1. Would-be teachers should be required to meet high educational standards, to demonstrate an aptitude for teaching, and to show their competence in an academic discipline. Colleges and universities offering teacher preparation programs should be judged by how well their graduates meet these criteria.

2. Salaries for teaching should be increased—and should be market sensitive and performance based. Pay, promotion, tenure, and retention should be tied to an "effective evaluation system that includes peer review so that superior teachers can be rewarded, average ones encouraged, and poor ones either improved or terminated."

3. School boards should adopt an eleven-month contract for teachers.

4. Career ladders should be established for teachers so they can gain in status and pay without leaving the classroom.

5. The country should make an urgent push to solve the math and science (and English) teacher shortages, including bringing "qualified individuals" into the classroom through unconventional paths.

6. Incentives should be created to attract outstanding students to teaching.

7. Master teachers should design teacher preparation programs and supervise novice instructors.

Note the image of teachers and their role in education that threads through the Excellence Commission's diagnosis and prescription. Though paying some heed to "professionalism," on the whole it was an instrumental view of teachers as crucial workers in an underperforming industry, namely U.S. schools. Bold steps were needed to boost that industry's efficiency and productivity, which naturally included attention to the quality and effectiveness of its workforce. But the Excellence Commission's conception of teachers was chiefly as the means to an important end, not as an end in themselves. We find in A *Nation at Risk* no clarion summons to "empower" teachers or place them in charge of key education decisions or reinvent schools around them. Their well-being and the enhancement of their profession were not the commission's foremost concerns. Rather, teachers were seen as a key ingredient in schools, an input that needed to be altered— along with time, curriculum, and standards—in order to make schools more effective. Keep this in mind when we turn to the different view of teaching that has shaped most activity in this domain over the past two decades.

And Then What Happened?

In a few policy realms, the Excellence Commission's recommendations were taken fairly seriously in the years after 1983. Certainly that was the case with respect to standards and curriculum. When it came to teachers, however, twenty years later the most striking reality is the degree to which the same problems remain with us. In this sphere, perhaps more than any other, U.S. education hasn't even tried very hard to take the Excellence Commission's advice—and those who did try found themselves facing stubborn resistance.

It's not that the Excellence Commission was wrong. Indeed, its analysis still rings true today. For example, in laying out the "highly qualified teachers challenge" in a June 2002 report to Congress, U.S. education secretary Rod Paige emphasized four problems that echoed (while updating) those of two decades earlier: the failure of most states to tie their standards for teachers to those for students; low academic standards for new teachers; "alternative routes" into teaching that, while numerous, are "still larded with a variety of requirements"; and the employment, via waivers, of too many teachers (especially in high-poverty schools and in math, science, and special education classes) who lack any certification or other qualifications.[1]

These problems are now widely recognized, and not just by Secretary Paige. Any governor giving a state-of-education speech today, upon reaching the part about teaching and teachers, is apt to identify these same problems, very likely in words that echo the Excellence Commission's urgent 1983 summons. Some of these problems, in fact, are worse now—or at least we understand them more vividly. We're more mindful of shortages of competent instructors in key fields and more sensitive to problems like out-of-field teaching. As the baby-boom generation retires in large numbers, we face replacement needs that loom larger than anyone could have imagined back in 1983. At the same time, class size reduction programs (combined with renewed enrollment growth) have heightened the demand for teachers and exacerbated shortages. Perhaps above all, we're more keenly aware of how important teachers are to children's education, particularly for the most sorely disadvantaged youngsters. Consider, for example, William Sanders's powerful evidence from Tennessee demonstrating how severely children's progress is retarded by a succession of weak teachers and how marvelously it is advanced by several excellent instructors in a row.[2]

Though the teacher-related problems that the Excellence Com-

mission identified remain very much with us, the solutions urged in
A Nation at Risk have not been widely embraced. As a country, we've
really just toyed with some of them. Prodded by then-governor Lamar
Alexander, for example, Tennessee established a teacher "career ladder." Several communities and states make incentive payments to new
math and science teachers. A few give bonuses and other incentives
to beginning teachers. A handful of districts have haltingly experi-
mented with performance-based compensation systems. Some states
have formally abolished the undergraduate education major, in the
hope that teachers will instead immerse themselves in the fields they
intend to teach. Most states have developed "alternate routes" to
certification, meant to ease the entry of nontraditional candidates into
public school classrooms.

Yet nearly all of these innovations were small or transient or turned
into Potemkin-style reforms as the old arrangements were gradually
reinstated behind a facade of change. Once Alexander left the state-
house in Nashville, Tennessee's teacher unions chewed away at the
career ladder until it collapsed. The performance-based pay experiments in places like Denver, Cincinnati, Minneapolis, and Douglas
County, Colorado, turn out to be linked primarily to supervisor or
peer judgments, not to one's track record in producing student learning.[3] States with the capacity to engage in "value-added" analysis of
teacher effectiveness refrain from doing so or—if they do it at all—
don't use such data for personnel actions or compensation decisions.
Many alternative-certification programs have slid back into the
clutches of the education schools, such that candidates end up eventually taking and doing essentially all the same things as "traditional"
candidates, the chief difference being that they do it later or part-time
and can earn a salary while doing so. (That's still a worthy change that
cuts the opportunity cost of becoming a teacher, but it doesn't transform our concept of what new teachers must take and what experiences they must have—or at whose hands.) Universities have also
proven adept at relabeling courses so that the "abolition" of the edu-

cation major may be illusory—for example, "math education" classes are dubbed "math" classes with no real change to their content or professors.

What Went Wrong?

Why hasn't more happened by way of serious reform in this area? Why have the Excellence Commission's recommendations not charted our actual course? I find two main explanations: intense resistance from powerful forces, plus the emergence of an alternative conception of teachers, teaching, and the reform thereof, a conception that carried the strong backing of the very forces opposed to the Excellence Commission's policy course.

Doing what the Excellence Commission urged with respect to teachers would mean altering deeply entrenched practices and challenging the sturdiest bastions of the "education establishment": teacher unions, colleges of education, and state education bureaucracies. It would mean training people differently, licensing them differently, paying them differently (and differentially), judging them differently. For the most part, this simply hasn't happened. The forces arrayed on behalf of such changes were not half as strong as those massed to repel reform.

Indeed, once the Excellence Commission delivered its report in 1983, it went out of business. Though the federal education department published a follow-up report (A Nation Responds), the policy reforms that the Excellence Commission had urged were largely out of Washington's hands. And after the Excellence Commission folded its tent, there was no organized force to do battle on its behalf. Yet plenty of organized forces stood ready to oppose such changes. It didn't take long for that resistance—particularly to the Excellence Commission's salary recommendations—to surface.

A year and a half after A Nation at Risk was issued, Gerald Holton, who had drafted much of the report, wrote a memoir of the experience and its immediate aftermath. In it, he noted that "criticism by certain teacher groups [presumably he meant the unions] . . . focuses chiefly on the recommendation to make 'salaries professionally competitive, market sensitive, and performance based.' The fear is fundamentally one of seeing too great a differentiation in pay and status simply on the basis of 'merit,' as defined by others."[4]

Holton understood this anxiety: "Unless there is a marked upgrading of salaries across the board," he wrote, "with the present low level in many cities and states corrected, any policy concentrating on differentiation of pay must mean, in practice, that most teachers will experience cutbacks when the inadequate pool is reapportioned, often by criteria that the teachers themselves do not trust."

In fact, however, the pool grew. Since Holton wrote those words, teachers have enjoyed an across-the-board boost in their pay. Real (inflation-adjusted) teacher pay rose 12 percent from 1982 to 2000 (see figure 17 in chapter 3 by Caroline Hoxby). Some of that money presumably could have been "reapportioned" to the kind of differential-pay scheme the Excellence Commission had recommended without causing the "cutbacks" that Holton feared. But this didn't happen. It was the nature of the Excellence Commission's recommendations that posed the tough political challenge, not national stinginess toward schoolteachers. Instead of raising their pay at a faster clip, states and communities have tended to expand their numbers, both in order to reduce class size and, some analysts suggest, to compensate for their lackluster quality—and the comparatively greater cost of recruiting better ones.[5]

At the same time, we must note that educated workers in other fields found their income rising faster than that of teachers, meaning that the financial rewards of teaching declined in relative terms, a development sure to worsen the teacher-quality problem that had exercised the Excellence Commission (see figure 18 in Hoxby's chapter). Registered nurses, for example—another unionized, state-li-

censed, mostly female profession that requires a college degree—
enjoyed a constant-dollar increase of 16 percent from 1982 to 2000.

A Rival Is Born

On balance, of the Excellence Commission's seven recommendations
for solving the teacher-related parts of the education risk facing the
nation in 1983, numbers two through seven have been only dabbled
in. That there has been more action with respect to the first
recommendation[6] is due largely to the fact that it harmonized with
another teaching-reform impulse, one that has turned out to have
greater traction, in large part because it arose from within the education establishment itself.

Call it the "teacher professionalism" agenda. Though it had earlier
incarnations, for present purposes it can be traced mainly to another
prominent report of the eighties entitled *A Nation Prepared: Teachers
for the Twenty-First Century*. This did not emerge from the government and had no "official" standing, yet it carried considerable weight.
Its sponsor was the Carnegie Corporation of New York, via a program
called the Carnegie Forum on Education and the Economy led by
foundation president David A. Hamburg. At its maiden session, the
Carnegie Forum spun off a "Task Force on Teaching As a Profession,"
chaired by Lewis Branscomb, then IBM's chief scientist (now a Harvard professor). In 1986, the fourteen-member Carnegie task force
issued its report.

A Nation Prepared's most notable feature was a subtle yet profound
change of focus: from teachers as instruments of school improvement
to teachers as *shapers* of school improvement. From teachers as means
to teachers as ends. From teachers as staff in an education system run
by others, to teachers as key decision makers about the purpose and
operations of the system itself. One might almost say from teachers
as workers to teachers as bosses.

Accompanying this shift of power and emphasis were different idcas about the nature of schooling itself, away from the view that teachers should impart particular knowledge and skills to youngsters and toward the constructivist view that the teacher's foremost mission is to help children become learners. Here is how *Education Week* depicted this transformation:

> In 1986, a landmark report issued by a task force of the Carnegie Corporation of New York called for radical changes in teaching to make it a true profession. The authors envisioned a different kind of teacher—flexible, up-to-date, able to lead children into deeper learning. The next step was for teachers to be mentors and coaches rather than dispensers of facts. Students would take more responsibility for their own education, and teachers would collaborate with them in a search for knowledge and understanding. The school structure would change so that teachers would be deeply involved in decision making: Within broad curricular frameworks, teachers would decide how best to meet their goals. They would participate in the development of new performance-based assessments. They would be empowered to make decisions that affect instruction, budget, personnel, and scheduling. At the same time, though, the teachers would be much better educated and would be eased into their jobs with help from experienced mentors.[7]

Carnegie's view of teaching and teachers could coexist with one or two of the Excellence Commission's teacher recommendations, but on the whole it was rooted in dramatically different core beliefs about who should make key education decisions, and it advanced a markedly different view of the organizational and policy framework within which teachers work—or should work.

This altered focus had much to do with who was focusing. The Excellence Commission included educators but could in no way be termed a creature of the teaching profession or public-school establishment. For example, it had no organization heads, union chiefs, or college of education deans. By contrast, the Carnegie Task Force included a generous representation of public education's political establishment: the presidents of both national teacher unions (the

NEA's Mary Hatwood Futrell and the AFT's Albert Shanker), a governor (New Jersey's Tom Kean), a once and future governor (North Carolina's James B. Hunt), two state education superintendents (California's Bill Honig, Minnesota's Ruth Randall), an education school dean, prominent black and Hispanic academics, a businessman, a legislator, the New York Times's lead education columnist (Fred Hechinger) and the ubiquitous John W. Gardner. This deftly balanced group was staffed by Marc S. Tucker, who later went on to cofound the New Standards project and the National Center on Education and the Economy.

At least as important as—and probably because of—their differing compositions, the two panels began with divergent notions of the key education problems needing to be solved. The Excellence Commission took as its solitary challenge the weak performance of U.S. schools. The Carnegie task force acknowledged the need for stronger student performance but added a second, equivalent challenge: "creating . . . a profession of well-educated teachers prepared to assume new powers and responsibilities to redesign schools for the future." A Nation Prepared thus recast the country's education problem as a dearth of duly empowered teachers and formulated its solution in terms of making the teaching occupation more "professional." Its authors yearned to shift power from "those who would improve the schools from the outside" to educators themselves. They envisioned a "fundamental redesign" of schooling itself, not a simple boosting of the present system's efficiency and productivity.

The task force sought to change the teaching occupation in three crucial ways: raising standards for new entrants; finding ways "to retain in our schools those teachers with the needed skills"; and redesigning "the structure of the system . . . to take maximum advantage of those highly skilled teachers, so that the most efficient use is made of the additional funds required."

Those reforms overlapped a bit with A Nation at Risk's recommendations, but their basic thrust was quite different. The Carnegie group was bent on empowering teachers, boosting their status, influence, and control over the primary-secondary education field in general and schools in particular—and did so with serene confidence that doing this would also boost pupil performance. The Excellence Commission mostly wanted existing schools to work better. It sought to take their essential components and make these more effective. It didn't seek to reengineer schools per se. In a sense, the Excellence Commission trusted the existing system more than the Carnegie crew did, even though the latter were mainly card-carrying participants in that system. The key difference is that the Carnegie team sought to shift more control (and resources) into the hands of educators and their interest groups, while the Excellence Commission seemed content with the "civilian control" arrangements that traditionally characterized the system's governance.

Unlike the Excellence Commission, the Carnegie task force had powerful allies, including people and organizations with great staying power, notably the teacher unions themselves. The campaign that it launched also had access to ample private and public dollars. Much of this money came from Carnegie and other wealthy foundations such as Rockefeller—as became even clearer in 1994, when those two foundations teamed up to provide funds for the new (and seemingly permanent) National Commission on Teaching and America's Future (NCTAF), also drawn from the heart of public education's political establishment.

In time, the teacher-empowerment campaign also won federal funding—far more, ironically, than anything done about teaching in the name of the federally chartered Excellence Commission—and gained much sway in Washington, D.C., as well as state capitals. While it would oversimplify to ascribe this to partisanship, it cannot have hurt those advancing the Carnegie agenda that for eight crucial years during this period the federal executive branch was home to an administration that was politically in sync with teachers and their unions and philosophically comfortable with the professionalism agenda. (GOP policy makers are more apt to think of teaching as a problem area that needs to be set right, even when this entails changes that the unions don't like.) In the end, though, the main explanation for teacher professionalism's leverage at federal and state levels was the old-fashioned, many-splendored political clout of its architects and builders.

The Rival Prospers

Between 1986, when A Nation Prepared was issued, and 1994, when the NCTAF was formed, several related entities were born or strengthened in pursuit of the professionalism goal. Foremost among these was the National Board for Professional Teaching Standards (NBPTS), founded in 1987 and the recipient of much foundation and federal largesse, chiefly orchestrated by North Carolina's Jim Hunt, who had helped to draft A Nation Prepared. The NBPTS offers a special, advanced credential to superior teachers, whom it identifies largely through a peer-review process. In other words, it recognizes teachers whose ideas and practices find favor with other educators. (There is, as yet, no proof that their students learn more than those of other teachers.)[8]

Also launched in 1987 was the Interstate New Teacher Assessment and Support Consortium (INTASC), composed of state education departments, universities, and national education groups, which seeks to reform teacher preparation, licensure, and professional development.

Another key player is the National Council for Accreditation of Teacher Education (NCATE), long a sleepy, voluntary accrediting body whose transformation began in 1991, when Arthur E. Wise took its helm. A tireless, smart, and politically sophisticated veteran of both academe and Washington, Wise dedicated himself to advancing the professionalism agenda, particularly by persuading many states that they should view NCATE as a partner in deciding which teacher-preparation programs deserve state approval. (This effort got a further boost in 1992 when the National Education Association committed itself to requiring all teacher preparation programs to obtain NCATE certification.)

While the Excellence Commission had no organizational progeny to carry on its bloodline, the Carnegie task force sired a whole family of descendants, including the NBPTS, the INTASC, the NCTAF, and a reenergized NCATE. Three of those entities have come to wield much leverage over the means by which one gets trained for teaching, is licensed to teach, and advances through the profession. The fourth, the National Commission on Teaching and America's Future, has functioned as cheerleader, coach, and intellectual arsenal for the others, as well as campaign manager for the broader agenda advanced in *A Nation Prepared* and a host of subsequent reports. All these efforts gained further clout (and access to human, fiscal, political, and public relations resources) from their close affiliation with the teacher unions, the American Association of Colleges of Teacher Education (AACTE), and other mainstream groups comprising what former education secretary William J. Bennett once termed "the blob." And they benefited hugely from the emergence of a loose interlocking directorate among them, such that many of the same organizations and people are engaged in the policy direction, political advancement, and funding of them all.

Others joined the crusade for teacher professionalism. For example, in 1986, a cadre of prominent education-school deans formed a body called the Holmes Group to rethink teacher education. Its debut report, *Tomorrow's Teachers*, emphasized new and ostensibly more professional ways to prepare teachers, which it embellished four years later in *Tomorrow's Schools*, a report full of talk of radically restructuring schools, ensuring that learning would become lifelong for both teachers and students, creating "learning communities," "professional development schools," and so forth. The Holmes Group took teacher preparation as seriously as student learning—not too surprising, considering its constituency. Like Carnegie and its offspring, the Holmes Group placed teachers at the center of the education solar system, not as a satellite orbiting within that system.

Besides Carnegie and Holmes, in 1987 the Milken Family Foundation began its annual educator awards (of $25,000 per teacher) as a way of recognizing outstanding teachers and principals and fostering their professionalism. A decade later, Milken launched the Teacher Advancement Program, a promising way to restructure the entire teaching profession.

The Rival Prevails

Teacher professionalism has a mom-and-apple-pie aura. Americans are fond of their teachers and tend to respect people described as professionals. As a result, the quest for teacher professionalism has largely trumped the push for improved teacher performance. It has become a policy goal in its own right, one that now obscures the view of teachers as instruments for producing more learning in children and better performance by their schools. And it's become a goal on which much policy activity has centered. Indeed, the teacher-professionalism agenda has had enormous influence over the policies and practices of American public education during the past fifteen years, dwarfing any impacts attributable to the Excellence Commission in terms of both scale and durability.

It did not take long. Within months of A *Nation Prepared*'s 1986 release, the American Federation of Teachers and the National Governors Association (NGA) endorsed it, and the NGA incorporated some of its principles into that organization's own influential *Time for Results* manifesto, prepared under the leadership of future U.S. education secretary Lamar Alexander. At least seven states launched school-restructuring programs attuned to those same principles, as did a number of large school systems.[9] And as the professionalism agenda gained traction at the national level, it affected more and more state policies. Three examples illustrate the point.

First, heeding the professionalism rhetoric and responding to the teacher unions' (and education schools') political clout, by 2001, sixteen states had created teacher professional standards boards that were entirely autonomous of the state education agency and thus largely beyond the influence of elected policy makers, voters, and taxpayers. Such boards wield immense power through their control of teacher and principal preparation standards and certification decisions, so it matters greatly who is on them and what their members value. Three other states had semiautonomous boards of this kind—and a number of legislatures are considering moves in this direction. Seductive and reasonable as it sounds to wrest teacher standards and licensure from the bureaucratic grip of the state—after all, lawyers do much the same thing through the state bar associations—in reality, these structures nearly always turn out to be dominated by teacher unionists and education school faculty. This tends to lock in the professionalism agenda while rendering states markedly less hospitable to alternative certification, subject-centered preparation programs, and kindred reforms of teaching.

Second, the "professionalizers" have put great pressure on states to mandate NCATE accreditation for their teacher-preparation programs. Though this is a major departure from the theory of voluntary accreditation that launched the NCATE, it's consistent with the post-Carnegie view that government instrumentalities at every level should be bent to the service of teacher professionalism. Nearly every state now has some sort of partnership with this accrediting organization and, in half of them, the NCATE wields joint power in determining which preparation programs get state approval for purposes of teacher certification. (In eighteen others, the NCATE advises the state education agency on which programs to approve.) Four states require full NCATE accreditation before a teacher-training program can operate within their borders. Three more have imposed this requirement on their public colleges and universities. The upshot is that the NCATE's ideas of what comprises a sound program—its content, its methods, its faculty, its philosophy—have immense influence on state decisions about who will teach in the public schools and how they will be prepared for the classroom.[10]

Third, the National Board for Professional Teaching Standards has succeeded in persuading many states and districts to reward, recognize, or assist those teachers who secure its stamp of approval. Twenty-five states now offer ongoing (or multiyear) salary increases to NBPTS-certified teachers. Four provide one-time bonuses and twenty more offer other recognitions or subsidies (such as paying the NBPTS's hefty application fee for candidates from their states). Moreover, several hundred school districts have their own versions of salary boosts, bonuses, subsidies, and recognitions for NBPTS-certified teachers.

The professionalism agenda also proved influential in some localities, of which the best-known example is Rochester, New York, where Marc Tucker's National Center on Education and the Economy was long based. As Tucker and former U.S. labor secretary Ray Marshall recount the beginning of a long saga,

> In the fall of 1986, the Rochester City School District . . . and the Rochester Teachers Association announced a new contract that caught the country by surprise. The contract incorporated the salary recommendations of the Carnegie report, raising average teachers' salaries by more than 40 percent . . . ; incorporating . . . a career ladder for teachers . . . ; an agreement to develop a site-based management system that would empower teachers to make many more of the key decisions about instruction . . . ; a provision involving the teachers' union in working to improve the performance of weak teachers . . . ; and an agreement to develop a system for increased teacher accountability. . . .[11]

Considering all this activity and the immense political, legislative, and budgetary resources that it has consumed, one might say that the teacher professionalism agenda has functioned like a black hole in space, sucking in much of the available energy, attention, and funds and leaving little for other reforms—not just other teacher-related reforms (such as those urged by the Excellence Commission) but also a very different list of changes (for example, in technology, competition, preschool, new curricula) that might prove more effective and economical as strategies for boosting pupil achievement. Along with salary increases and class-size reductions, we can conclude that the reforms associated with teacher professionalism have been the principal policy preoccupation of educators themselves during the period since A *Nation at Risk*.

The Rival Is Doubted

So ardent a push for teacher professionalism might be warranted if we were confident that its full flowering would yield the desired results for students and schools as well as for teachers and their advocates and organizations. Perhaps the Excellence Commission's proposals were faulty and the Carnegie strategy is superior. Then we would have no reason to object to its consuming the available education-reform oxygen.

But there are significant reasons to doubt that the professionalism agenda is succeeding from the standpoint of children, parents, taxpayers, and public officials, however much it may point to changes that teachers favor.

First, it rests on a shaky evidentiary and research base concerning its ability to solve the problems identified by the Excellence Commission. There is little evidence that it will boost student learning or address either the quality or quantity challenges that the current teaching force poses. In other words, it is a weak—and costly—solution to the problems at hand.[12] In Rochester, for example, within five years, the Carnegie-inspired reform plan had succeeded in boosting teacher pay but had induced little change in school operations or student results.[13]

Second, the professionalism agenda rests on a philosophy of education that flies in the face of what most Americans believe to be essential in the schooling of their daughters and sons. This leads to friction, dissension, and confusion. In hindsight, it was inevitable that professionalism would eschew basic skills and knowledge and instead hook up with constructivism. They share kindred intellectual and institutional origins.[14] Yet most parents want their children's teachers to impart specific skills and knowledge, and that's also how many policy makers view the mission of the schools that they are asked to fund. However much one may wish it were not so, the skills-and-knowledge view of student learning is best advanced by treating teachers as expert technicians who are skillful at implementing others' designs. They also must be held accountable to others outside the profession for educational outcomes that are also largely shaped outside the priesthood of experts. Stating it simply: The public's push for basic skills and knowledge clashes with educators' press for greater professionalism.

Third, in institutional and organizational terms, the professionalism agenda is deeply conservative. It seeks to strengthen monopolies, to maintain established practices and orthodoxies, to retain power and prestige within a tight fraternity of experts, to fend off structural changes, and, of course, to deter radical education innovations that do not hinge on a vast cadre of "professional" teachers (for example, distance learning, virtual schooling).

Fourth, owing in part to its conservatism and in part to its constructivism, the professionalism agenda keeps running afoul of the two dominant education-reform strategies in America today. One of these, usually termed "standards-based reform," owes much to the Excellence Commission but is not popular with educators, who insist that many state standards are mindless, that "teaching to the test" cramps their style and makes a mockery of true learning, and that they ought not be held to account—especially to laymen—for pupil results that are substantially beyond their control. Thus, for example, most of the major K–12 education groups voiced serious misgivings about the federal No Child Left Behind legislation, never mind its attempt to mandate "highly qualified" teachers in every U.S. classroom.[15] (Though that measure made it through Congress, the public education "blob" succeeded in greatly weakening Bush's original proposal.)

The other prominent reform strategy, based on marketplaces, school competition, and parental choice (for example, charter schools, vouchers, privately managed public schools), owes little to the Excellence Commission, but is even more repugnant to established education groups. They see it as letting anybody into the classroom—not just members of their certified priesthood—while shifting power from experts to laymen and from producers to consumers.

As both of these strategies moved forward, the professionalizers found themselves on the defensive more often and discovered that some of their long-sought policy conquests were blocked or slowed by these newer notions of education reform.

Fifth, key elements of the professionalism agenda turn out to be less than fully welcome within the ranks of its strongest political allies, notably the teacher unions. Though they have carried its banner and in some cases (for example, the NBPTS) have been key agents of its advancement, their basic orientation to the work of teachers has more in common with fifties-style smokestack industries than with any normal notion of professionalism. The unions' top-priority issues are uniform salary levels, benefits, class size, and job security, none of which is compatible with traditional concepts of professionalism. Moreover, their focus on these issues tends to consume the available resources of money and political energy, resources that otherwise could go to the quest for greater professionalism and to the school reform campaigns that are most apt to advance the professionalism agenda. Moreover, there is plenty of evidence that education resources, when consumed in these ways, do little to boost school effectiveness and productivity.

For the most part, the unions have also ignored good advice about how to professionalize their own operations; they remain stuck in the steelworkers' mode of job actions, districtwide collective bargaining, the defense of mediocrity, and insistence on uniform treatment for all their members.[16] While there have been a handful of exceptions, mostly within the American Federation of Teachers and notably including that organization's respected longtime leader, the late Albert Shanker, the unions' general aversion to actually behaving—and encouraging their members to behave—as professionals is squarely at odds with the professionalism agenda itself. Indeed, as recently as July 2002, outgoing NEA president Bob Chase pleaded with his members not to "go backward" on the "new unionism" agenda that he had sought (with very limited success) to advance during his tenure.

Sixth, and finally, some of the changes sought by the professionalizers end up worsening other education problems. Notably, the push to raise standards for entry into the public school classroom aggravates teacher shortages, boosts opportunity costs for career-switchers and others who would be willing to try teaching, and strengthens the public education cartel that resists other reforms. NCATE accreditation standards militate against innovations in teacher preparation. Financial rewards for teachers who get certified by the NBPTS not only absorb scarce state and local education dollars, but they also impede the move to judge educators' effectiveness by how much their students learn.

The Rival Is Opposed

These are heavy burdens for the professionalizers, major impediments to reshaping the education world around their model, and they haven't gotten any easier to skirt. Indeed, resistance to the professionalism agenda has stiffened in recent years. Four developments warrant mention.

First, standards-based reform turned out to have staying power, which has placed greater pressure on teachers and other educators to demonstrate their effectiveness. It has also incorporated efforts to set external standards for educators themselves. More states are testing their teachers—new teachers, rarely veterans—and in 1998, California congressman George Miller spearheaded a successful move in Congress to require states to report the pass rates of their various teacher-preparation programs. (This was, in fact, a recommendation of the Excellence Commission.) Although the present version of this rule proved easy for universities to foil and states to manipulate, Congress will likely revisit it in 2004. Most important, the advent of more student testing, especially the spread of value-added measures of pupil and school performance, and the arrival of high-stakes test-based accountability, has underscored the idea that teachers should be evaluated based on the results they produce, a far cry from everything the professionalizers cherish. Worse (from their standpoint), Uncle Sam has gotten deeper into the act, first with a pair of 1994 statutes and more recently with the No Child Left Behind act, which further prods schools, districts, and states to moor their education policies to results-based accountability. (The legislation also mandates that, by 2006, every child in American schools be taught by a highly qualified teacher, which one might think would please the professionalism crowd but which seems to be having the opposite effect!)[17]

Second, the education marketplace has been strengthened; new providers have entered and consumers have been empowered. With some 2,700 charter schools in operation, choice-based education reform has gained traction despite the unions' opposition—and may gain more in the aftermath of the Supreme Court's June 2002 decision in the Cleveland voucher case. Though nothing says that a school of choice ought not be staffed by top-notch education professionals (and many are), the bottom-up, deregulatory, consumer-driven nature of the choice movement inevitably weakens the government-centered, regulation-based, educators-in-charge strategy of the professionalism agenda. Many schools of choice—charters, private schools, outsourced schools, and certainly home schools—are even exempt from state teacher-licensure requirements, meaning that, in effect, the school may select whomever it likes to instruct its pupils. That's a grave blow to Carnegie-style professionalism—and becomes more potent as evidence emerges that such schools perform just as well as, and possibly better than, traditional public schools with all their certified teachers and principals. Because most such schools of choice are also free from mandatory collective bargaining, their proliferation weakens the unions, education schools, and other cartel institutions from which the professionalizers draw most of their political oomph.

Third, bona fide supply and demand considerations, other demographic and school-policy changes (for example, class size reduction), and secular macroeconomic trends have made it impossible for states, districts, and schools to meet their teaching needs exclusively through mechanisms favored by the professionalizers. So they have made pragmatic exceptions to and alterations in those mechanisms when recruiting, compensating, and licensing teachers. In the process, they have often found that the exceptions work at least as well as the rule. Moreover, programs such as Teach for America and Troops to Teachers have come into being, grown, and been vindicated by evaluations, even though these, too, fly in the face of the professionalizers' assumptions and advice. The upshot is that policy makers and citizens alike have observed good results being obtained without jumping through all of the hoops of professionalization.

Fourth, besides those practical problems, an alternative theory has begun to win adherents, one that says the strategy favored by the professionalizers and advanced by their organizations is wrong—or, at least, that it hasn't proved right and therefore should not be mandated throughout the land.

The alternative theory favors deregulation of many aspects of teaching, freer entry into public school classrooms, greater flexibility in personnel management, and more alternatives. Among the groups espousing this heterodox view are the National Council on Teacher Quality, the Education Leaders Council, the Progressive Policy Institute, the Thomas B. Fordham Foundation, and the Abell Foundation. In June 2002, these organizations were joined by none other than U.S. education secretary Rod Paige, whose report on teacher quality alarmed the NCTAF, the NCATE, the American Association of Colleges of Teacher Education, and others habituated to federal backing for the professionalism agenda.[18] Instead, Paige has on several occasions urged states to raise the bar on teacher academic standards while lowering barriers to classroom entry by people without conventional pedagogical preparation. "Raising teacher standards," he said, "is only half of the equation. . . . [S]tates must also tear down the wall that is keeping many talented individuals out of the profession." Paige particularly deplores "mandated education courses, unpaid student teaching, and the hoops and hurdles of the state certification bureaucracy." Instead, he said, "states will need to . . . focus on the few things that really matter: verbal ability, content knowledge, and, as a safety precaution, a background check of new teachers. States need to tap into the vast pool of potential teachers who today are discouraged by the bureaucratic hoops and hurdles but tomorrow might be willing to fill their classrooms."[19] The education secretary has little patience for talk of teacher shortages, contending that this is a policy-induced problem that can be solved by policy changes.

For the Future

How do we go forward? When it comes to teachers, in the years since *A Nation at Risk* a large dichotomy has surfaced between two views of their place in education reform: as instruments—along with many others—for boosting student achievement and school effectiveness or as ends in themselves? Though the real world seldom poses the choice so starkly, we do well to acknowledge that different policy conclusions flow from these rival conceptions of the teacher's role.

Though nothing is gained by papering over these differences, let us also acknowledge that neither approach has the might to vanquish the other. Nor has either yet proven itself so effective that it should be imposed across a large and varied nation. In other words, political prudence and intellectual honesty argue for experimenting with both approaches and with some of their amalgams and combinations. Let's try other plausible ideas and approaches, too. And let's carefully appraise the costs and benefits of them all.

What might this mean in practice?

First, we must agree on a common metric by which to gauge the effectiveness of these several approaches, and it seems clear that this must center on student achievement and, even more, on the value that is added to student achievement by various policy regimens and intervention strategies. Though the value-added methodology for gauging teacher effectiveness is far from fully developed, it is sure to improve and is surely the fairest way to measure the impact of teachers and schools (and education reforms) upon students. Teacher contentment is a welcome secondary outcome—and possible prerequisite—for greater student learning, but it's not the central point or the right barometer of progress. Student learning must be our primary focus and chief tracking system.

Second, because many different strategies have the potential to boost student learning, including some that have not yet been fully tried or examined, we should be open-minded and experimental rather than doctrinaire about teacher-related education reforms. Nobody should have the power to veto a promising approach that might benefit students on grounds that it doesn't appeal to adults who work in schools (or to other interest groups).

Third, among the strategies worth trying are some that flow from the teacher-professionalism agenda: place teachers in charge of schools, employ and compensate them on terms that they like, and let them decide who is qualified to teach in those schools. Encourage the teacher-professionalism organizations and the unions to run schools of their own—an opportunity made readily available by the spread of the charter-school movement. Encourage some school systems and states to embrace the professionalism agenda—so long as it is accompanied by high-quality, long-term, objective evaluations focusing primarily on pupil achievement.

Fourth, among other strategies worth trying are some that do not obey the dictates of the professionalism agenda, including some that remain to be tested from the days of the Excellence Commission. Let charter schools violate the dictates and experiment with alternative approaches to personnel and everything else. Let districts and states experiment, too—field-testing, for example, performance-based pay keyed to the academic value that teachers add to their pupils. Let distance-learning ventures get properly tested despite their profound implications for the role of teachers. Evaluate them, too.

Fifth, when it comes to teacher preparation, we should try both approaches. Let some teachers be trained by NCATE-accredited programs, certified through INTASC-approved means and reviewed by the NBPTS. Let others enter the classroom through alternate routes and programs such as Teach for America. Evaluate both.

Sixth, let us also try some promising hybrids, such as the Teacher Advancement Program developed by the Milken Family Foundation, which enhances teacher professionalism in ways that also recall a number of the recommendations of A Nation at Risk and the latter-day alternative view of teacher quality reform.[20]

This list could easily be extended, but the point is clear. Too many of today's education reform debates are conducted as if they were winner-take-all contests that must leave a single reform strategy standing. That would make sense only if we were certain that a single strategy will succeed everywhere—and if there were any realistic political prospect of that single strategy prevailing everywhere. As yet, however, that case simply cannot be persuasively made. So let's try multiple approaches. Let's try them seriously, with adequate funding and over a long enough period of time. Let's try them with proper control or comparison groups, and let's make sure they are evaluated according to the best available methods—and chiefly in relation to their impact on student achievement. To make that possible, let us declare a truce in the "teacher wars" for a decade or so, while we try to figure out what works best. Perhaps it will turn out that many different approaches are effective. Perhaps none will work well enough. But we'll be better off if we take seriously the job of trying to learn this from the children's standpoint instead of fussing endlessly over the allocation of adult interests.

Notes

1. U.S. Department of Education, Office of Postsecondary Education, Office of Policy Planning and Innovation, *Meeting the Highly Qualified Teachers Challenge: The Secretary's Annual Report on Teacher Quality*, Washington, D.C., 2002.
2. William L. Sanders and June C. Rivers, "Cumulative and Residual Effects of Teachers on Future Student Academic Achievement," University of Tennessee Value-Added Research and Assessment Center, 1996. For a more recent analysis, based on Texas data and conducted by prominent economists, see Steven G. Rivkin, Eric A. Hanushek, and John F. Kain, "Teachers, Schools, and Academic Achievement," National Bureau of Economic Research Working Paper 6691, revised July 2002, which can be found on the Internet at http://edpro.stanford.edu/eah/papers/basic.july2002.PDF.
3. At this writing, the Cincinnati teacher union has backed away from even that and the superintendent who spearheaded the program has resigned.
4. Gerald Holton, *The Advancement of Science, and Its Burdens* (Cambridge, Mass.: Harvard University Press, 1998), 265.
5. Darius Lakdawalla argues that the rising price of skilled labor in the U.S. economy has contributed both to a decline in teacher quality and to the class-size reduction strategy by which the public education system has tended to substitute more (but lower-paid) teachers for fewer, abler but pricier teachers. Of course, teachers' and parents' preferences for smaller

classes must also be considered, as must the teacher unions' preference for larger membership rolls and more dues. See Lakdawalla, "Quantity over Quality," *Education Next* 2, no. 3 (Fall 2002):67.

6. "People preparing to teach should be required to meet high educational standards, to demonstrate an aptitude for teaching, and to demonstrate competence in an academic discipline. Colleges and universities offering teacher preparation programs should be judged by how well their graduates meet these criteria." U.S. Department of Education, The National Commission on Excellence in Education, *A Nation at Risk: The Imperative for Educational Reform*, Washington, D.C., April 1983.

7. *Education Week*, "Teaching As a Profession," 2000. http://www.nationalissues.com/education/teacher_issues/overview_article.html.

8. It must be noted that the NBPTS's emphasis on "peer review" partially adheres to the Excellence Commission's second recommendation concerning teachers. The Commission never really explained what else besides peer review should be part of the teacher evaluation system. Note, too, however, that the review system contemplated in *A Nation at Risk* included "improving or terminating" "poor" teachers, not just rewarding good ones.

9. Ray Marshall and Marc Tucker, *Thinking for a Living* (New York: Basic Books, 1992), especially chapter 8, "Restructuring the Schools for High Performance: Tough Road to Excellence."

10. In the past several years, the NCATE has been challenged, albeit not strongly, by the advent of the Teacher Education Accreditation Council, about which more can be learned at http://www.teac.org/about/index.asp.

11. Marshall and Tucker, op. cit., 113–14.

12. See, for example, the review of this body of research by Kate Walsh, *Teacher Certification Reconsidered: Stumbling for Quality* (Baltimore: The Abell Foundation, 2001). http://www.abell.org/TeacherCert Reconsidered.pdf.

13. See Marshall and Tucker, op. cit., especially 114–124. Eric Hanushek notes that the effects of the Rochester school reform effort have never been seriously evaluated. See Eric A. Hanushek, "Outcomes, Costs, and Incentives in Schools" in *Improving America's Schools: The Role of Incentives*, ed. Eric A. Hanushek and Dale W. Jorgenson (Washington, D.C.: National Academy Press, 1996), 44.

14. For expert renderings of this convoluted story, see E. D. Hirsch Jr., *The*

Schools We Need and Why We Don't Have Them, (New York: Doubleday, 1996); and Diane Ravitch, *Left Back: A Century of Failed School Reforms* (New York: Simon & Schuster, 2000).

15. Prominent exceptions included the American Federation of Teachers and the Council of Great City Schools.

16. See for example, Charles Kershner, Julia Koppich, and Joseph G. Weeres, *United Mind Workers: Unions and Teaching in the Knowledge Society* (San Francisco: Jossey-Bass, 1997).

17. After much debate, Congress ended up with a blurry and evasive definition of "highly qualified" that still defers substantially to the traditional "inputs" approach.

18. For one account of their reaction, see Julie Blair, "Critics Claim Missteps on Execution of Title II," *Education Week,* 7 August 2002, 30,35.

19. U.S. Department of Education, op. cit., 40. See also Secretary Paige's interview with Lawrence McQuillan, "Nonteachers Suggested for U.S. Shortage," *USA Today,* 17 September 2002.

20. More about the Teacher Advancement Program can be learned at http://www.mff.org/tap/. Also see Lowell Milken, *Growth of the Teacher Advancement Program: Teaching As the Opportunity* 2002 (Santa Monica: Milken Family Foundation, July 2002). http://www.mff.org/publications/publications.taf?page?03.

8

The
Curricular
Smorgasbord

Williamson M. Evers
and
Paul Clopton

Introduction

In *A Nation at Risk*, the members of the National Commission on Excellence in Education (Excellence Commission) argued that much of America's decline in academic achievement could be traced to the "cafeteria-style curriculum" or "curricular smorgasbord" offered to high-school students.[1] The report said that the presence of so many nonacademic courses in the curriculum—such as preparation for adulthood, off-campus work experience, and physical and health education—was compromising America's commitment to high-quality academics. This was the result of society placing a "multitude of often conflicting demands" upon the schools, which were regularly asked, according to the Excellence Commission, to solve "personal, social, and political problems" that the home and other societal institutions

The authors wish to acknowledge the research assistance of Kate Feinstein.

were failing to solve. These demands, the report said, have placed burdens on the schools that are both educational and monetary.[2]

A *Nation at Risk* argued that academics should be the core mission of the schools. The report was significant not only because it pointed to the abysmal state of American education. This finding was merely factual. The report was more important for taking on a reigning idea: that American schools, especially high schools, should be multiservice agencies catering to all aspects of the whole child and his or her future adult life. The proponents of this idea believe that the high school curriculum should be substantially, perhaps predominantly, nonacademic. It should include personal and developmental courses (Bachelor Life, for example) as well as vocational courses. Within this scheme, some talented students might be allowed to take difficult academic courses, but most students would take watered-down academics and a substantial load of nonacademic courses. A *Nation at Risk* and its prestigious panel of commissioners declared war on all of this.

In this chapter, we review what has happened to curriculum and achievement in the twenty years since A *Nation at Risk*. We first show that students are taking more academic courses today than in 1983 (as recommended by A *Nation at Risk*), but that these courses may be academic in name only, since student achievement has remained stagnant.

The second half of this chapter considers the historical trends and philosophical traditions that led to the prevalence of the cafeteria-style curriculum in American public high schools by the early eighties. We examine the ideological beliefs of educators and the bureaucratic tendencies of school systems that have encouraged—then and now—watering down the academic curriculum and the proliferation of nonacademic courses. We also explore why those who oppose academic rigor show such passion, persistence, and self-confidence. We conclude by speculating on the future of the academic curriculum and educational achievement in light of the impact of A *Nation at Risk*.

Changes in Curriculum and
Achievement Since A *Nation at Risk*

High School Coursework

Since the publication of A *Nation at Risk*, U.S. Department of Education studies of high school transcripts have shown that school officials have heeded the plea for greater academic coursework, at least in mathematics and science.[3] The studies detail the number of Carnegie units[4] earned by high school graduates in various subject fields for selected graduation years. Because increasing the number of courses overall could artificially bolster the tally of academic courses,[5] we present coursework summaries here as a percentage of total Carnegie units. Figure 1 summarizes these findings.

The share of the curriculum devoted to vocational and "personal" coursework declined from 33 percent in 1982 to 27 percent in 1998. Most of this decline (about 6 percentage points) was in the vocational education category. The average high school graduate had 0.63 fewer Carnegie units in vocational courses in 1998 than in 1982. Meanwhile, the personal coursework category stayed essentially stable over this same period, at 12 pecent of the curriculum. The personal category includes personal and social courses and other nonacademic, nonvocational courses.

At the same time, coursework in higher mathematics and science was increasing. Figure 1 combines mathematics and science coursework into lower math/science and higher math/science. The lower math/science category (which includes mathematics below the algebra level and general science) decreased from 8 percent to 6 percent of the curriculum while the higher math/science category (mathematics courses in algebra and above and biology, chemistry, and physics) increased from 15 percent to 20 percent. Since the other categories in the figure have been relatively stable, it appears that some vocational

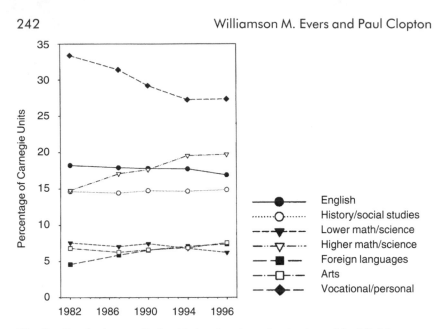

Fig. 1. Curriculum units for high school graduates by subject field

Notes: Values are Carnegie units in specific content areas as a percentage of total Carnegie units. Lower math and science is the sum of mathematics less than algebra and general science. Higher math and science is the sum of mathematics algebra or higher and biology, chemistry, and physics. The vocational and personal categories have been combined.

Source: U.S. Department of Education, National Center for Education Statistics. *Digest of Education Statistics, 2001*, NCES 2002-130, by Thomas D. Snyder. Production Manager, Charlene M. Hoffman. (Washington, D.C.: 2002) 158–59.

coursework has been replaced by courses in higher mathematics and science.[6]

Completion rates for specific mathematics and science courses increased dramatically over this same period.[7] The percentage of graduates who completed geometry increased from 47 percent to 75 percent and the completion rate for algebra 2 increased from 40 percent to 62 percent. The completion rate for math analysis/precalculus increased from 6 percent to 23 percent. Completion rates in each science course increased more than 13 percent.

A Nation at Risk defined a New Basics curriculum for high school graduates that included a minimum of four years of English, three years of mathematics, three years of science, three years of social studies, and a half-year of computer science. College-bound students were also advised to study a foreign language for two years. The completion rate for this series of courses increased from 2 percent in 1982 to 29 percent in 1998. This growth is not an artifact of the increases in computer usage and availability over the same time period. Without the computer science requirement, the increase was from 10 percent to 44 percent. Gains were reported for both boys and girls as well as for each of the ethnic groups studied.[8]

It should be noted, however, that the New Basics curriculum stipulated the number of years of coursework, but not the specific content to be learned. Therefore, some of the reported gain may be deceptive. Not all seemingly academic courses necessarily have solid content or cover the advanced aspects of an academic discipline. Furthermore, the New Basics completion rates still fall short of the college enrollment rates. Of all high school graduates in 1998, 65 percent had enrolled in college by the following October, compared with 51 percent in 1982.[9] An increased proportion of students are going on to college, but not always having taken the New Basics course sequence.

High School Achievement

Given that students are completing more academic courses in mathematics and science today than in 1983, one would expect to find corresponding increases in achievement. But long-term trend data from the National Assessment of Educational Progress (NAEP) show only small increases in mathematics and science scores since 1983, when scores for seventeen-year-olds reached their nadir.[10]

The increase in mathematics scores from 1982 to 1999 was 10 points. The increase in science scores over the same period was 12 points. Since NAEP long-term trend scores are not given in a familiar metric, it is necessary to find a way to characterize the size of these gains. Perhaps the most widely recognized characterization of effect sizes is that provided by Jacob Cohen, who has quantified the definitions of small, medium, and large effects.[11] For NAEP mathematics scores, small, medium, and large effect sizes correspond to differences of about 6, 15, and 24 points, respectively. The corresponding values for NAEP science scores are about 8, 20, and 33 points. Therefore, NAEP gains since 1982 in both mathematics and science are clearly small.

Even more worrisome is the fact that these achievement levels on the NAEP are considerably lower than would be expected from students who are taking reasonably rigorous academic classes. Consider the performance level description for a NAEP mathematics score of 350, which is substantially above the actual mean achievement level:

> Students at this level can apply a range of reasoning skills to solve multistep problems. They can solve routine problems involving fractions and percents, recognize properties of basic geometric figures, and work with exponents and square roots. They can solve a variety of two-step problems using variables, identify equivalent algebraic expressions, and solve linear equations and inequalities. They are developing an understanding of functions and coordinate systems.[12]

This definition is not describing work at the precalculus level or even at the algebra 2 level; it is in fact describing some of the less difficult content from algebra 1 and geometry coursework. Yet even the average for the upper quartile of students has never reached this level.[13]

Changes in achievement levels over time can be seen by looking at results on the SAT college entrance examinations.[14] From 1982 to 2001, the verbal score increased by 2 points, while the mathematics score increased by 21 points. Small, medium, and large effects on both scales would be 20, 50, and 80 points, respectively. Therefore, SAT scores show little change in verbal achievement and a small increase in mathematics achievement since 1982. These findings are reasonably consistent with the NAEP results reported above.

In summary, achievement gains in mathematics and science are detectable but small. The magnitude of these gains is disappointing, particularly in light of increased participation in courses that are categorized as academic.

Other Disappointments

The relative weakness of even our most advanced students is confirmed by results from the 1996 Third International Mathematics and Science Study (TIMSS). Scores for the physics and advanced mathematics component of TIMSS reflect the achievement levels of only the subgroup of students who have taken courses in these advanced subjects. In physics, the United States scored significantly lower than fourteen of the fifteen participating countries. In advanced mathematics, the U.S. scores were significantly lower than those of eleven of fifteen participating countries. On neither exam was the United States' score significantly higher than the score for any other nation.[15] These findings failed to demonstrate improvement over the disappointing U.S. results on the Second International Mathematics Study (SIMS) conducted in the early eighties.[16]

Another disappointment is that remediation rates for incoming college students appear to be increasing. Data for the entire California State University system illustrate this point.[17] Students who fail the placement exams in mathematics and English are required to complete remedial coursework. In 1989, 23 percent of incoming students required remedial mathematics. By 1998, the figure had jumped to 54 percent. It should be noted that part of this increase is due to a change in the test in 1992. Nonetheless, the proportion of students failing the placement test has increased each year and has more than doubled over this period. The remedial instruction rate for English also increased substantially over the same interval.

Academic Coursework Revisited

The divergent trends—of increased enrollment in academic courses while achievement remains stagnant—suggest a hypothesis: In the process of increasing enrollments, the academic content of courses has been watered down. This may be an inevitable consequence of policies that stress equal academic treatments for all students. When schools place nearly all eighth-graders in algebra courses, this placement policy may seriously affect the rigor of algebra courses.[18] This effect may be mirrored throughout the academic curriculum.

Data from the Standardized Testing and Reporting (STAR) program in California can be used to examine the consequences of simply placing more students in algebra courses.[19] This analysis is possible because California has put in place both a national, norm-referenced achievement test and standards-based, course-specific tests in various content areas.

Figure 2 presents data for individual schools in California. The mean achievement of schools in eighth-grade algebra classes on a standards-based test is shown as a function of the percentage of eighth-graders enrolled. The algebra scores are adjusted (using simultaneous multiple linear regression) for mean achievement in the same school in seventh-grade mathematics the prior year as measured by the nationally normed test.

The impact of what appear to be district-level or school-level policy decisions is quite large. A partial correlation of −.67 was found between enrollment and algebra achievement. Small, medium, and large effects for correlations are .10, .30, and .50, respectively.[20] The observed effect greatly exceeds the criterion for a large effect size.

It is not surprising that higher enrollments in more advanced courses would result in lower achievement in those courses overall. It is quite surprising that placement policy decisions could have such a dramatically adverse effect on achievement. As schools and districts feel the need for more "accessible" curriculum materials to accom-

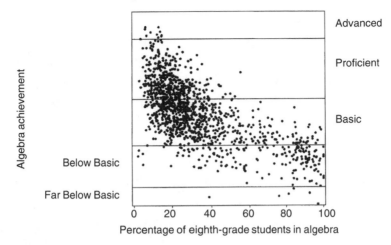

**Fig. 2. Consequences of placement strategies in
8th-grade mathematics**

Notes: Data are for 1,265 individual schools in California. Grade 8 algebra
achievement is based on California Standards Test in algebra 1 in 2001, adjusted for
grade 7 mathematics achievement in the same school in 2000 as measured by SAT9
(Stanford Achievement Test Series, Ninth Edition) mathematics scale scores. Algebra
placement is the proportion of students with scores on the algebra exam as a percentage of reported enrollment in 2001.

Source: California Department of Education, Standardized Testing and Reporting
Program, *STAR Results for 2001* and *STAR Results for 2000.* See http://star.cde.ca.
gov/.

modate less-prepared students, they deliberately seek out programs
with less rigorous content. Meanwhile, expectations for achievement
in these courses fall lower and lower. Flooding academic courses with
unprepared students has the net effect of taking the rigor out of these
courses. Ironically, the district or school policy decisions for eighth-
grade mathematics may ultimately have been motivated, in part, by
the emphasis on academic coursework per se in *A Nation at Risk.* More
recent reports also promote this policy decision by stressing student
completion of algebra courses in eighth grade.[21]

The supposed conflict between achievement goals and reducing
the socioeconomic achievement gap has received much attention in

the literature. In 1961, John Gardner suggested that achieving both excellence and equity simultaneously is possible,[22] as counterintuitive as this might sound. Put bluntly, however, the United States has been rather unsuccessful on both counts. The algebra results above suggest that merely placing large quantities of students in more academic courses may have undesirable consequences.

In the wake of *A Nation at Risk*, several studies emerged showing that reducing the number of low-level course offerings and increasing enrollment in more advanced academic courses improved educational outcomes.[23] Greater enrollment in academically rigorous courses within a school leads to greater achievement for the school as a whole. That said, however, greater individual differences in progress through the series of academic mathematics courses was also found to lead to greater achievement overall.[24]

In other words, the best course of action is for high schools to increase academically rigorous course offerings and graduation re-quirements while at the same time differentiating among students with respect to the extent and rate of progress through the rigorous subject-matter content. A policy of rigorous content but retaining grouping to allow differing rates of progress is in sharp contrast to the differentiated curriculum (rigorous content for the college-bound, watered-down content for the rest) that *A Nation at Risk* warned against. However, it is also in sharp contrast to the policy that all students should be enrolled in the same lockstep sequence of academic courses.

Course Rigor Versus Course Names

Transcript studies use course names to measure rigor, but this measure may not accurately reflect course content. Perhaps, even while aca-demic course completion has been increased, the actual curriculum hiding beneath these course identifiers has been declining. As then U.S. secretary of education William J. Bennett was already warning five years after A *Nation at Risk*: "We need to pay more sustained attention to the content of courses, in addition to the number and type of course scheduled. Time on task is not a meaningful yardstick of achievement if students are not being given a challenging, rich curriculum."[25]

The notion that the strength of the curriculum is declining is nothing new. It underlies the lament in A *Nation at Risk* that "[w]e have, in effect, been committing an act of unthinkable, unilateral educational disarmament."[26] The serious deterioration of textbook content appears to have begun in the sixties.[27] Indeed, achievement declines (reflected in NAEP scores) followed the deterioration of the curriculum immediately preceding the publication of A *Nation at Risk*.[28] Jeanne S. Chall and Sue S. Conrad studied widely used textbooks covering the period from 1945 to 1975 and noted that, "On the whole, the later the copyright dates of the textbooks for the same grade, the easier they were, as measured by indices of readability level, maturity level, difficulty of questions, and extent of illustration."[29]

There is reason to believe that curriculum materials have continued to deteriorate since the publication of A *Nation at Risk*. Indeed, it was the weakness of curriculum materials that precipitated the turmoil that has come to be known as the "math wars." In "A Brief History of American K–12 Mathematics Education in the 20th Century," David Klein notes, "The immediate cause of the math wars of the '90s was the introduction and widespread distribution of new math textbooks with radically diminished content and a dearth of basic skills."[30]

One of the leading textbooks for introductory algebra, originally written by Mary P. Dolciani, has gone through multiple editions during this time period. A comparison of the 1973 version[31] with the 2000 version[32] reveals some of the changes that took place over this period. For example, the 1973 edition included some introductory geometry and trigonometry, but this was eliminated in 2000. At the same time, the text itself has increased from 596 pages to 744 pages. The increased page count is not the result of changing to a larger typeface. Rather, sections have been inserted that would fit under a banner of "thinking skills" and "real-world applications" to make the textbook more palatable to those who stress these features over actual mathematics content. This includes sections called Explorations and Technology and Special Topics at the end of each chapter.

However, the changes in this classic textbook are minor compared to those that stimulated the math wars. The release of newer texts seen as grossly inadequate stimulated the growth of parent-led protest organizations for mathematics reform such as HOLD (Honest Open Logical Debate) and Mathematically Correct.[33] Many of these new mathematics programs were sponsored by the National Science Foundation (NSF).[34] A review of NSF influence in mathematics education states:

> At the high school level, there is a continuing emphasis on discovery learning and a significant deemphasis of algebraic skills and logic. Indeed, one program, Interactive Mathematics Program, has candidly noted that all items listed for "less emphasis" in the NCTM [National Council of Teachers of Mathematics] standards, such as manual calculation and proof, were completely eliminated. Many key topics are presented in ways that are unlikely to lead to a high level of mastery, while introduction of the quadratic formula, a topic fundamental to high school algebra, is delayed until the twelfth grade. *Integrated Math I, II, and III* has been criticized as being seriously lacking in key content areas, ill-designed for mastery learning, full of contrived problems, and unlikely to prepare students for mathematics-based science courses or college mathematics. The Core-Plus Mathematics Project generated massive resentment among the students who were the experimental subjects during early implementation. Many students found themselves ill-prepared for college, even though they came from highly educated homes and had a high likelihood of success.[35]

A comparison between the 1973 Dolciani text noted earlier and the 1998 Core-Plus text[36] mentioned above illustrates just how dramatic these differences are. The 1973 Dolciani text contains an entire chapter on factoring and special products. The 1998 Core-Plus text has no section on factoring. The index of the two texts confirms this (see Table 1). The striking difference between the two listings reflects the dramatic loss of rigor in many newer texts—a loss of rigor that provoked the math wars of the nineties.

Another example from mathematics is the textbook *Algebra: Themes, Concepts, Tools*.[37] Motohico Mulase, professor of mathematics at the University of California at Davis, provided a review of this program, stating:

> When I volunteered to read the book, I never expected to take poison. The feeling I received from reading the student edition was irritation, frustration, and pain. This is the feeling I receive from the world news these days, but as a mathematician, I usually enjoy reading math books with pleasure. At first I couldn't quite articulate the reason for my feeling. So I checked out the teacher edition . . . from a local district teacher and started to read. I then exploded. . . . The book is full of destruction and discouragement to students. The teacher edition treats readers as fools and encourages them to remain fools. A curriculum based on the book is a pure poison to the young mind. No matter how it is used, I do not believe that one can run a reasonable algebra 1 course out of this book. The only message I obtained from the teacher edition is, do not teach mathematics![38]

Similar changes are occurring in science education. Here again the NSF has sponsored instructional programs. An example is *Active Physics*, which consists of a series of curriculum modules from It's About Time, Inc.[39] School officials in San Diego, California, mandated that ninth-graders take the program, and the turmoil that resulted is well documented:[40]

> At the high school level, things are also in disarray. The district has mandated that all ninth-graders take physics. And just to make sure it's "successful," the district has watered down the curriculum, say many teachers and parents. . . .

Table 1. Mathematics introduction then and now, illustrated by index listings under "F"

1973 *Modern Algebra:* *Structure and Method,* Book 1 (also known as Dolciani Algebra 1)	1998 *Contemporary Mathematics in* *Context: A Unified Approach,* Course 1 (also known as Core-Plus)

Factors
  Greatest common, monomial,
  polynomial, prime
Factoring
  Applications of, the difference of
  two squares, polynomial products,
  product of a binomial sum and a
  binomial difference, products of
  binomial sums or differences,
  quadratic trinomials, trinomial
  squares
Fallacies
Finite decimal
Finite set
Flow charts
  Loops in, open sentences in,
  problems
Formula(s)
  Quadratic
Fractions
  Adding, complex, decimal form of,
  dividing, multiplication property of,
  multiplying, reducing to lowest
  terms, subtracting
Fractional equations
Functions
  Arrow notation, cosine, described
  by tables, domain, graphs,
  linear, quadratic, range, sine,
  tangent, value of, values of
  trigonometric
	Families
	  In poverty data, income measure
	  of center, number of children
	Fast food nutrition data
	Fat in fast food
	Feasibility study, scheduling
	Feeding tours, scheduling
	Ferris wheel, height of car
	Fish, population growth
	Fishing, boat rental
	Flags, symmetry
	Flea treatment, half-life
	Flight
	  Aircraft, baseball
	Floor plan, best path
	Flower beds, managing conflicts
	Food
	  Concession profit, fast food costs
	Football
	  Athletes and homework, Nielsen
	  ratings, quarterbacks statistics
	Ford Mustang, price data
	Franchises, start-up costs
	Free-throw game, planning
	Frequency, radio, assigning
	Fuel, amount in plane
	Fuel economy
	  Auto ratings, mpg model
	Fuller, R. Buckminster
	  Geodesic dome, globe net
	Fund raising carnival, moon walk

Sources: Mary P. Dolciani and William Wooton, *Modern Algebra: Structure and Method*, Book 1, rev. ed. (Boston: Houghton Mifflin, 1973); and A. F. Coxford, J. T. Fey, C. R. Hirsch, H. L. Schoen, G. Burrill, E. W. Hart, and A. E. Watkins, *Contemporary Mathematics in Context: A Unified Approach*, Course 1 (Chicago: Everyday Learning, 1998).

"It costs $14,000 per class to buy the materials, and it's all junk stuff," says [physics teacher Martin] Teachworth. "The smart kids are bored to death. . . .

San Diego administrators pointed to Fairfax, Va., where *Active Physics* was reportedly getting glowing results. When Teachworth contacted Fairfax teachers, he was told, "The only students who used *Active Physics* were the lowest of the low. If they couldn't pass any other physics class for high school graduation, they took *Active Physics*. . . ."

"*Active Physics* only covers 20 percent of the state standards," says Teachworth. "However, I'm being told that if I don't teach this curriculum, I will be documented and fired. My job has always been to teach real physics to kids who want to go to college. I could find myself in a lot of trouble."[41]

Physics achievement scores are now available from the 2002 California Standards Test in physics.[42] Out of 232 school districts with data available, only eight districts had mean scores lower than San Diego City Schools. This places San Diego among the bottom 4 percent of districts statewide. In the state as a whole, achievement in biology, chemistry, and earth science improved in 2002, and only the physics test showed a decline. However, this statewide decline in physics scores changes to an increase if the San Diego data are eliminated.

Thus, in both mathematics and science, programs have recently been established that are seen by critics as drastically watered down. These are not just isolated reports. An Internet search for "dumbed-down education" yields thousands of hits.[43] Most of these protests come from parents who first notice that their children's textbooks are inadequate. These protests are no longer isolated, scattered, and merely local, and the parents have acquired some prestigious allies.[44]

It is important to note that while *A Nation at Risk* focused on the academic nature of the high school curriculum, recent protests over declining academic rigor cover the full spectrum from kindergarten through college. In elementary school, we may have course names no more glamorous than Grade 3 Mathematics, but attentive parents are noticing a dearth of content even in the schoolwork of young children.

Thus, we suggest that the academic rigor sought in A *Nation at Risk* and the twin goals of excellence and equity have been largely achieved—but achieved in name only. Academic course enrollments are up but achievement is not, because the rigor of the academic core is evaporating—perhaps throughout the K–16 experience.

David L. Angus and Jeffrey E. Mirel used a somewhat different research focus to arrive at a similar conclusion. They looked in depth at the content of mathematics and science courses in Detroit and Grand Rapids, Michigan, to see how local districts have responded to policies calling for tougher coursework. They concluded that educators have poured old wine into new bottles. The educators invented courses "to meet the letter but not the spirit" of more rigorous graduation requirements. Angus and Mirel say that policy makers who oppose an academic curriculum are adept at discovering ways to "give the appearance of toughening standards without actually doing so." According to Angus and Mirel, the antiacademic educators use a variation on the unethical sales technique of "bait and switch." They fill the high school schedule with classes that have academic titles, but "unchallenging content."[45]

Grade Inflation and Teacher Preparation

An increase in academic coursework without a corresponding increase in achievement may be largely caused by weaker curriculum materials, as suggested above. However, there are other contributing causes that must be noted. Two salient factors are highlighted here—grade inflation and the inadequate preparation of teachers.

If achievement drops in rigorous courses, it may be obscured by lowered grading standards—grade inflation. Lenient grading can be detected when objective tests are given at the end of specific courses, as shown by the data from Texas for a statewide end-of-course algebra exam.[46] While only 2 percent of the students failed the course yet passed the state exam, 36 percent of the students passed the course but failed the exam. Grading standards were lower for schools with greater numbers of students from racial and language minorities and students from poor households. Thus, relaxed grading criteria can obscure both low achievement per se and an achievement gap, in a phenomenon President George W. Bush has called the "soft bigotry of low expectations."[47]

The need for an adequately prepared core of teachers is critical if real increases in academic rigor are to be achieved. In 1996, the National Commission on Teaching and America's Future stated:

> When it comes to widespread change, we have behaved as though national, state, and district mandates could, like magic wands, transform schools. But all the directives and proclamations are simply so much fairy dust. Successful programs cannot be replicated in schools where staff lack the know-how and resources to bring them to life.[48]

Reports of inadequate teacher preparation are too numerous to review. However, the U.S. secretary of education recently released one such report.[49] This report focuses on the implementation of new legislation designed, in part, to increase teacher preparation in content areas:

> . . . the focus of the law is on "content knowledge." Congress has made it clear that it considers content knowledge to be of paramount importance. The law also implies, through these detailed definitions, that Congress suspects that current state certification systems are not doing enough to ensure preparation in solid content knowledge . . . [As both research and compliance data from schools of education show], these concerns are well founded.[50]

Both grade inflation and inadequate teacher preparation have surely contributed to America's less-than-expected student achievement. Nonetheless, curriculum materials that have declined in rigor, and courses that sound academic but aren't, have played a major role in creating a seeming paradox: gains in students' academic coursework and, at the same time, little in the way of gains in academic learning.

Ideology and Bureaucracy

In the twenty years since A *Nation at Risk* was published, more students are taking nominally academic courses, but gains in student achievement have been modest at best. Although students have a more academic-sounding course load, they don't appear to be learning in a manner commensurate with what they are supposedly doing in the classroom. At least part of the explanation is that beneath the academic labels on all too many courses is watered-down content.

The interesting question is: Why is this going on? Why hide watered-down content behind academic labels? Indeed, why did non-academic courses have such a large role in the curriculum for most of the twentieth century? Why have high schools had differentiated curricula that downplayed serious academics for many students? Is there a reason educators have clung to this reigning idea with such zeal and determination? Is there something in the very life of bureaucracies (and public schools *are* government agencies) that encourages them to take on multiple missions (including, in the case of schools, nonacademic missions)? To answer this, we need to delve into the mindset of educators and examine the nature of bureaucracies.

Ideology and Moral Energy

The story of American education in the past century has been the story of Progressive education. Progressive educators have been the most influential figures in American education. Historians have noted their enthusiasm, energy, moral earnestness, and sense of mission.[51] Even when Progressive educators did not succeed in getting everything they wanted, they have set the terms of the debate. As the name suggests, Progressive educators first flourished in the reform period called the Progressive Era that began in the last decade of the nineteenth century and continued up until U.S. entry into the First World War.

The ideology of Progressive education combined an anti-intellectualism and devotion to naturalness inherited from the romantic era; the rhetoric, jargon, and sometimes the methods of the social and behavioral sciences; and often-secularized religiosity committed to transforming the world through schooling.[52] Indeed, one of the features of Progressive education brought over from Protestantism backgrounds was an intellectual tendency to unify things that were logically disparate.[53] The fusing of these disparate currents (romanticism, behavioral science, and religious millennialism) into Progressive educational doctrine is a conspicuous example of just such a monistic approach to philosophical problems.

The pietist millennialists and their secular successors contributed to Progressive education an animating spirit of confidence and righteousness. From their pietist background, many Progressive educators brought along a rhetoric of pious good intentions and, their critics would charge, a sense that such intentions were more important than actual scientific rigor and effectiveness. Indeed, in their enthusiasm for reform, Progressive educators often embraced rather odd notions of what constituted a scientific approach to educational reform in general and to curricular change in particular.

Educational reformers of the Progressive Era believed in or were heavily influenced by pietist Protestant millennialism. Religious adherents—in particular, millennialist religious adherents—are usually highly motivated and morally strenuous. Kingdom-of-God-on-Earth millennialists want to change the world and sometimes succeed in doing so. Even when such beliefs are transformed into a more secular form, these beliefs retain much of the impetus they had when they were explicitly religious. When considering modern Progressive and radical politics, Martin Buber speaks of a "secularization of eschatol-

ogy," and Eric Voegelin speaks of the "immanentization of the escha-
ton."[54] The practices and way of life of the pioneering capitalists in
the early modern era, the romantic movement in the late eighteenth
and early nineteenth centuries, and Marxian socialism in the late
nineteenth and the twentieth centuries all were secular transformations of beliefs that were originally pietist or millennialist.[55] Each in
their different ways is testimony to the power of such beliefs.

American pietist millennialists at the onset of the Progressive Era
were not End-of-the-Worlders in beard and smock looking for a sud-
den Second Coming of Jesus. Instead, these millennialists soberly but
fervently sought to rid America of perceived societal ills as necessary
preparation for the Second Coming. They wanted to build a New
Jerusalem, moral brick by moral brick, in order to usher in Christ's
earthly reign. They believed it was their duty to construct an earthly
kingdom of righteousness.

Strenuous human effort over the course of history would create
this realm, not an instantaneous supernatural miracle. These Kingdom-of-God-on-Earth millennialists strove to use any means necessary
(including all levels of government) to create edifying institutions,
extirpate sin, and develop a citizenry of saints.[56] Sin to these pietists
included not only succumbing to temptation and violating God's law,
but also allowing ignorance or wrong thoughts to stand in the way of
salvation of oneself or others.[57]

In his book on Progressive Era reform and alcohol prohibition,
James Timberlake succinctly encapsulates the Kingdom-of-God-on-
Earth millennialist outlook:

> Unlike those extremist and apocalyptic sects that rejected and with-
> drew from the world as hopelessly corrupt, and unlike the more
> conservative churches, such as the Roman Catholic, Protestant Epis-
> copal, and Lutheran, that tended to assume a more relaxed attitude
> toward the influence of religion in culture, evangelical Protestantism
> sought to overcome the corruption of the world in a dynamic man-
> ner, not only by converting men to belief in Christ but also by

Christianizing the social order through the power and force of law. According to this view, the Christian's duty was to use the secular power of the state to transform culture so that the community of the faithful might be kept pure and the work of saving the unregenerate might be made easier. Thus the function of law was not simply to restrain evil but to educate and uplift.[58]

By the 1830s, this doctrine predominated in Protestant churches in New England and in areas settled by New Englanders. It was particularly influential among the New England crusaders for common schools.[59] When common-school advocate Horace Mann became secretary of the Massachusetts Board of Education in 1837, Boston Unitarian minister William Ellery Channing declared: "If we can but turn the wonderful energy of [the American people] into right channels, what a new heaven and earth might be realized among us."[60] By the 1890s, Kingdom-of-God-on-Earth millennialism was in the ascendancy nationwide. During the Progressive Era, those who sought to reform education and the rest of American life came from this Protestant Kingdom-of-God-on-Earth millennialist milieu.

From the Progressive Era on through the thirties, someone who was a leader in the Progressive education movement was usually either an earnest, committed millennial pietist or else a fallen-away pietist, whose parents and upbringing had been pietist.[61] John Dewey, for example, proclaimed in his "Pedagogic Creed" that the teacher is "the prophet of the true God and the sharer in the true kingdom of God."[62] Many school reformers may have shucked off overt religiosity, but even they held onto their moral fervor and their belief that theirs was a providential (if now secular) mission.[63] The educational progressives blended, as historians David Tyack and Elizabeth Hansot put it, the values of their small-town pietism with what the Progressives considered an objective "science of education."[64]

Ellwood P. Cubberley, the dean of the Stanford school of education and promoter of progressive policies of school administration, spent his childhood and youth in a pietist small town and taught briefly at a Baptist college. Charles Judd, the dean of the school of education at the University of Chicago, was the son of a Protestant minister and had once planned to become a minister. G. Stanley Hall, the founder of the child-study movement and pioneer advocate of what are today called "developmentally appropriate practices" and "differentiated instruction," had likewise studied for the ministry. Other preachers' sons included two top leaders of different strands of the Progressive education movement: Edward L. Thorndike, the founder of the field of educational psychology, and William Kilpatrick, the Teachers College professor who popularized child-centered education and the project method. George Counts, the founder of the social-reconstruction strand of Progressive education, testified that his major inspiration had been "the Methodist Church and its social gospel."[65]

The Progressive educators who specialized in curriculum development also shared this same Kingdom-of-God-on-Earth millennial pietist background. Thomas Jesse Jones, the Progressive who influentially argued for channeling American blacks into nonacademic courses of study, had studied education at the graduate level at Columbia. But he also had a divinity degree from Union Seminary and had worked briefly for the Federation of Churches of New York City.[66] Clarence Darwin Kingsley, the Progressive educator who headed and gave intellectual direction to the commission that wrote the 1918 *Cardinal Principles* report, studied for the Baptist ministry.[67] *Cardinal Principles* advocated nonacademic courses and a curriculum designed to encourage social adjustment. The report that Kingsley guided into existence supplanted a previously widely accepted set of K–12 curriculum guidelines: the 1893 report of the Committee of Ten, which had advocated an academic course of study for all students.[68]

The Progressive educational reformers from pietist backgrounds retained their righteous certainty and zeal even as they combined that sense of certainty with what they considered to be the objective, value-free practices of a secular social science.[69] At the same time, they secularized the religious project of building a sinless utopia as preparation for the Second Coming of Jesus. For some of them, the social reconstructionists, the secular substitute was building a new socialist society through transformation of the school curriculum.[70] But most progressive educators concentrated their certainty and zeal on advocating process-oriented instruction, administrative centralization, and changes in the curriculum so that it would (in their opinion) help students adjust to the existing American society. Some Progressive educators described these curricular changes in terms of life adjustment, others in terms of social control. Sociologist Edward A. Ross, for example, explicitly connected schooling and social control and wrote that education can "help in 'breaking in' the colt to the harness."[71]

Armed with moralistic self-assurance, scientific-sounding rhetoric, and an anti-intellectualism inherited from the romantic movement, Progressive educators have consistently resisted academic rigor in the school classroom. Pioneering Progressive educators were born in a scientific age, often saw themselves as scientific and often wanted others to see them that way. But Progressive education's roots in nineteenth-century pietist millennialism and in romanticism (which itself was rooted in an earlier millennialism) have made scientific habits of mind uncongenial to Progressive educators. Intellectual content has always been secondary to a program of remolding the child and the society.

The American pietist millennialists endeavored to extirpate perceived societal ills to ready society for the Second Coming. They sought to rescue sinners and build a New Jerusalem for Christ's earthly reign. The heirs of these pietist millennialists—the twentieth-century Progressive educators—developed parallel secular goals. They sought to minister to the whole child and build a progressive society. These goals shaped the Progressive curriculum and shoved aside academic subject-matter. Those Progressives who focused more on the child called for children reliving reconstructions of mankind's learning processes or for attending to children's interests or child psychology in various ways. Those Progressives who focused on society called for teaching children to adjust to society or using the schools to build a new political order or to fine-tune the adult labor market. Whatever their focus, Progressives had a tendency to resist academic rigor and to deemphasize content.

In short, millennialism lived on in missionary zeal, in a less than scientific approach, and in secularized goals of a regenerate child and regenerate society. To see how this manifested itself in Progressive curricular proposals, we have to look at the specific approaches of the various strands of Progressive education.

Ideology and the Nonacademic Curriculum

The ideology of the Progressive Era reformers and of their intellectual heirs today offers four different rationales for emphasizing the nonacademic and watering down the academic in the curriculum. Proponents of the nonacademic in the present day draw on these rationales and do so with the fervor and moral certainty of the nineteenth-century pietists and the twentieth-century secular reformers.

Developmental appropriateness and the child-centered curriculum

The most invoked name in the history of American educational thought is that of John Dewey, who endeavored to make instruction a problem-solving, experiential process linked to the present-day child's interests and natural development. When John Dewey was first starting out as an educational theorist he associated with a circle of American followers of the German philosopher Johann Freidrich Herbart. The American Herbartians believed, as Dewey did, that educational curricula should reflect the natural development of the child. The American Herbartians also believed, again as Dewey did, that child development recapitulated the cultural evolution of mankind (and school curriculum should do likewise).[72] Thus, in kindergarten, the Herbartians would have the student learn about the life of primitive peoples, whose fears and superstitions the Herbartians likened to those of young children. There might be a year in which students studied literature on hunting and gathering, then perhaps a year studying works on agriculture and farm life. By high school, students should be studying the literature of advanced civilization.[73]

Dewey did have some differences with the Herbartian approach to the curriculum. He agreed with the Herbartians that the curriculum should be naturalistic and that it should mimic the cultural evolution of mankind. But Dewey wanted the curriculum to be experiential, rather than literary or strictly historical. The student would learn from an artificially created environment that would resemble that confronted by humans along the different stages of cultural development. Students would learn through experience the ways of knowing that were developed in each cultural epoch. Thus, in kindergarten, students would face the problems (in artificially reconstructed form) that the cavemen faced and learn from them. By high school, students would face the problems of advanced contemporary civilization and, again, learn from them.[74] As Dewey saw it, the key was having the child directly experience, to the extent possible, the activities that were common to a historical epoch or way of life: "[T]he agricultural instinct requires . . . to be fed in just the same way in the child in which it was fed in the [human] race—by contact with earth and seed and air and sun and all the mighty flux and ebb of life in nature."[75]

Dewey's specific curriculum proposals were not widely adopted, though variations on them can be found in a few private progressive schools, past and present.[76] But his curriculum is notable for reasons other than wide acceptance of its details. It is significant because in adopting it, Dewey showed that he had a rather odd idea of what constituted an objective science of education. He had no empirical basis for believing that children learn best by being put through a recreation of cultural evolution. Furthermore, because Dewey took as his curriculum every sort of still-relevant learning through experience that had happened in the course of human civilization, he left nothing out. There were no limits in principle to what should be taught. Thus, to the extent that Dewey was broadly influential on curricular issues, the logic of his ideas backed large-scale inclusion of nonacademic topics.[77]

Life-adjustment

An even odder idea of science was associated with the life-adjustment strand of Progressive education.[78] The advocates of life-adjustment sought to make the curriculum functionally efficient in preparing the student for adult life. Thus, they studied adult life, then created the curriculum by working backward. Of course, different people held different roles in adult life, and these curriculum planners wanted their curriculum to be scientific. Therefore, they called for both differentiating the curriculum and predicting the future occupational status of students. With the student's future "scientifically" predicted, the student would be assigned to appropriate curriculum.

With all of adult life and all of adult skills, knowledge, and problems on the agenda, nonacademic topics loomed large in the life-adjustment curricula. As historian Herbert Kleibard points out, the aims set forth in the 1918 *Cardinal Principles* report, a famous and influential document drafted by life-adjustment progressives,

> . . . gave secondary schools license to expand the curriculum almost indefinitely. . . . Almost no activity that human beings engage in could not be subsumed under one of those [aims]. Thus, almost anything that the human imagination could conceive of became fodder for the secondary-school curriculum.[79]

If the overarching goals were quite vague and all-encompassing, the curriculum planners were deliberately quite specific in formulating the curriculum in operational terms. This specificity left a tempting target for critics who wondered out loud whether "How to Bake a Cherry Pie" should be a high school curriculum requirement. Thus, a program that aimed at social engineering and functional efficiency became an object of mockery for its use of scientific lingo.

More importantly, the life-adjustment movement encouraged watering down of content while retaining course titles. In actuality, the practitioners of life-adjustment (and their intellectual heirs today) all too often assigned children from poor households or from racial and language minorities to nonacademic courses and to academic courses with reduced content.[80]

Social reconstruction

The social reconstructionists were the political socialists within the Progressive education movement.[81] Like other educational Progressives, social reconstructionists were opposed to an academic humanities-and-sciences curriculum. But in their case it was because they believed such a curriculum wasn't preparatory for the struggle for socialism or life in a future socialist society. Like the other educational Progressives, the social reconstructionists favored organizing the curriculum around problems and problem-solving. But unlike the other Progressives, the social reconstructionists were not interested in life-adjustment and social control within the existing exploitative society. The reconstructionists wanted students to scrutinize social and economic problems with a view to how they could be solved through a planned economy and government ownership.[82] Organizing the curriculum around social problems gave a green light to importing some nonacademic topics into the curriculum.

But more than this, social reconstructionists also sought to reorient the existing courses. They had a particular interest in preserving the labels on history and social studies courses, while changing the political character of the content. The curricular changes that the reconstructionists earnestly worked for were rooted in their radical political ideology. It would be odd to say that their curricular proposals were rooted in an objective science of education.

Holding youth off the labor market

During the thirties, child-advocacy groups and educational interest groups began to argue that young people should be held off the labor market and kept in school.[83] The quasi-ideological message from social workers and child-welfare advocates was that young people needed training and preparation for adult work. They should not enter the workforce at a young age and learn on the job. Young people, it was argued, deserve an extended period of youth before they take on adult responsibilities, and they deserve training from professionals before they enter the world of work. Most importantly, some argued that high wages cause prosperity and that holding young people off the labor market was necessary to maintaining high wages.[84] While this high-wage argument would certainly be challenged by many economists, one can see how it would resonate with the public, both during the Great Depression and later on.

Once many policy makers became convinced that young people needed to be held off the labor market, the question was what government agency would have control of these young people's lives. In the thirties, educational interest groups saw that this field of endeavor could expand the size, scope, and budget of K–12 schools, and they struggled with various rivals over jurisdiction and government money. The rivals were youth community-service agencies and similar bodies. By the forties, the schools had largely won the jurisdictional battle, and they were multiple-service agencies in charge of young people. As educators saw it, with that multiple-service mandate came a need to stress nonacademic topics in the curriculum and to water down the academic.

Whatever one thinks of the dubious high-wages-create-prosperity argument, policy considerations of this sort should not relegate young people to make-work activities and content-free courses. By the time of *A Nation at Risk*, a consensus was emerging in American society at

large that this treatment of young people was wrongheaded and counterproductive.

The Progressive education movement sprang from its early leaders'
pietist Protestant milieu and, after its secular transformation, produced the notion of the comprehensive high school and the differentiated curriculum. The high schools could ". . . serve democracy by
offering usable studies to everyone, rather than dwelling on academic
abstractions that would interest only a few."[85]

But not all schools deserted the academic curriculum under the
influence of Progressivism. Catholic educators tended to withstand
Progressive education, with its utopian millennialist fervor and Protestant roots. Catholic schools resisted abandoning the academic curriculum.[86] The comparisons of student achievement between the public schools (where the Progressive influence has been pervasive) and
Catholic schools favor the Catholic schools on both excellence and
equity. Catholic school students performed one full grade level above
public school students from a similar family background.[87] Education
scholars, in particular James Coleman, were noticing this "Catholic
school effect" in the same time period that A Nation at Risk was being
drafted.[88] Attention to the "Catholic school effect" contributed to
discontent with public-school performance in the early eighties.

Bureaucracy and Multiple Services

The history of public-school curriculum shows that educators actively
sought and fought to have schools take on nonacademic tasks. A
Nation at Risk had suggested that society imposed nonacademic burdens on the schools. In truth, the schools eagerly took on these burdens.

Many political scientists study bureaucrats and bureaucracy using
the same scholarly premises and tools that economists use to study
economic activity. These "public choice" political scientists have

found that bureaucrats who are in charge of a government agency tend to strive to expand that agency's size and budget. In addition, bureaucrats have an incentive to transform a government agency with a single mission by adding additional missions. Not only does this add to the agency's size and scope, but providing multiple services also allows the agency to pad its budget in a way that gives the agency spending flexibility as new contingencies arise.[89]

Indeed, the quasi-autonomy traditionally enjoyed by school boards has allowed them (once the national educational interest groups had beaten back the rival youth agencies) to pursue expansionist dreams more successfully than many government agencies. Educational interest groups fought to obtain a monopoly of control over young people's civilian lives in the forties and subsequently expanded the activities and objectives of schools in actuality, going beyond what Progressive educators had been able to achieve on behalf of their beliefs.

Although there were four different major reasons for Progressive educators to oppose an academic humanities-and-sciences curriculum, the proponents of these different rationales had much in common:[90]

- All of them caricatured the nineteenth-century high school as elitist and dominated by wishes of college officials.

- All of them believed that to make high schools more "democratic" the curriculum needed to be expanded beyond its academic content.

- All of them believed that the expanded curriculum needed a multitude of practical, problem-solving courses, and they sought to modify high-school graduation requirements and college-entrance requirements in line with these curricular changes.

- All of them sought to make the curriculum relevant to what educational professionals perceived to be the needs of students.

- All of them believed that education professionals, not lay boards of education, should be making curricular decisions.

- All of them retained something of the zeal and certainty of millennialist crusaders and had an odd notion of what constituted a scientific approach to education in general and the curriculum in particular.

The same rationales are used by adherents of the present-day variants of Progressive education. Although the Progressive education movement no longer shows obvious indications of its roots in pietist millennialism, the movement remains fervent and is alive and well in colleges of education, complex public-school bureaucracies, and even the National Science Foundation. Progressive rhetoric of egalitarianism translates today into coursework with "accessibility" as its key feature—meaning that reliance on prior learning is to be avoided. "Accessible" courses are courses that sound academic but where no one expects that students have learned (or previous teachers have taught them) the prerequisite academic content. A *Nation at Risk* helped mightily in convincing policy makers and the public to do away with the differentiated curriculum of the early eighties. The issue then became what to replace it with. Proponents of solid education want to replace it with an academically rigorous curriculum; the present-day Progressives want an undifferentiated curriculum without rigor.

Conclusion

The publication of A *Nation at Risk*, like the launch of Sputnik before it, served as a wake-up call for the complex political machinery that guides education in the United States. Significant gains in academic course completion rates have followed, at least in mathematics and science. On the other hand, the growth rate in achievement indicators has been disappointing. Worse yet, there are indications that the content of heretofore rigorous academic courses is at risk. Can we hope that greater gains lie ahead? Or will this limited progress fade away with the next round of fads in education?

Today, the standards and accountability movement that was ignited by *A Nation at Risk* acts as something of an ideological counterweight to proponents of nonacademic topics and of less thorough coverage of academic topics. It is more difficult to disguise a lack of rigor in an era of standards and accountability measures than it is to attach an academic label to a less-than-rigorous course offering.

In addition, pluralism has emerged in the delivery of schooling. Magnet schools and other public-schools-of-choice, charter schools, privately managed charter and public schools, and parents with vouchers usable in public or private schools are likely to put pressure over time on comprehensive high schools with differentiated curricula. This pluralism may check the ideological desires of educators to hang onto a nonacademic curriculum when parents don't want it, and it may limit the expansionist tendencies of school bureaucrats.

Yet the thinking that unites the variations of Progressive education is still with us today. Standards that are both demanding and explicit are called "elitist" and are therefore difficult to implement. Nonacademic courses are on the decline, but nonacademic content is being infused into traditionally academic courses. Math problems without obvious real-world applications (such as factoring a trinomial) are shunned while those that relate to the student world (such as selecting the best video-rental contract) are praised. Parents and professors alike are told to leave matters of education to the education "experts," while what passes for research in education all too frequently lacks scientific rigor.

Given the changes that have followed the publication of *A Nation at Risk*, it appears that further real gains will be slow in coming, if they materialize at all. There is every reason to assume that the effort required to produce real gains will be tremendous. Easy solutions, like simple changes in placement practices, will not be sufficient. Yet there is little hope for the future of the academic curriculum without continuing and refining the efforts stimulated by *A Nation at Risk*.

Notes

1. National Commission on Excellence in Education, *A Nation At Risk: The Imperative for Educational Reform* (Washington, D.C.: U.S. Government Printing Office, 1983), 18–19, http://www.ed.gov/pubs/NatAtRisk/.
2. Ibid., 6.
3. U.S. Department of Education, National Center for Education Statistics. *Digest of Education Statistics, 2001*, NCES 2002-130, compiled by Thomas D. Snyder (Washington, D.C., 2002).
4. A "Carnegie Unit" is one year of study or the equivalent in a secondary-school subject.
5. William H. Clune and Paula A. White, "Education Reform in the Trenches: Increased Academic Course Taking in High Schools with Lower Achieving Students in States with Higher Graduation Requirements," *Educational Evaluation and Policy Analysis*, 14 (1992), 1, 2–20.
6. See chapter 3 by Caroline Hoxby, figures 1 through 4, for more data on curricular changes since 1983.
7. *Digest of Education Statistics, 2001*, 161.
8. Ibid., 161; see also chapter 3 by Caroline Hoxby, figure 5.
9. U.S. Department of Education, National Center for Education Statistics, *The Condition of Education 2002*, NCES 2002-025 (Washington, D.C.: U.S. Government Printing Office, 2002), 166.
10. U.S. Department of Education. Office of Educational Research and Improvement. National Center for Education Statistics. *NAEP 1999 Trends in Academic Progress: Three Decades of Student Performance*, NCES 2000-469, compiled by J.R. Campbell, C.M. Hombo, and J. Mazzeo (Washington, D.C.: 2000). [Hereafter *Three Decades*.]
11. Jacob Cohen, *Statistical Power Analysis for the Behavioral Sciences*, 2nd Ed. (Hillsdale, N.J.: Lawrence Erlbaum Associates, 1988). Cohen's effect sizes can be related to NAEP long-term trend scores by estimating the standard deviations of NAEP scores. The standard deviations are estimated from the means for quartiles published in *Three Decades* on pages

11–15. These are then multiplied by the coefficients provided by Cohen (0.2, 0.5, and 0.8) to get effect size estimates in NAEP score terms.

12. *Three Decades*, 18.

13. Ibid., 13.

14. Paul Peterson presents a more detailed review of SAT scores in chapter 2 of this volume (see especially figures 1 and 3). Data here are from *Digest of Education Statistics, 2001*, 153.

15. Ibid., 30.

16. Curtis C. McKnight, F. Joe Crosswhite, John A. Dossey, et al., *The Underachieving Curriculum: Assessing U.S. School Mathematics from an International Perspective* (Champaign, Ill.: Stripes Publishing, 1987).

17. California Legislative Analyst's Office, February 8, 2001, *Improving Academic Preparation for Higher Education*, prepared by Jennifer Kuhn, reviewed by Buzz Breedlove. http://www.lao.ca.gov/2001/remediation/ 020801_remediation.html.

18. See Jay Mathews, "Algebra = X in One School, Y in Another; Teaching Inconsistent as Standards Waver," *Washington Post*, August 19, 2002 (comparing algebra course content in Virginia and Maryland).

19. California Department of Education, Standardized Testing and Reporting Program, STAR *Results for 2000* and STAR *Results for 2001*, http:// star.cde.ca.gov/.

20. Cohen, 79–80. The unit of sampling for these effect sizes is the school, not the individual student, since the variation of individual scores is not reported. The effect here is best interpreted as an effect of policy on school performance.

21. This includes the influential briefing paper "Mathematics Equals Opportunity," White Paper prepared for U.S. Secretary of Education Richard W. Riley, October 20, 1997, http://www.ed.gov/pubs/math/, and National Center for Education Statistics, "Do Gatekeeper Courses Expand Education Options," *Statistics in Brief*, February 1999.

22. In the early sixties, this assertion was made in the context of higher education. John W. Gardner, *Excellence: Can We Be Equal and Excellent Too?* (New York: Harper, 1961).

23. See, for example, Valerie E. Lee and Anthony S. Bryk, "Curriculum Tracking as Mediating the Social Distribution of High School Achievement," *Sociology of Education*, 61 (1988), 78–94.

24. U.S. Department of Education. National Center for Education Statistics.

High School Curriculum Structure: Effects on Coursetaking and Achievement in Mathematics for High School Graduates—An Examination of Data from the National Education Longitudinal Study of 1988, Working Paper No. 98-09, by Valerie E. Lee, David T. Burkam, Todd Chow-Hoy, Becky A. Smerdon, and Douglas Geverdt. Jeffrey Owings, Project Officer. Washington, D.C., 1998.

25. William J. Bennett, *American Education: Making It Work. A Report to the President and the American People*, ED 289 959 (Washington, D.C.: U.S. Government Printing Office, April 1988), 17.

26. A *Nation at Risk*, 5

27. Diane Ravitch, *Left Back: A Century of Failed School Reforms* (New York: Simon & Schuster, 2000), 404.

28. See, for example, Charles J. Sykes, *Dumbing Down Our Kids* (New York: St. Martin's Griffin, 1995), 130.

29. Jeanne S. Chall and Sue S. Conrad with Susan Harris-Sharples, *Should Textbooks Challenge Students? The Case for Easier or Harder Textbooks* (New York: Teachers College Press, 1991), 2.

30. David Klein, "A Brief History of American K-12 Mathematics Education the 20th Century," in James M. Royer, ed., *Mathematical Cognition* (Greenwich, Conn.: Information Age Publishing, 2002). http://www.csun.edu/~vcmth00m/AHistory.html.

31. Mary P. Dolciani and William Wooton, *Modern Algebra: Structure and Method*, Book 1, rev. ed. (Boston: Houghton Mifflin, 1973).

32. Richard G. Brown, Mary P. Dolciani, Robert H. Sorgenfrey, and William L. Cole, *Algebra: Structure and Method*, Book 1 (Evanston, Ill.: McDougal Littell, 2000).

33. See Klein, "Brief History," for an account of these events.

34. Michael McKeown, David Klein, and Chris Patterson, "The National Science Foundation Systemic Initiatives," in Sandra Stotsky, ed., *What's at Stake in the K–12 Standards Wars: A Primer for Educational Policy Makers* (New York: Peter Lang, 2000).

35. Ibid., 326.

36. Arthur F. Coxford, James T. Fey, Christian R. Hirsch, Harold L. Schoen, Gail Burrill, Eric W. Hart, and Ann E. Watkins, *Contemporary Mathematics in Context: A Unified Approach*, Course 1 (Chicago: Everyday Learning, 1998) (also known as Core-Plus).

37. Anita Wah and Henri Picciotto, *Algebra: Themes, Concepts, Tools* (Mountain View, Calif.: Creative Publications, 1994).

38. Motohico Mulase, 1996 book review of *Algebra* by Wah and Picciotto, http://www.mathematicallycorrect.com/pinkbook.htm.

39. See http://www.its-about-time.com/htmls/ap.html.

40. Sherry Posnick-Goodwin, "Isn't It Time to Treat Teachers As Professionals?" *California Educator*, vol. 6, no. 6 (March, 2002).

41. Ibid., 11, 15.

42. Data extracted from the California Department of Education website (http://www.cde.ca.gov) on August 31, 2002.

43. About 8,500 on google.com and about 4,500 on altavista.com on July 15, 2002.

44. Support from the mathematics community is indicated by a letter that appeared November 18, 1999, as a full-page advertisement in the *Washington Post* that was signed by more than 200 individuals, mostly university mathematicians. A copy of the letter is available at http://www.mathematicallycorrect.com/riley.htm.

45. David L. Angus and Jeffrey E. Mirel, *The Failed Promise of the American High School, 1890–1995* (New York: Teachers College Press, 1999), 195. See also 186–95, for the authors' detailed analysis of mathematics and science courses in Grand Rapids and Detroit.

46. Texas Education Agency, Student Assessment Division, *Performance on Algebra I EOC Test Compared to Performance in Algebra I Course*, Spring 2000. http://www.tea.state.tx.us/student.assessment/resources/conferences/tac/2000/algperf.html.

47. "Bush Warns Against the 'Soft Bigotry of Low Expectations,'" *Education Week*, Sept. 22, 1999, 18.

48. National Commission on Teaching and America's Future, *What Matters Most: Teaching for America's Future* (New York, 1996), 5.

49. U.S. Department of Education, Office of Postsecondary Education, Office of Policy, Planning and Innovation, *Meeting the Highly Qualified Teachers Challenge: The Secretary's Annual Report on Teacher Quality* (Washington, D.C., 2002).

50. Ibid, 6.

51. Lawrence A. Cremin, *The Transformation of the School: Progressivism in American Education, 1876–1957* (New York, Vintage Books, 1964), vii ("enthusiasm," "energy"); David Tyack and Elisabeth Hansot, *Managers*

of Virtue: Public School Leadership in America, 1820–1980 (New York: Basic Books, 1982), 3 ("moral earnestness and sense of mission").

52. Ravitch; E. D. Hirsch Jr., *The Schools We Need and Why We Don't Have Them* (New York: Doubleday, 1996); Williamson M. Evers, "From Progressive Education to Discovery Learning," in Evers, ed., *What's Gone Wrong in America's Classrooms* (Stanford, Calif.: Hoover Institution Press, 1998), 1–21.

53. Sydney E. Ahlstrom, *A Religious History of the American People* (New Haven, Conn.: Yale University Press, 1972), 780–81.

54. Buber, *Paths in Utopia* (London: Routledge & Kegan Paul, 1949), 10; Voegelin, *The New Science of Politics: An Introduction* (Chicago: University of Chicago Press, 1952), 188.

55. Max Weber, *The Protestant Ethic and the Spirit of Capitalism*, trans. Talcott Parson (New York: Charles Scribner's Sons, 1930), chap. 5; M. H. Abrams, *Natural Supernaturalism: Tradition and Revolution in Romantic Literature* (New York: W. W. Norton, 1971), 325–72, 416–18, 445; Robert C. Tucker, *Philosophy and Myth in Karl Marx*, 2nd ed. (Cambridge, Eng.: Cambridge University Press, 1972). The background to modern political millennialism lies in Western European history. See Norman Cohn, *The Pursuit of the Millennium: Revolutionary Millenarians and Mystical Anarchists of the Middle Ages*, rev. ed. (New York: Oxford University Press, 1970). We have benefited from discussions with and suggestions from David Gordon and Jonathan Reider on the topic of secularized religion.

56. See Ahlstrom, chaps. 39, 44, 46, 47; Ernest Lee Tuveson, *Redeemer Nation: The Idea of America's Millennial Role* (Chicago, University of Chicago Press, 1968); Cushing Strout, *The New Heavens and New Earth: Political Religion in America* (New York: Harper & Row, 1973); Paul Boyer, *When Time Shall Be No More: Prophecy and Belief in Modern American Culture* (Cambridge, Mass.: Harvard University Press, Belknap Press, 1992). In "World War I as Fulfillment: Power and the Intellectuals," Murray N. Rothbard discusses the influence of Kingdom-of-God-on-Earth millennialism on other noneducational areas of Progressive reform, in John V. Denson, ed., *The Costs of War* (New Brunswick, N.J.: Transaction Publishers, 1997), pp. 203–53.

57. Ahlstrom, 779; Tuveson, 58.

58. James H. Timberlake, *Prohibition and the Progressive Movement, 1900-1920* (Cambridge, Mass.: Harvard University Press, 1963), 7–8.

59. Tyack and Hansot, 3.

60. Quoted in Ahlstrom, 641.

61. Col. Francis W. Parker, the father of modern progressive education in America, said: "Feed the lambs of God [i.e., instruct the schoolchildren], and the gates of glory shall be lifted up, and the King of Glory shall enter in." Parker, "The Child," *Journal of Proceedings and Addresses of the National Education Association*, 1889, 482. When New York began to require that teachers be trained, Parker was jubilant. The new regulation led him to declare that he believed in the "resurrection in this life" and "the coming of a new spirit" and to proclaim: "Mine eyes have seen the glory of the coming of the Lord." See "The Instruction and Improvement of Teachers Now at Work in the Schools: Discussion," *Journal of Proceedings and Addresses of the National Education Association*, 1895, 191–92.

62. John Dewey, "My Pedagogic Creed" (1897), in Dewey, *The Early Works, 1882–1898* (Carbondale: Southern Illinois University Press, 1972), vol. 5, 95. Tyack and Hansot (197–98) write of Dewey's "naturalistic ethics blended laced with millennial Christian and democratic values."

63. "[Liberal Protestants] were fervently optimistic about the destiny of the human race. Supported by the apparent success of democratic governments and the evidence of scientific and technological advances, their confidence in the future outran even that of the Enlightenment's apostles of progress. The Kingdom of God was given a this-worldly interpretation and viewed as something men would build within the natural historical process." Ahlstrom, p. 780. Most evangelical Protestants and all liberal Protestants believed that the Kingdom of God would develop as part of the historical process. P. 811.

64. Tyack and Hansot, 6–7, 114–15.

65. Ibid., 114–15, 122. As an undergraduate, Kilpatrick went to Mercer University, a Baptist college. He later taught there and served as Mercer's acting president. Samuel Tenenbaum, *William Heard Kilpatrick: Trail Blazer in Education* (New York: Harper, 1951), 11. Counts went to Baker University, a Methodist college. Gerald L. Gutek, *George S. Counts and American Civilization* (Macon, Ga.: Mercer University Press, 1984), 5.
   On the concluding page of his Social Gospel classic *Christianity and*

the Social Crisis, Walter Rauschenbusch writes: "If at this juncture we can rally sufficient religious faith and moral strength to snap the bonds of evil and turn the present unparalleled economic and intellectual resources of humanity to the harmonious development of a true social life, the generations yet unborn will mark this as *that great day of the Lord for which the ages waited. . . .* " *Christianity and the Social Crisis* (New York: Macmillan, 1907), 422 (italics added). As Ahlstrom points out, the Social Gospel was "a form of millennial thought." Ahlstrom, 786. Ahlstrom also describes the Social Gospelers as the "praying wing of Progressivism." 804.

On the interrelationship between Progressive political thought and the Social Gospel, see Eugene McCarraher, *Christian Critics: Religion and the Impasse in Modern American Social Thought* (Ithaca, N.Y.: Cornell University Press, 2000), chap. 1.

66. Herbert M. Kliebard, *Changing Course: American Curriculum Reform in the 20th Century* (New York : Teachers College Press, 2002), 25.

67. Ibid., 33.

68. Charles W. Eliot, the president of Harvard University and chairman of the Committee of Ten, had argued that school administrators had no business predicting students' futures and then using their administrative authority to make those predictions come true by assigning certain students (namely, the ones for whom lesser futures were predicted) to nonacademic courses of study. See Eliot, "The Fundamental Assumptions in the Report of the Committee of Ten (1893)," *Educational Review*, 60 (1905): 330–31. See also Kliebard, *Changing Course*, 58.

69. Tyack and Hansot, 3–4, 6–7, 116–17.

70. "The social reconstructionists had a radical vision of using public schooling to transform society into a planned cooperative commonwealth." Ibid., 202. See also Ravitch, chap. 6.

71. Edward A. Ross, *Social Control and the Foundations of Sociology: Pioneer Contributions of Edward Alsworth Ross to the Study of Society*, ed. Edgar F. Borgatta and Henry J. Meyer (Boston: Beacon Press, 1959), 72. See also Herbert M. Kliebard, *Forging the American Curriculum: Essays in Curriculum History and Theory* (New York: Routledge, 1992), 11; Christopher Lasch, *The New Radicalism in America, 1889–1963: The Intellectual as a Social Type* (New York: Alfred A. Knopf, 1966), 170–77.

72. Cremin, 102 n. 5.

73. For the American Herbartians' literary approach, see Charles De Garmo, *Herbart and the Herbartians* (New York: Charles Scribner's Sons, 1896), for example, 209–13 (on the history curriculum).

74. Kleibard, *Forging*, 68–82. See also Cremin, 119, 141.

75. Quoted in Kleibard, *Forging*, 74.

76. Ibid., 78; Ravitch, 171. For a brief description of the curriculum at Dewey's Laboratory School, see Cremin, 139–40.

77. Compare the similar effect of the G. Stanley Hall's criterion of child-centeredness. Cremin writes: "[I]t opened the pedagogical floodgates to every manner of activity, trivial as well as useful, that seemed in some way to minister to 'the needs of children.'" 104.

78. See Kleibard, *Forging*, chap. 5; Ravitch, 163–69.

79. Kleibard, *Changing Course*, 47.

80. In another variation, Progressive educators today often oppose teacher-led instruction as unsuitable for girl students and students from racial and language minorities while insisting on watered-down content and "discovery-learning" instruction as more suitable for these students. David Klein, "Big Business, Race, and Gender in Mathematics Reform," in Steven G. Krantz, ed., *How to Teach Mathematics*, 2nd ed. (Providence, R.I.: American Mathematical Society, 1999), 221–32.

81. See Kleibard, *Changing Course*, chap. 5.

82. See Cremin, 229–30.

83. Angus and Mirel, see esp. 3–4, 59, 69. See also W. Norton Grubb and Marvin Lazerson, "Education and the Labor Market: Recycling the Youth Problem," in Harvey Kantor and David B. Tyack, eds., *Work, Youth, and Schooling: Historical Perspectives on Vocationalism in American Education* (Stanford, Calif. : Stanford University Press, 1982), 110–41 (on the Progressive Era and the 1970s).

84. The erroneous theory that high wages cause prosperity had a prominent adherent in Depression-era president Herbert Hoover: "The very essence of great production is high wages and low prices, because it depends upon a widening . . . consumption, only to be obtained from the purchasing-power of high real wages and increased standards of living." *Memoirs of Herbert Hoover* (New York: Macmillan, 1937), vol. 2, 108. President Hoover was by no means alone in adopting this idea; it was widespread in the twenties.

In reality, increased productivity and capital investment cause higher real wage rates, not the other way around (as President Hoover would have it). On the economics of a high-wage policy, see Alfred Marshall, *Elements of Economics of Industry*, 4th ed. (London: Macmillan, 1907), 401–2; Richard K. Vedder and Lowell E. Gallaway, *Out of Work: Unemployment and Government in Twentieth-Century America*, 2nd ed. (New York: New York University Press, 1997). We are indebted to Joseph Fuhrig for the reference to Alfred Marshall.

85. Arthur G. Powell, Eleanor Farrar, and David K. Cohen, *The Shopping Mall High School: Winners and Losers in the Educational Marketplace* (Boston: Houghton Mifflin, 1985), 260.

86. See, for example, Anthony S. Bryk, Valerie E. Lee, and Peter B. Holland, *Catholic Schools and the Common Good* (Cambridge, Mass.: Harvard University Press, 1993). Laurence J. O'Connell argues that in Progressive education, activities are given an almost exclusive place of importance, at the expense of intellectual learning and reasoning. O'Connell, *Are Catholic Schools Progressive?* (St. Louis: B. Herder Book Co., 1946), 129–30, 131, 155.

   James S. Coleman and Thomas Hoffer point out that Catholic schools were able to hold off "the curriculum watering-down and course-content watering-down" that took place in American high schools in the seventies. See Coleman and Hoffer, *Public and Private High Schools: The Impact of Communities* (New York: Basic Books, 1987), 94.

87. For a review, see James S. Coleman, Thomas Hoffer, and Sally B. Kilgore, *High School Achievement: Public, Catholic, and Private Schools Compared* (New York: Basic Books, 1982).

88. The Catholic school effect was not caused by smaller class size, larger teachers' salaries, or better buildings and equipment. Coleman attributed the Catholic school effect to "social capital"—namely, shared values within the students' families and between the families and the schools. Coleman and Hoffer, *Public and Private High Schools*. See 39–50 for discussion of curriculum and coursework.

89. William J. Niskanen Jr., *Bureaucracy and Public Economics* (Aldershot, Eng.: Edward Elgar Publishing, 1994), 36–42, 106–12.

90. Angus and Mirel, 13–14.

9

Neglecting the Early Grades

E. D. Hirsch Jr.

A *Nation at Risk*, the report published by the National Commission on Excellence in Education (Excellence Commission) in 1983, was mainly concerned with the high school years and ignored for most of its length the first eight grades of schooling. Then, in its last pages, the report finally alluded to the early curriculum:

> The curriculum in the crucial eight grades leading to the high school years should be specifically designed to provide a sound base for study in those and later years in such areas as English language development and writing, computational and problem solving skills, science, social studies, foreign language, and the arts. These years should foster an enthusiasm for learning and the development of the individual's gifts and talents. (72)

A *Nation at Risk* assumed that the first eight years are devoted mainly to foundational skills and considered high school the arena for decisive educational improvement.

It was natural for the writers of A *Nation at Risk* to seek reform where the most notable declines had appeared. But when we take a longer historical perspective on the declining test scores of high schoolers during the sixties and seventies, it seems probable that the watering down of high school was less a cause of its lower scores than a consequence of a gradual decline of learning in the early grades. A *Nation at Risk*'s attitude toward the early grades reminded me of the comment many years ago of a repair man who came to fix a leak in our washing machine. He asked my wife where the leak was, and she replied, "At the bottom." He looked at her knowingly and said, "Yeah, that's what they all say." Because the writers of A *Nation at Risk* saw the problems manifest in high school, they assumed that high school was the source of the problems.

With the passage of years and further empirical research on our current educational system (a notable example is the work conducted by Keith Stanovich and his colleagues), we now know that a student's academic achievement in first grade predicts his academic achievement in eleventh grade.[1] As a result, reformers and legislators have begun to emphasize early literacy—a promising advance in thinking and policy. But this welcome new emphasis on the early grades may not yield the hoped-for improvements in equity and overall achievement if, while correcting for an earlier neglect, we persist in the same formal, skills orientation to early education that guided the writers of A *Nation at Risk*.

Guiding ideas have great practical significance in educational affairs—greater than is sometimes assumed. The unexamined assumptions of teachers, administrators, and reformers can play just as large a role in determining the quality and equity of educational outcomes as money, organizational structure, accountability, and competition. Consider just one striking bit of evidence on that score. Some high-performing systems of early education, such as those in Japan, do not follow the advice of A *Nation at Risk* in stressing formal "higher-order skills" in early schooling. They pay much closer attention to the sequence and coherence of the content a child receives in the early grades. Nonetheless, the scores of their eighth-graders on the so-called higher-order skills, such as comprehension and problem solving, are not only higher than ours but are also more equitably distributed among social classes.

This is not intended as a dismissal of current efforts to introduce more competition into American schooling. It's possible that Japan would elicit even better results by experimenting with the market-oriented schemes currently being tested in the United States. But the superior outcomes of nationalized, bureaucratic, nonmarket education systems suggest that, at least in these instances, organizational schemes have been less critical to student outcomes than the ideas that have governed teaching and learning. The questionable ideas about the early curriculum that permeated *A Nation at Risk* continue to dominate discussion in the United States, while among research psychologists a consensus has formed that points to a set of more accurate ideas.

Higher-Order Skills

The writers of *A Nation at Risk* believed that the goal of early grades is to gain proficiency in the skills of reading, writing, thinking, and reckoning in order to "provide a sound basis" for high school study. With this assumption—that the aim of early education is skill building—it was natural for the writers of *A Nation at Risk* to pay little attention to the curricular content of the early grades. They assumed that any sensible content that develops the necessary foundational skills would do.

I have elsewhere called this concept—of skill building through arbitrary content—"educational formalism," the notion that a chief aim of early education is the attainment of formal skills.[2] The educational experts who were consulted by the writers of *A Nation at Risk* explicitly stated that the purpose of early schooling was the development of "higher skills," and they cited with approval the consensus on this point that emerged from a hearing on Language and Literacy held in April 1982:

> A panel of five [Excellence] Commission members, chaired by Jay Sommer, foreign language teacher at New Rochelle High School in New York, and an audience of approximately 200 people heard testimony regarding the development of the higher-order language skills necessary for academic learning. Six invited speakers presented national perspectives on teaching reading, writing, and second languages and discussed related concerns with the [Excellence] Commission members. Sixteen other speakers presented their views on the hearing topics, predominantly from regional and local perspectives. The general theme provided by the witnesses was that the language skills that should be emphasized were the more sophisticated, integrated, concept-oriented skills of comprehension and composition. Each of the experts suggested that priority should be assigned to these high-level skills and that they can be taught through systematic instructional strategies requiring conscientious effort by teachers, administrators, and publishers. (55)

Throughout A *Nation at Risk*, the concern was expressed that comprehension and problem solving were being neglected in favor of merely basic skills such as number facts, phonics, and spelling. The writers implied that the battle for educational improvement in the early grades would be won when these grades went beyond the basics and emphasized higher skills. In that context, little needed to be said about the content of early schooling. The path to improvement was seen to lie not in the substance of what was taught in the first eight grades, but in the higher-order proficiencies that were systematically inculcated.

Two decades later, we can infer from the results of putting these formalistic ideas into practice that there was something wrong with that picture. For the past twenty years, our elementary schools have tried to follow the advice of the experts who contributed to A *Nation at Risk* by teaching such higher-order skills as critical thinking, problem solving, and looking for the main idea. Yet these turned out to be the very skills in which our students continued to decline compared with students in Asian and European countries that placed less emphasis on formal comprehension skills and more emphasis on coherent year-to-year subject matter. Cognitive psychology has long since reached a level of sophistication that enables it to explain why teaching higher-order skills explicitly as formal structures is highly ineffective.[3] This finding is the most plausible explanation for the historical paradox that national systems that stress content more than skills nonetheless inculcate these higher-order skills more effectively than systems that try to teach higher-order skills as such. To teach content *is* to teach higher-order skills; to teach higher skills as such is to pursue a phantom.

Content Is Skill, Skill Content

Literate adults already possess the reading skills that A *Nation at Risk* thought could be taught divorced from content. We can read the words of this chapter with comprehension, think critically about them, analyze their main import, and ultimately judge whether the argument contributes to solving an educational problem. We can congratulate ourselves that our schooling has done the foundational job that A *Nation at Risk* called for. But it is unlikely that we gained these proficiencies by being taught them directly as formal skills. Few of us learned to find the main idea by being taught explicitly to look for it (a favorite with the formalistic approach to comprehension skill). Few of us learned the skill of thinking critically about what we read by taking formal lessons in critical thinking. How then did we gain these complex skills, and what is their nature? These are questions that educational experts and policy makers need to be able to answer if we are to achieve better results in the next twenty years than we did in the post–A *Nation at Risk* period.

By the time A *Nation at Risk* was published in 1983, cognitive psychology had achieved a degree of consensus about the fundamental nature of academic skills. Yet the science of psychology was not often alluded to in *A Nation at Risk*. Even today, twenty years later, there is little crossover between cognitive science and educational policy. *A Nation at Risk* simply assumed that gaining an academic skill such as reading or reckoning is independent of the specific curricular content through which the skill is taught. This formalistic conception continues to dominate American educational circles. It is a misleading over-simplification that will have to be corrected if our schools are to teach higher skills successfully.

Five propositions neatly summarize the scientific consensus on the nature of academic skills:

1. The character of an academic skill is predetermined by the narrow limitations of working memory.[4]

2. Academic skills have two components: procedures and contents.[5]

3. Procedural skills such as turning letters into sounds must initially be learned as content along with other content necessary to higher-order skills.[6]

4. An advance in skill, whether in procedure or content, is correlated with an advance in speed of processing.[7]

5. A higher-order academic skill such as reading comprehension requires prior knowledge of domain-specific content; the higher-order skill for that domain does not readily transfer to other content domains.[8]

Understanding the Five Principles

These well-established principles, taken together, constitute a refutation of the formalistic conception of academic skills. They explain why national systems of early education that stress a coherent approach to content succeed in teaching higher-order skills such as problem solving in mathematics more effectively than does our system, which although it explicitly stresses higher-order skills, it does so on the incorrect assumption that they are formal procedures that can be learned through arbitrary contents and transferred to new content domains. This is a mistake of historic proportions. Let's take each principle in turn, and see how they each support the idea that the learning of higher-order skills is dependent on the coherence and content of an academic program.

1. The character of an academic skill is predetermined by the narrow limitations of working memory.

The conscious activity of the mind occurs within a narrow window of time, lasting a very few seconds, in which we can manipulate a very small number of mental objects before they disappear into forgetfulness. These limitations cannot be overcome directly. Acquiring a skill means acquiring ways of indirectly circumventing the limitations of working memory for the purposes at hand. This is the most fundamental and important principle for understanding the nature of academic skills.[9]

Consider the difference in mental capacity between a practiced reader and a beginning first-grader who is painstakingly parsing out T-H-E-C-A-T-I-S-O-N-T-H-E-M-A-T (we'll use the example of reading skills here, but the principles apply just as well to mathematics, and indeed to any subject). What is the difference in raw mental capacity between that child and practiced readers? We find that the child's functional mental operations are equal to or even exceed our own. For example, the child's ability to remember a set of unfamiliar sounds or shapes is equal to ours, and the child's reaction time may be even faster than ours. The child's basic operational machinery— the hardware, so to speak—is as good as or better than our own.

It follows that our ability to read "the cat is on the mat" is not a consequence of an enhanced raw ability that has made our mental muscles bigger and stronger or has given us a more powerful central processing unit. Our ability is the consequence of our acquiring some specific software that allows us to transform an arduous task for the child into a task that is as easy for us as falling off a log. Our ability to effortlessly convert visual symbols into words is an acquired system by means of which we are able to cleverly circumvent the still-unyielding constraints of working memory.

On this basic fact hang all the law and the prophets of educational doctrine relative to skills. The conscious mind, where higher-order skills mostly take place, is limited by a universal, highly democratic constraint called working memory whose narrow limits are on average the same for child and adult, rich and poor. It is the small window of present-tense consciousness and attention. It is the "place" where we put things together and create meaning, where we solve problems and process language. Within its small temporal extent, which lasts just a few seconds, we are able to manipulate only a very small number of sensations, sounds, or symbols.

In the fifties, George Miller wrote "The Magical Number Seven Plus or Minus Two," a famous article about the limitations of working memory. Miller pointed out that the number of chunks we can handle in the brief span of working memory is extremely limited—five to nine items at most.[10] (Some now believe that the true limit of working memory varies according to the temporal constraints of the number of syllables required to name the items.)[11] The enlargement of academic skills, including, notably, acquiring a big vocabulary, consists of building efficient mental systems that enable us, despite the very constrained bottleneck imposed by limited memory, to perform huge feats of analysis and synthesis.

A famous experiment conducted by Dutch psychologist Adrian de Groot illustrated this universal bottleneck in human processing skills.[12] He noticed that chess grand masters have a remarkable skill that we amateurs cannot emulate. They can glance for five seconds at a complex midgame chess position of twenty-five pieces, perform an intervening task of some sort, then reconstruct on a blank chess board the entire chess position without making any mistakes. Performance on this task correlates almost perfectly with one's chess ranking. Grand masters make no mistakes, masters a very few, and amateurs can get just five or six pieces right. (Remember the magical number seven, plus or minus two!)

On a brilliant hunch, de Groot then performed the same experiment with twenty-five chess pieces in positions that, instead of being taken from an actual chess game, were just placed at random on the board. Under these new conditions, the performances of the three different groups—grand masters, masters, and amateurs—were all exactly the same, each group remembering just five or six pieces correctly.

The experiment suggests the skill difference between a master reader who can easily reproduce the sixteen letters of "the cat is on the mat" and a beginning reader who has trouble reproducing the same letters: t-h-e-c-a-t-i-s-o-n-t-h-e-m-a-t. If, instead of providing expert and child with that sentence, we change the task and ask them to reproduce a sequence of random letters, the performance of the first-grader and the master reader will become much closer. If the sixteen letters had been "rtu kjs vb fw nqi pgf," the expert would exhibit little skill advantage over the novice, and on average neither will get more than a short sequence of the letters right.

Practiced readers, chess grand masters, and other experts do not possess any special, formal abilities that novices lack, and they do not perform any better than novices on formally similar yet unfamiliar tasks. Nonetheless, experts are able to perform remarkable feats of memory with real-world situations such as midgame chess positions and actual sentences. How do they manage?

The sentence "the cat is on the mat" consists of six words that are easily remembered, and expert readers can easily reproduce the sixteen letters not because the letters are individually remembered, but because they are reconstructed from prior knowledge of written English. What de Groot found, and what subsequent research has continually confirmed, is that the difference in higher-order skill between a novice and an expert does not lie in mental muscles but in what de Groot called "erudition," a vast store of available, relevant, previously acquired knowledge.

Despite the narrow limitations of working memory, the wealth of contents that can be manipulated by experts through this previously acquired "erudition" is immense. If I already know a lot about baseball, the term "sacrifice fly" can represent a page or two of exposition. Such shorthand representation is a chief timesaving technique of higher-order skills. A short manageable element (like a phrase) can represent a much larger complex of already-learned meaning. The phrase "World War II" is short and therefore easily remembered, but the content represented by the phrase is enormous. It cannot be grasped by those who, however skillful in other ways, lack that relevant knowledge. By the time someone had learned the content needed to grasp "World War II," the immediate task would have long disappeared from working memory. The phrase can be understood and communicated only by those who already share the relevant knowledge and associations.

I use this example as a rapid way of indicating why an academic skill like reading depends on learning much more than the foundational ability to form sounds from symbols, turn the sounds into words, and put the words together in sentences. While such formal skills are critically important, they are quite insufficient to comprehend a passage about World War II in the absence of relevant already-learned background knowledge. A shorthand way of saying this is that the skill of reading (and listening) depends on, among other things, a prior knowledge of what most of the words in a text mean and refer to.

This example can be generalized. A skill depends upon prior possession of specifically relevant content knowledge that enables the mind to circumvent the strict limits of working memory. Academic skills cannot be isolated from the possession of specifically relevant content knowledge.[13]

The subsequent four principles are clarifications of this essential insight.

2. Academic skills have two components:
procedures and contents.

Procedural skills correspond roughly to activities that have become automatic and unconscious; content skills correspond to activities that are conscious. A complex skill like reading is composed of both procedural elements like decoding and content elements like vocabulary knowledge.[14]

I type these words under a disadvantage. I never learned a system of touch typing. Still, because I have performed this activity so many times, I type fairly fast. Finding the right key takes up very little of my working memory. I never have to ask myself where a letter on the keyboard is; I just hit it without thinking. This is the very model of learning a procedural skill. The activity becomes automatic and unconscious because it is often repeated and nearly invariant. The letters on the keyboard do not move around from one typing session to the next. Similarly, the procedural skills of reading—rapid eye movements from left to right and from line to line, automatic calculation of the highest letter-sound probabilities (decoding)—remain fairly stable and repeatable from one reading event to another and are therefore good candidates for being turned into unconscious, procedural skills.

The so-called basic skills of reading and math are largely of this procedural sort. It is essential that these skills be mastered so that working memory can occupy itself with nonrepeated, content-based skills such as reading comprehension. Given the constraints of working memory, any mental space that is consciously concerned with decoding and identifying words will occupy space that could otherwise be used for higher-order skills.

It should be emphasized, however, that procedural skills are not inherently independent of content. They do not start out as part of a separate system. Before my typing became fast, automatic, and unconscious, it was conscious, slow, and error-prone. This is the usual pattern for learning procedural skills. Before a child masters the automatic decoding of print into speech sounds, he must slog through many hours of conscious and laborious content-filled activities. Such skills are contents before they are procedures. In the early grades, the regularities and probabilities behind the procedural skills are themselves an important content of schooling. But the fact that such pre-procedural skills are "basic" doesn't mean they are the only important content of early schooling—a point that deserves mention as a third principle.

3. Procedural skills such as turning letters into sounds must initially be learned as content along with other content necessary to higher-order skills.

Efforts to learn procedural skills such as the decoding of letters into words are at first slow and uncertain because of the narrow limitations of working memory. Some procedural skills, like decoding, become speedy and automatic only after years of practice. The case is different with content-based skills such as vocabulary knowledge.[15] These content elements can be learned rapidly, with few exposures, and are the chief components of higher-order abilities. Knowledge of the broad content that is relevant to the general reading demanded by the modern world should be gained steadily from the earliest years of schooling, along with procedural skills.

The complex skill of reading comprehension is a combination of both types of skills. Reading skill consists of a relatively small store of unconscious procedural skills accompanied by a massive, slowly-built-up store of conscious content skills (for example, vocabulary). If school time is to be spent effectively in the early grades, the massive buildup of content knowledge that is essential to higher-order skills must not be subordinated to the slow multiyear buildup of foundational procedural skills. To attain maximum effectiveness, both kinds of skill-learning should occur simultaneously.

The procedural/content distinction used by psychologists clarifies the dual, unconscious/conscious character of academic skills. The duality suggests why our schools have been mistaken in assuming that reading skill can be reliably built up simply by wide practice and frequent exposure to arbitrary sorts of content. This conception does work for procedural tasks like eye movements and decoding, which are relatively invariant from one occasion to another. But exposure to arbitrary content cannot reliably build up the knowledge and vocabulary that is the foundation of higher-order reading skill because these content elements are not the same from one task to another. They require conscious attention in working memory.

It is true that broad content knowledge can be built up over time simply from wide desultory reading. Given world enough and time, the reading of many and varied books over many years can yield a good general education. But achieving competence in higher-order, knowledge-based skills such as reading comprehension is a difficult and time-consuming process that the schools need to foster in a time-effective way. Exposing students to content in a hit-or-miss fashion leaves many behind. Exposing them to content in a coherent sequence, as many national systems do, securely provides all students with the content knowledge they need to be competent readers.

Bringing all students to competence in higher-order skills is a fundamental responsibility of the schools of a democracy. If we follow out the implications of the scientific consensus, our schools are duty-bound to adopt a coherent, rational, and sequenced approach to content and vocabulary knowledge—not the content-indifferent approach allowed by a mistakenly formal, purely procedural conception of higher-order skills.

4. An advance in skill, whether in procedure or content, is correlated with an advance in speed of processing.

For repeated, procedural activities such as translating visual symbols to sounds, speed is increased by "automaticity." For content skills such as reading comprehension, speed is increased by "chunking."[16]

An advance in skill requires an advance in speed because the contents of working memory begin to disintegrate and dissolve after a few seconds. Correlating what we are thinking or reading about has to be done fast before the elements disappear. Working memory imposes an unforgiving temporal limitation on what we can attend to before the elements of thought evaporate.

The magnitude of what we are able to accomplish in this small window of conscious attention depends first of all on our enabling the procedural aspects of the task to take up less and less mental time and space. We can attend only to a very few things at a time, so if we attend to the basic process, we can't attend to much else. The more automatically and rapidly we can turn letters into words and sentences, the more rapidly we can read. The beginner cannot remember the sixteen letters of t-h-e-c-a-t-i-s-o-n-t-h-e-m-a-t because his working memory gets filled up by the conscious process of attaching names and sounds to the visual symbols, leaving no mental space for active attention to the letter sequence itself. Speed is of the essence. The higher-order processes cannot begin to function well until these underlying processes have become fast and automatic.

Once the underlying processes of reading have become fast and automatic we must still be able to deal with the substance of what the decoded words signify. Being able effortlessly to turn w-o-r-l-d-w-a-r-I-I into World War Two doesn't count for much if we don't comprehend what the phrase means. In this sphere of content, speed also counts for a great deal. The rapid availability of a phrase's meaning enables us actively to combine that meaning with other meanings before the elements dissolve into oblivion.

The general skill of reading comprehension correlates very highly with the possession of a broad, quickly available general vocabulary, which is unsurprising since vocabulary knowledge is a component of the skill of reading comprehension.[17] A vocabulary item like World War Two can be unpacked by a comprehending reader into a large number of implicitly included meanings like Axis powers, Allies, 1939–1945, Holocaust, atom bomb, and so forth, and these can themselves be further unpacked. All these meanings are implicitly included in the phrase, but the phrase itself is so compact that it can be manipulated with other large complexes of meaning before the elements dissipate.

The concentration of complex meaning into a simple, small packet that can be accommodated in working memory is the chief trick of the mind in higher-order skills. When psychologists first began experimenting with the limits of working memory, they found that a chief device for improving performance was "chunking," that is, turning a large number of discrete items into a small number of chunks. If you want to remember the telephone number 7265346519, you will do well to turn these eleven discrete items into three chunks: 726-534-6519.

In order for we humans to think effectively, the elements that we attend to must be grasped rapidly and therefore must be few in number. Later on, the numerous implications of those few elements can be unpacked and analyzed at leisure. It was rapid concentration of meaning that de Groot's chess masters engaged in—a kind of chess vocabulary, whether or not formed into words—when they observed a midgame position. They immediately identified a familiar structure that could have been named, say, "Queen's Pawn Gambit Declined, Lasker Variation." Later, they could unpack this quasi-vocabulary item and reconstruct the position with perfect fidelity. The fundamental need of the mind for such speedy meaning-concentration explains why higher-order skills require the possession of relevant prior knowledge and its associated vocabulary.

5. A higher-order academic skill such as reading comprehension requires prior knowledge of domain-specific content; the higher-order skill for that domain does not readily transfer to other content domains.

De Groot showed that being an expert in chess does not improve one's memory for randomized chess positions. Tracing the implications of that discovery, psychologists have found that being expert in chess is even less likely to improve one's skills in areas that are still more remote from chess, like math problem-solving or the ability to think logically about politics.[18] A famous example was Bobby Fisher. He was one of the greatest chess grand masters America has produced, with unparalleled critical thinking skills for analyzing chess strategy—but he had famously poor critical-thinking skills in the affairs of everyday life.

Being good at one mental skill does not necessarily train the mind to be skilled in other domains.[19] This could be called the principle of nontransferability. It is one of the most solid findings in psychology, confirmed and reconfirmed many times, tested so often possibly because it has been such a surprising and unwelcome finding. People who have just finished a course in logic are barely more logical than those who have never taken such a course.[20] People who have been carefully trained how to solve a problem in one domain are rarely able to solve a problem that has identical structure but lies in a different domain. Those who are skilled at diverse tasks in various domains are people who have managed to acquire broad general knowledge that includes knowledge relevant to those diverse domains. Such generalized skill is in fact a practical aim of a broad, general education. Students who score well on the verbal SAT invariably possess a broad vocabulary that represents broad general knowledge—which is hardly surprising since the verbal SAT is essentially an advanced vocabulary test.[21]

The so-called higher-order skills are therefore those that are least susceptible to transfer. They are the most dependent upon domain-specific knowledge. All of the examples and analyses in this chapter hint at why higher skills are so dependent upon specific knowledge. They show that problem solving and critical thinking are not mental muscles. They are not abstract rules of operation. If remembering chess positions had been based on internalized rules, then the grand masters would have been able to apply them to a completely random chess position. There do exist internalized rules of operation in a skill, of course, but these never concern aspects that we call higher-order skills. They are more like the rules of grammar in a language. These stable grammar rules transfer from one sentence and domain to another, because they are relatively invariant. But they are also relatively basic. A six-year-old has already internalized most of the intricacies of grammar rules. What the six-year-old lacks is world knowledge and its associated vocabulary. Such knowledge is not imparted by schools that place their educational faith in the power of formal skills and the assumption that they will empower a child to acquire knowledge and vocabulary on her own.

For practical purposes, there are no such things as transferable higher skills of problem solving and reading comprehension. The ability to solve a math problem depends on having a specifically relevant and available math vocabulary. The ability to comprehend a printed text depends on having a specifically relevant and available linguistic vocabulary that comprises at least 90 percent of the words of the text.[22] The vague hope that students will be able to apply what they know in depth about supermarkets to new domains is not sustained by experience or psychological theory.

That is not to say that the mental transfer of structure from one problem to another never occurs. On the contrary, one of the features of expert performance in a domain (after about ten years of practice) is the ability to intuit the deep structure of problems and their connections with other problems in that domain. But this is a kind of skill that comes after long experience.[23] The hope that skilled intuition of deep structural similarities among superficially dissimilar problems can be successfully taught to novices has been shown to be incorrect. Some improvement in reading can come from making students aware of the need to look for the main idea or to ask questions and make inferences, but this improvement levels off very quickly after about six lessons and yields an initial and unchanging effect size that is the same as that yielded by twenty-five such lessons. There are no significant shortcuts to gaining structural skills in a domain.[24]

If mental transfer is difficult among problems within a domain, it is exceedingly difficult from one domain to another. Such analogous thinking is rare; it represents the pinnacle of human thought, the epitome of creative thinking. When it happens, a new art form or field of thought is born. The great physicist Erwin Schroedinger wrote a little book entitled *What Is Life?* in which he suggested that life is a kind of crystal that enables the living molecule to replicate itself, as do the molecules of a crystal.[25] This thought transfer from physics to biology was so captivating that it caused a whole generation of physicists to turn their attention to biology, resulting in the Crick-Watson discovery of DNA and, ultimately, in the transformation of modern biology and medicine. For most of us, though, most of the time, such leaps of thought are very rare precisely because they are so difficult.

Our American faith that teaching students biology will teach them the nature of science or that teaching students to think critically about the Civil War will teach them how to think critically about current affairs is a misplaced faith that is supported neither by large-scale results nor by the laboratory. The practical result of our faith in the transferability of higher skills has been an incoherent curriculum that is especially damaging to those students who have not gained broad academic knowledge outside of school.

Needed: A Coherent and Specific Curriculum

There are clear policy implications to be drawn from understanding the domain- and content-specific character of higher-order skills.

These do not include continuing to follow popular slogans about local control of curriculum and letting a thousand flowers bloom. The goal of a literate citizenry can be reached only by offering ideas for educational reform that specify a coherent curriculum. The writers of *A Nation at Risk* did not recommend a coherent, grade-by-grade-specific elementary curriculum because its writers did not understand as fully as we do now the degree to which higher skills are dependent upon a sound base of general knowledge. Schools cannot be sure of offering all students a sound base of general knowledge until the states *specify* the core content of the early curriculum.

A beginning has been made in the state-standards movement. Currently most state standards are vague and fail to offer grade-by-grade guidance. State tests are not effectively tied to specific, grade-by-grade knowledge. The few states, like Virginia and Massachusetts, that are farthest along that path, have made significant progress in both excellence and equity. The many states that lag behind in setting specific grade-by-grade standards have shown little educational progress. I believe that our best hope for widespread improvement in K–12 education lies in the standards movement, which potentially offers a more effective educational arrangement than any we have had, not least because by defining the knowledge that students need we also implicitly specify the knowledge that teachers should possess. We need a good core curriculum for each state. Our best hope for succeeding where the generation that wrote *A Nation at Risk* failed is to act on this unavoidable yet still unpopular implication of the content-ridden nature of higher-order skills.

Notes

1. Anne E. Cunningham and Keith E. Stanovich, "Early Reading Acquisition and Its Relation to Reading Experience and Ability 10 Years Later," *Developmental Psychology* 33 (November 1977): 934–45.

2. E. D. Hirsch, *Cultural Literacy*, (Boston: Houghton Mifflin, 1987), 110–13; see also *The Schools We Need* (New York: Doubleday, 1996), 218–22.

3. The up-to-date psychological literature on problem solving and other higher-order skills is summarized in Daniel B. Willingham, *The Thinking Animal* (Upper Saddle River, N.J.: Prentice-Hall, 2001), 382–478. Another excellent overview is Rosemary J. Stevenson, *Language, Thought and Representation* (New York: John Wiley & Sons, 1993).

4. George A. Miller, "The Magical Number Seven, Plus or Minus Two: Some Limits on Our Capacity for Processing Information," *The Psychology of Communication*, Basic Books, 1967. See also Alan D. Baddeley, *Human Memory: Theory and Practice* (revised edition), (Needham Heights, Mass.: Allyn & Bacon, 1998).

5. Daniel B. Willingham, *The Thinking Animal*, 318–25.

6. Alan D. Baddeley, *Human Memory: Theory and Practice*, 120–25, 149–51, 299–300. See also Rosemary J. Stevenson, *Language, Thought and Representation*, 231–56.

7. Robert Kail, "Development of Processing Speed in Childhood and Adolescence," *Advances in Child Development and Behavior* (v. 23, 1991), 151–85.

8. Walter Kintsch, *Comprehension: A Paradigm for Cognition* (New York: Cambridge University Press, 1998), 287–90.

9. George A. Miller, op. cit. Alan D. Baddeley, *Human Memory: Theory and Practice*.

10. See note 4.

11. Alan D. Baddeley, *Human Memory: Theory and Practice*, 29–32.

12. A. de Groot, *Het Denken van den Shaker*, 1946. English: *Thought and Choice in Chess*, Mouton, The Hague, 1965.

13. Rosemary J. Stevenson, *Language, Thought and Representation*, 231–56.

14. Walter Kintsch, *Comprehension: A Paradigm for Cognition*.

15. Rosemary J. Stevenson, *Language, Thought and Representation*, 231–56.

16. "Chunking" was first used by Miller in "The Magical Number Seven, Plus or Minus Two: Some Limits on Our Capacity for Processing Information."

17. W. E. Nagy, and J. Scott, "Vocabulary Processes" in Kamil, M., et al., *Handbook of Reading Research, Volume III* (Mahwah, N.J.: Erlbaum, 2000), 269–84.

18. S. E. Newstead, and J. Evans, eds., *Perspectives on Thinking and Reasoning* (Hillsdale, N.J.: Erlbaum, 1995).

19. Rosemary J. Stevenson, *Language, Thought and Representation*, 231–56.

20. W. H. Klaczynski, and J. S. Laipple, "Role of Content Domain, Logic Training, and IQ in Rule Acquisition and Transfer," *Journal of Experimental Psychology. Learning, Memory and Cognition* (v. 19, 1993), 653–72.

21. John B. Carroll, "Psychometric Approaches to the Study of Language Abilities," in Fillmore et al., *Individual Differences in Language Abilities and Language Behavior* (New York: Academic Press, 1979), 29.

22. W. E. Nagy and J. Scott, "Vocabulary Processes."

23. K. A. Ericsson, K. A. and N. Charness, "Expert Performance: Its Structure and Acquisition," *American Psychologist* (v. 49, 1994), 725–47.

24. Barak, Rosenshine, and Carla Meister, "Reciprocal Teaching: A Review of the Research," *Review of Educational Research* (v. 64, 1994), 479–530.

25. E. Schroedinger, *What Is Life? With Mind and Matter and Autobiographical Sketches* (Cambridge, Eng.: Cambridge University Press, 1996, 1967, 1944).

PART THREE

GETTING SERIOUS

10

Real Accountability

Herbert J. Walberg

By 1985, the concerns of policy makers and the public were increasingly shifting to achievement outcomes. A *Nation at Risk* showed American students lagged behind those in other countries. A *Nation at Risk* argued that the best jobs and industries of greatest growth required general knowledge, language mastery, and mathematical, scientific, and technical skills. It seemed obvious that voting, serving on juries, and other duties of citizenship require such knowledge and skills as well as mastery of American history, civics, and geography.

To meet the crisis of mediocrity, legislators and school boards continued to spend substantially more money on schools,[1] and educators reformed policies and practices. But ever more pointedly, legislators, citizens, and parents asked how much students were actually learning. They wanted accountability for results.

These concerns were warranted. Indeed, A *Nation at Risk* underestimated the problem because we now know that American students fall further behind the longer they remain in U.S. schools even though, when they begin school, they are just as able as students in other countries.[2] Before and after A *Nation at Risk*, moreover, both per-student spending and students' mental abilities rose steadily and substantially, but students' achievement in the standard school subjects stagnated at low levels. Perhaps most worrisome, more than $125 billion dollars of federal money spent on students in poverty failed to eliminate or even reduce the gap in achievement between them and more-advantaged students.

Failed schools have debilitating effects on the economy: An estimated 78 percent of our nation's institutions of higher learning offer remedial courses for first-year students who are unready for college work. About half of American firms provide training to make up for inadequate schooling, perhaps a considerable fraction of the estimated annual $55 billion spent on employee training. A U.S. Department of Labor study estimated that illiteracy in one year cost eight southern states $57.6 billion in lost productivity, substandard work, unrealized taxes, unemployment claims, and social problems.[3]

Accountability Milestones

A *Nation at Risk* encouraged national, state, and local deliberations and many policy reforms. A consequence was an effort to hold educators accountable for outcomes, particularly achievement test scores. Policy makers, businesspeople, the public, and parents increasingly insisted on having better measures and improvements of actual outcomes. As shown in table 1, accountability reforms grew slowly at first but later swelled into the crescendo of state and federal legislation we now see.

One significant accountability milestone took place in 1989, at the National Governors' Association Education Summit in which then President George H. Bush, the nation's governors, and business leaders gave impetus to business-style accountability for schools. "Systemic

Table 1. Significant accountability events

Year	Event
1983	• During President Reagan's term of office, a panel of citizens issues *A Nation at Risk* that declares a "rising tide of mediocrity in education." Influenced by poor U.S. standings on achievement tests, the panel calls for core curriculum subjects, higher learning expectations, more time in school, and better teaching. Business leaders complain of poor employee academic-skill preparation for work.
1988	• Twenty-five states pass legislation intended to raise education spending. • Congress creates the National Assessment Governing Board, composed of elected state officials, school board members, business leaders, scholars, and others, to develop assessments and standards for national, regional, and state comparisons of achievement in reading, mathematics, science, and other subjects.
1989	• President Bush calls National Education Summit of state governors to establish education goals for 2000. Arkansas governor and future president Bill Clinton plays a leading role.
1991	• The U.S. Department of Education funds efforts to draft national curriculum standards for core curriculum subjects. • National Assessment Governing Board releases first-ever valid state achievement comparisons. • The Governing Board also releases the first-ever percentages of students meeting the standards of Advanced, Proficient, Basic, and Below Basic levels; poor performance levels continue in subsequent years.
1994	• President Clinton signs Goals 2000: Educate America act, mandating creation of the National Education Standards and Improvement Council. Congress voices opposition and no one is appointed to the council.
1995	• National curriculum standards are released to widespread criticism from Congress and other groups.
1996	• The second National Education Summit of governors pledges to set standards at the state and local levels. • The Southern Regional Education Board releases report showing that states around the country have much lower standards than the National Assessment.
1998	• Thirty-eight states have adopted state standards in core academic subjects.
2001	• A report commissioned by Congress shows that approximately $120 billion in spending and detailed regulations of state and local districts over more than 20 years have failed to reduce the gap between children in poverty and other children.

Table 1. (*continued*)

Year	Event
2002	• President Bush signs No Child Left Behind act, which is to approximately double spending and impose further regulations; states to develop challenging standards for students to meet by twelfth grade. • U.S. Department of Education reports that only nineteen states meet the 1994 federal Elementary and Secondary Act requirements. • All states but high-scoring Iowa have adopted curriculum standards in core subjects, but most are neither well measured nor enforced. • U.S. history again stumps seniors; almost 60 percent score Below Basic.

reform," as recommended by the attendees, meant aligning the chief components of education: goals, curricula, instruction, and tests.

Like the accountability of business executives, school accountability was thought to require simultaneous centralization and decentralization: centralization of standards at the state level and decentralization of operational responsibilities to the district or school level. State policy makers were to set goals and measure progress, but, unlike in the past, they were to leave local school districts and schools to develop and execute effective practices.

State officials could then set high targets for achievement and maintain more objectivity in evaluating the results, at least more than in the past when they tried to determine both goals and means. Without this division of labor, local districts might set easy-to-reach, unmeasurable, or obfuscated goals. Concern for achievement accountability was bipartisan, and surveys show that the public strongly supported and still supports objective testing, higher standards, and greater specificity about what students should learn.[4]

Another milestone was the congressional creation of the National Assessment Governing Board to develop achievement standards. The board's reports showed that few American students could meet the Advanced standards level roughly comparable to that of Asian and European students. Dismayingly few could even reach the Proficient level, roughly indicating the knowledge and skills required to proceed to the next grade level. The Governing Board's comparisons of states created even greater reform momentum, since state legislators could see how education systems for which they are responsible compare with others.

In 1994, the National Governors' Conference's resolve to develop measurable national education goals built further momentum. More and more states began testing programs and began setting standards. Though per-student costs of tests were small, they provided both school accountability information and useful data on the progress each student needed to make to attain standards. States that instituted more rigorous accountability programs, moreover, made better achievement progress.[5]

The Rise of State Accountability Systems

For most of the century, nearly all schools employed a variety of commercial tests that made accountability difficult since scores on different tests cannot be readily compared. A *Nation at Risk*, other reform reports, and rising concerns changed this substantially. The most important development is that most states have initiated accountability systems and have begun aligning their tests to state learning standards. Evaluation of the evidence in 2001 suggested that tests had been aligned at least in part to learning standards for the school subjects in the following numbers of states:

English	45 states
Mathematics	43 states
Science	29 states
History and social studies	23 states

Nearly all states employed multiple-choice tests, and about two-thirds used essay tests and short-answer questions. Only two employed portfolios of student work. To create school ratings, fourteen states employed only student test scores; the others employed dropout rates, attendance, and other indicators in addition to test scores.[6]

Lack of Achievement Progress

Despite such accountability milestones and state testing programs since A *Nation at Risk*, achievement progress has been disappointing. As shown in table 2, not even one of the eight Year 2000 National Educational Goals set in 1989 has been accomplished. Some results were even worse after a decade or so of effort.

As shown in table 3, few states rose to the standards of the National Assessment Governing Board, which Congress created to set forth national standards and measure their degree of attainment. Only six of twenty-two surveyed states claimed that more than half their students were proficient by their own state standards. Only one state, Connecticut, could show that more than one-third of its students met the standards of the National Assessment Governing Board.

Contrary to the long-standing goal of the federal legislation, moreover, vast amounts of extra spending for poor children failed to break the link between poverty and achievement. As shown in table 3, relatively poorer southern states such as Tennessee, Arkansas, and Louisiana ranked much lower than northern states such as Connecticut, Massachusetts, and Oregon.

Progress in Accountability Research

Even though the nation and individual states and schools have not reaped the full potential benefits of testing and accountability, considerable progress has been made in identifying effective and efficient practices of testing and accountability for improving students' learning. The most important and promising are discussed in this section.

Table 2. Achievement of the eight Year 2000 national education goals set in 1989

Goal	Indicator	Baseline	Update	Achieved?
All children in America will start school ready to learn.	Percentage of 3- and 5-year-olds whose parents read to them regularly	66%	69%	No
High school graduation rates will increase to at least 90 percent.	Percentage of 18- to 24-year-olds with a high school credential	86%	85%	No
All students will leave grades 4, 8, and 12 having demonstrated competency over challenging subject matter including English, mathematics, science, foreign languages, civics and government, economics, arts, history, and geography.	Percentage of students at National Assessment of Educational Progress proficient level	12% to 40%	16% to 40%	No
The nation's teaching force will have access to programs for continuing improvement of their professional skills.	Percentage of secondary school teachers who hold an undergraduate or graduate degree in their main teaching assignment	66%	63%	No
U.S. students will be first in the world in mathematics and science achievement.	U.S. rank of first on international assessments	No	No	No
Every adult American will be literate and will possess the knowledge and skills necessary to compete in a global economy.	Percentage of adults who score at the three highest literacy levels	52%	No update	No

Table 2. (*continued*)

Goal	Indicator	Baseline	Update	Achieved?
Every school will be freed of drugs, violence, and the unauthorized presence of firearms and alcohol.	Student reports	17% to 63%	16% to 63%	No
Every school will promote parental partnerships.	Parent reports that they participated in two or more school activities per year	63%	62%	No

Source: Adapted from *National Education Goals Panel, The National Goals Report: Building a Nation of Learners 1999*, vi, 17–21.

Examinations for Accountability

Frequent testing with essay and short-answer questions and multiple-choice tests leads to higher achievement. Students prepare more regularly, and frequent tests provide more information to both teachers and students about their strengths and weaknesses. Teachers may also observe and rate their students' performance in class. They may assign, for example, laboratory exercises in science, physical measurements in geometry, and essays in history and literature. Then they may judge or rate the quality of the resulting work. For additional assessment and feedback, teachers may also check their students' homework and either grade or comment upon it. Such assessments may be termed "teacher-aligned" or integrated with instruction because they correspond to the content of the lessons being taught.[7]

For several reasons, such teacher assessments do not serve well in large-scale surveys of achievement intended to provide information on how students, schools, districts, and states compare with one another, how they compare with established standards, or how achievement is changing over time. Tests intended for this purpose are "standardized" in that the conditions and timing of the tests are nearly

Table 3. Percentages of students meeting state and national proficiency standards for 8th-grade mathematics

	State	National	Difference
Connecticut	55	34	21
Massachusetts	34	32	–2
Oregon	49	32	17
Vermont	32	32	0
Indiana	64	31	33
North Carolina	81	30	51
Maryland	50	29	21
Idaho	15	27	–12
Illinois	47	27	20
New York	40	26	14
Virginia	61	26	35
Wyoming	32	25	7
Rhode Island	20	24	–4
Texas	26	24	2
Missouri	14	22	–8
Kentucky	25	21	4
Georgia	54	19	35
Oklahoma	71	19	52
South Carolina	20	18	2
Tennessee	40	17	23
Arkansas	16	14	2
Louisiana	8	12	–4

Source: Education Week, February 20, 2002; Internet www.edweek.org.ew/newstory.cfm?slug=23profchrt2.h21.

identical for all students. Standardized tests can widely sample many aspects of the subject matter. In this respect, they are like national voter and consumer surveys that sample, say, a thousand people, to provide information on the entire adult population with a probable sample error of less than a few percentage points. Sample surveys provide information quickly, efficiently, and cheaply. So, too, can thirty to sixty multiple-choice questions tap what a student knows about a broad subject constituted by thousands of facts and ideas.

So that aspects of the subject may be sampled in a short time, achievement surveys generally employ multiple-choice examinations.

Thirty items may be administered in as much time as would be required to answer a single essay question. Multiple-choice questions afford a much larger sample of students' knowledge and skills than do long essay questions. They are also fairer to students, since their scores do not depend heavily and arbitrarily on whether they happened to have concentrated on only one narrow aspect of the subject, which happens to be on an essay examination.

A final reason that multiple-choice tests are preferred in large-scale achievement surveys is that "constructed response" tests requiring essays, laboratory equipment, calculators, and the like usually add little value to the information provided by students' scores on objective tests. So, the large extra cost of essay examinations is usually unwarranted by the marginal information they may provide (except possibly, as pointed out above, when educators want to encourage and measure essay writing as separate from knowledge and skills in a subject such as history, literature, or science).[8]

Cost of Tests, Standard Setting, and Accountability

Given the positive effects of testing on learning and their uses in accountability, they are one of the most cost-effective means of improving education. Though some educators have protested the costs of accountability systems, as Caroline Hoxby pointed out, their costs are surprisingly small, representing a miniscule percentage of school budgets.[9] The payment to commercial firms for standardized testing, standard setting, and accountability in 2000 was $234 million, which was less than 0.1 of 1 percent of K–12 school costs; it amounts to $5.81 per American student. For the twenty-five states with available information, these per-student testing costs run between $1.79 and $34.00.

These costs, moreover, will undoubtedly decline in the longer run since they were estimated as states were developing accountability systems; after development and initial revision, much of the activity can be routinized at lower costs. Few states require tests more than once a year, but, given their positive effects and small costs, there is good reason to administer them more frequently to measure the progress of teachers, schools, districts, and states. In addition, value-added measures or gains over time (discussed in a subsequent section) are more reliable when based on more than two test administrations.

Curriculum-Based External Examinations

Tests contribute to greater achievement when they are geared toward learning standards to be mastered. Curriculum-based external examinations have the common elements of being externally composed and geared toward agreed-upon subject matter that students within a certain nation, state, or province are to learn. Usually given at the end of related courses, they have substantial positive effects on learning.[10] Cornell economist John Bishop has intensively studied the effects of curriculum-based external examination on learning. He analyzed the examination effects on learning by studying surveys of the U.S. Advanced Placement program, the New York State Regents, and U.S. state and Canadian provincial systems. He also analyzed examination effects on learning in the United States in comparison with effects in Asian and European nations. He has consistently found their effects on learning to be positive.

When made publicly available, curriculum-based external evaluations allow policy makers, educators, parents, and students to assess and compare achievement standings and progress. Schools that perform poorly are pressured to make progress. When students can choose schools to attend, failing schools risk losing students and even closing.

Division of Labor and Competition

Such external examinations may benefit from the ways that other nations organize their school systems. The largest and most sophisticated international comparative analysis of national achievement, performed by Ludger Woessmann of the Kiel Institute of World Economics, corroborates Bishop's and related findings.[11] Using data from thirty-nine countries that participated in the Third International Mathematics and Science Study, his analysis showed that the following four factors consistently promote learning:[12]

1. External, curriculum-based examinations and close, outside monitoring of achievement progress
2. School autonomy over personnel and operations
3. Teacher discretion over teaching methods
4. Competition from privately governed schools

How and why should these factors yield striking national effects? Despite variations in design, the examinations cover uniform subject matter in humanities and sciences. Since the exams are graded by educators other than the students' own teachers, students have little incentive to challenge their teachers about difficult course content and standards. Instead, students and teachers work together toward the common goal of meeting examination standards. Because of examination and course uniformity, moreover, teachers can concentrate not on what to teach but how to teach, and the students' subsequent teachers can depend on what students have been taught.

Accountability Effects

A decade ago, few states specified what students should know and be able to do, but forty-nine states now do so at least for some subjects and grade levels, and the number of states with adequate academic standards has increased. The more sustained and comprehensive the accountability system, moreover, the better states' learning progress appears. A study commissioned by the National Educational Goals Panel revealed these reasons for North Carolina and Texas making the largest gains on the National Assessment of Educational Progress:

- Grade-by-grade standards with aligned curricula and textbooks

- Expectations that all students would meet the standards

- Statewide assessments linked to the standards

- Accountability for results, with rewards and sanctions for performance

- Deregulation and increased flexibility in ways the standards can be met

- Computerized feedback systems and achievement data for continuous improvement[13]

Employing standard economic principles, legislators are designing increasingly refined accountability systems and tying incentives to test results.[14] For example, states increasingly "disaggregate" test scores to be sure that various groups are well served. Texas, for example, reports separate results for boys and girls, and for whites, blacks, and Hispanics. This disaggregation is the precedent, discussed below, for the federal No Child Left Behind act. Similarly, the National Assessment of Educational Progress reports percentages of students that meet Advanced, Proficient, Basic, and Below Basic standards, which encourages improvement at all levels rather than on only a single standard that is too easy for some students, schools, and districts and too challenging for others.

Improving Accountability

Despite such promising scholarly and policy breakthroughs, achievement has yet to improve. Has accountability failed in principle or in practice? Chester Finn and Marci Kanstoroom suggest that state practice is flawed. Designated as "irresponsible" in table 4, twenty-one states have weak accountability and either weak or no standards. Only five states—Alabama, California, North Carolina, South Carolina, and

Texas—make the table 4 honor roll in having both solid standards and strong accountability.

Strong accountability means the state employs report cards and ratings of schools, rewards successful schools, has authority to reconstitute or make major changes to failing schools, and exercises such authority. Solid standards are clear, measurable, comprehensive, and rigorous. The twenty-one irresponsible states and other twenty-four states have much work to do to catch up with the five on the table 4 honor roll.

Exemplary Standards

What do good standards look like? The Massachusetts History and Social Science Curriculum Framework[15] is particularly notable, not only in exemplifying the Finn-Kanstoroom criteria but in representing principled content. The framework begins with three convictions: that democracy is the worthiest form of government, that its spread cannot be taken for granted, and that its survival depends on each new generation acquiring loyalty to the American founders' vision.

In seven Guiding Principles, the framework sets forth requirements for all K–12 history and social science content: (1) emphasis on the development of political principles and institutions of Western civilization, (2) recognition of each person as an individual while developing a common American civic identity, (3) need for understanding the world outside the United States, (4) learning of social science through current events and public policy, (5) continuous study of history and social science from prekindergarten through high school, (6) integration of content, concepts, and skills in a coherent course of study, and (7) drawing upon non–social science disciplines such as fine arts, literature, and mathematics.

These principles are exemplified in the framework's ten Concepts and Skills for Grade 2. They are shown on page 320.

Table 4. States classified by quality of standards and accountability

Account-ability/ standards	Solid standards A or B	Mediocre standards C	Inferior standards D or F
Strong account-ability	*Honor roll* Alabama, California, North Carolina, South Carolina, Texas	*Shaky foundations* Florida, Illinois, Indiana, Kansas, Maryland, Nevada, New York, Oklahoma, Virginia, West Virginia	*Trouble ahead* Kentucky, New Mexico
Weak account-ability	*Unrealized potential* Arizona, Massachusetts, South Dakota	*Going through the motions* Delaware, Georgia, Louisiana, Mississippi, Nebraska, New Hampshire, Ohio, Utah, Wisconsin	*Irresponsible states* Alaska, Arkansas, Colorado, Connecticut, Hawaii, Idaho, Iowa, Maine, Michigan, Minnesota, Missouri, Montana, New Jersey, North Dakota, Oregon, Pennsylvania, Rhode Island, Tennessee, Vermont, Washington, Wyoming

Source: Chester E. Finn and Marci Kanstoroom, "State Academic Standards," in *Brookings Papers on Education Policy, 2001,* ed. Diane Ravitch (Washington, D.C.: Brookings Institution Press, 2001), 51, 131–80.

Accountability Principles

Table 5 explains a dozen accountability principles that, when implemented, are likely to improve achievement. They may be applied not only by states but by local districts to school administrators and, to some extent, by school administrators to teachers and teachers to students. Several of these overlap the Finn-Kanstoroom criteria. Others emphasize the importance of timeliness, fairness, balance, the expression and disaggregation of test scores, and the need to design accountability reports for the convenience and ready understanding

History and Geography

1. Use a calendar to identify days, weeks, months, years, and seasons.
2. Use correctly words and phrases related to time (now, in the past, in the future), changing historical periods (other times, other places), and causation (because, reasons).
3. Explain the information that historical timelines convey, then put in chronological order events in the student's life (such as the year he or she was born, started school, or moved to a new neighborhood) or in the history of countries studied.
4. Describe how maps and globes depict geographical information in different ways.
5. Read globes and maps and follow narrative accounts on them.
6. Identify cardinal directions (north, east, south, and west) and apply them to maps, locations in the classroom, school, playground, and community.

Civics and Government

7. Define and give examples of some of the rights and responsibilities that students as citizens have in the school (for example, students have the right to vote in a class election but have the responsibility to follow school rules).
8. Give examples of fictional characters or real people in the school or community who were good leaders and good citizens, and explain the qualities that made them admirable (for example, honesty, dependability, modesty, trustworthiness, courage).

Economics

9. Give examples of people in the school and community who are both producers and consumers.
10. Explain what buyers and sellers are and give examples of goods and services that are bought and sold in their community.

of those held accountable as well as of those who hold them accountable.

Few states, districts, and schools follow the twelve principles. But some do,[16] which suggests that others can.

Value-Added Accountability

One of the principles in table 5 deserves further discussion: value-added achievement scores, which can also be called gain or progress

Table 5. Twelve accountability principles

Independence	To avoid bias and conflicts of interest, information should be sought from sources other than staff and institutions being evaluated.
Results-focused	Though indexes of inputs and processes may be useful, the chief focus of accountability should be on the attainment of intended and measured results.
Comprehensible	Written and oral accountability reports should be readily understandable.
Timeliness	Other things being equal, accountability value is proportional to how quickly it can be reported.
Incentive-driven	Consequences, preferably prespecified, should follow good and bad results.
Objective	Quantifiable information such as examination results should be preferred over anecdotes, public hearings, and the like.
Fair	Prespecified goals and content and curriculum-based external examinations should be favored.
Value-added	Accountability should include progress or gains in learning as well as end results.
Balanced	The scoring of multiple indicators should reflect the intended range and priority of subjects, topics, and skills.
Expressive	Success and failure should be displayed in ways that are readily comprehended by those responsible for policies and decisions.
Disaggregated	Results should be reported for girls and boys, poor and not, and various ethnic and language groups of concern.
Consumer-informed	What citizens, parents, and others are concerned about and their opinions about the quality of provided services should be included in accountability indicators.

Source: Herbert J. Walberg, "Principles for Accountability Designs," in School Accountability, ed. Williamson Evers and Herbert J. Walberg (Stanford, Calif.: Hoover Institution Press, 2002), 155–183.

scores, in contrast to scores that reflect a student's status on only one occasion. In their simplest form, value-added scores are the gains from one test administration to another, say, over the span of one year.

Value-added scores are important for several reasons. Status scores may be deceptive, since accountability consumers may attribute them

only to recent education experiences (say, the past year) when they
are also determined by earlier schooling and extramural experiences
including those in early childhood and peer groups. Thus, schools
serving children in poverty may make excellent value-added progress
even though their status scores are poor. Similarly, status scores in rich
neighborhoods may misleadingly suggest that schools are effective
even though the scores may have been largely determined by social
advantages.

Despite such obvious appeal, value-added scores are not without
controversy. Scholars do not completely agree on how they should be
calculated and employed. They may provide a somewhat unreliable
indication of a school's or a teacher's progress. Even so, the perfect
should not be the enemy of the good. In science and practical affairs,
an approximate answer to the right question is better than a precise
answer to the wrong question. In holding institutions and people
accountable, it is useful to know both their status and their progress,
even though neither indication is precise.[17]

No Child Left Behind:
Will the Federal Act Work?

Table 6 shows eight provisions of the act that directly concern or relate
to accountability. All the provisions are mandated, and states that do
not comply risk losing federal funds.

Will the mandated requirements be well implemented? Will the
requirements be implemented at all? As the last column in the table
shows, many states would have to expend considerable effort to be in
nominal compliance. As pointed out above, in 2001 only nineteen
states had complied with 1994 federal education requirements. Such
previous noncompliance may suggest that the state departments of
education may not move forward quickly. Indeed, as of September
2002, at least five states had the mistaken impression that they need
not meet a key requirement of the No Child Left Behind Act for

Table 6. No Child Left Behind: State provisions, requirements, and recent state status

Provision	Man-dated	Conse-quences	Recent (2000–2002) state status
State academic standards and student achievement standards in reading, mathematics, and science	Yes	Yes	All states but Iowa have reading and mathematics standards; most states have science standards.
Adequate yearly progress	Yes	Yes	At least 22 states have analytic methods; the other states were adopting methods.
Annual student testing of grades 3 through 8	Yes	Yes	Between 7 and 24 states have at least one or various combinations of reading, mathematics, and science assessments for one or more grades.
Participation in bi-ennial NAEP in grades 4 and 8 reading and mathematics	Yes	Yes	Between 36 and 40 states have recently participated in each examination.
State report cards	Yes	Yes	Many states do not report at the state, district, and school level; 32 states report graduation rates and 8 report the number or percentage of certified teachers; the number varies of states reporting separate results by ethnicity, gender, economic disadvantage, English-language learners, disability, and migrant status.
Consequences for low-performing schools/school improvement	Yes	Yes	Between 5 and 25 states sanctioned schools, districts, or both, including required improvement plans, dis-accreditation, funding withdrawal, imposed staff dismissals or reorganization, and takeovers
School support	Yes	Yes	Between 3 and 13 states provide support to schools, districts, or both.
School recognition	Yes	Yes	Nine states reward districts for performance; 20 reward schools.

Source: Adapted from Education Commission of the States; Internet posted February 2002 as http://www.ecs.org/ecsmain.asp?page=/search/default.asp.

school year 2002–03: to provide tutoring and other supplemental services for students in failing schools.[18]

It remains to be seen, of course, whether the federal government
will withhold education funds from congressional districts. And will
the provisions actually raise achievement?

Whatever the fifty state departments discover about No Child
Left Behind in the many complex pages of federal legislation, then
promulgate as official policy to local districts and schools, teachers
may continue as they please. Despite the policy crescendo of state
standards, tests, and accountability since *A Nation at Risk,* a gulf
remains between what teachers teach and what is called for in standards-based reform such as No Child Left Behind. In the preface to a
national survey of what fourth- and eighth-grade teachers actually
teach, Chester Finn calls attention to the key findings:

> First, a majority of teachers in both fourth and eighth grade opt for
> "student-directed learning" rather than "teacher-directed learning."
> . . . Second, three-quarters of teachers have embraced the college-
> of-education dogma that the purpose of schooling is to help young-
> sters "learn how to learn" rather than to acquire specific information
> and skills. . . . Third, not even two out of five teachers in fourth
> grade base their students' grades primarily on a "single, classwide
> standard," while the majority place heavier emphasis on individual
> children's abilities. . . . Fourth, teachers do not seem to have terribly
> high expectations for their pupils when it comes to how much and
> how well they will end up learning. . . . Finally, and most bluntly,
> one-third of fourth-grade teachers and 30 percent of eighth-grade
> teachers do not agree that "a teacher's role is primarily to help
> students learn the things that your state or community has decided
> students should know."[19]

Finally, aside from nominal compliance, quality is at issue: As
indicated in table 4, only five states recently had strong accountability
and solid standards. Can the other forty-five states be expected to
improve their own work while simultaneously coordinating their pol-

icies with the No Child Left Behind act? Prediction is difficult especially if it involves the future, but it is hard to be sanguine about the prospects of the new federal legislation unless powerful sanctions and incentives are employed, such as closing failing schools and introducing market competition so that parents can choose their children's schools.

Conclusion

A *Nation at Risk* and subsequent reform reports led to the current primacy of interest in accountability for school outcomes, particularly achievement as measured on objective examinations. The public, parents, and legislators increasingly recognized the importance of knowledge and skills for individual and national welfare, but accountability proceeded only slowly and fitfully. In the meantime, scholarship and policy analysis showed that the application of accountability policies, principles, and standards can help promote educational outcomes effectively and efficiently.

Even though all states have made serious efforts, only five or so have solid standards and strong accountability systems. Perhaps none is well prepared to meet the accountability challenges of the federal No Child Left Behind act, which in principle threatens to withhold federal funds from noncomplying states, may require extramural tutoring for students in failing schools, and may force closure of failing schools.

The Public Agenda and Business Roundtable national surveys show that the public, parents, teachers, and students strongly support accountability and see a pressing need for more rigorous standards.[20] President Bush and Congress agreed on strong accountability provisions in the No Child Left Behind act, and legislators in fifty states have passed bills requiring new standards and testing. And we now have much better evidence that accountability works and how it best works. In a nation still at risk, it behooves us to design the best accountability systems we can and implement them as well as we can.

Notes

1. On spending and other resource trends, see Caroline M. Hoxby's chapter in this volume and Erik Hanushek's and my chapters in Terry Moe's, edited, *A Primer on America's Schools*, edited by Terry M. Moe (Stanford, Calif.: Hoover Institution Press, 2001), 43–68 and 69–88.

2. On outcome trends, see Paul E. Peterson's chapter in the present volume, my chapter in the Koret Task Force report, *A Primer on America's Schools*, edited by Terry M. Moe (Stanford, Calif.: Hoover Institution Press, 2001), and my *Spending More While Learning Less* (Washington, D.C.: Thomas B. Fordham Foundation, July 1998).

3. Milton Goldberg and Susan L. Traiman, "Why Business Backs Education Standards," in *Brookings Papers on Education Policy 2001*, ed. Diane Ravitch (Washington, D.C.: Brookings Institution Press, 2001), 81–90.

4. Diane Ravitch, ed., Introduction to *Brookings Papers on Education Policy 2001* (Washington, D.C.: Brookings Institution Press, 2001), 1–8.

5. On testing costs, see Caroline Hoxby's chapter in *School Accountability*; on constructive effects of accountability, see the chapters by Julian Betts and Robert Costrell, Herbert Walberg, Milton Goldberg and Susan Traiman, Chester Finn and Marci Kanstoroom, David Grissmer and Ann Flanagan, and John Bishop in the Ravitch-edited Brookings 2001 volume.

6. The brief account in this section draws on Eric A. Hanushek and Margaret E. Raymond, "Sorting Out Accountability Systems" in Williamson M. Evers and Herbert J. Walberg, editors, *School Accountability* (Stanford, Calif.: Hoover Institution Press, 2002), 75–104.

7. See Herbert J. Walberg and Jin-Shei Lai, "Meta-Analytic Effects for Policy" in Gregory J. Cizek, *Handbook of Educational Policy*. (San Diego, Calif.: Academic Press), 419–52.

8. See Williamson M. Evers and Herbert J. Walberg, editors, *Testing Student Learning, Evaluating Teaching Effectiveness* (Stanford, Calif.: Hoover Institution Press, 2003).

9. Caroline M. Hoxby, "The Cost of Accountability," in *School Accountability*, ed. Williamson M. Evers and Herbert J. Walberg (Stanford, Calif: Hoover Institution Press, 2002), 47–74.

10. For a summary, see John H. Bishop, "The Impact of Curriculum-Based External Examinations on School Priorities and Student Learning," *International Journal of Educational Research*, 1996, 653–752.

11. Ludger Woessmann, "Why Students in Some Countries Do Better," *Education Next*, Summer 2001, 65–74.

12. The study also indicated that the influence of teacher unions on curriculum had negative effects and that spending variations made no difference in achievement.

13. The authors also attributed the gains in the two states to the intensity and stability of business support for the reforms but not to per-pupil spending, pupil/teacher ratios, proportion of teachers with advanced degrees, and average of teacher experience. See David Grissmer and Ann Flanagan, "Searching for Indirect Evidence for the Effects of Statewide Reforms" in *Brookings Papers on Ed___:ion Policy 2001*, ed. Diane Ravitch (Washington, D.C.: Brookings Institution Press, 2001), 181–229.

14. Julian R. Betts and Robert M. Costrell, "Incentives and Equity Under Standards-Based Reform," in *Brookings Papers on Education Policy 2001*, ed. Diane Ravitch (Washington, D.C.: Brookings Institution Press, 2001), 9–74.

15. Massachusetts Department of Education, *History and Social Science Curriculum Framework, Final Draft* (Malden, Mass.: Author, 2002). Internet version: http://www.doe.mass.edu/frameworks/history/hss_draft_0926.pdf. Diane Ravitch kindly called this framework to my attention.

16. See my chapter "Principles for Accountability Designs" in the Evers-Walberg volume for further explanation of these principles and examples from districts and states.

17. Averaging value-added scores over two or more years, over several school subjects, and over large numbers of students yields more trustworthy accountability indexes. Four useful papers on value-added calculations and uses appeared in *Education Next* (Summer 2002), vol. 2, no. 2, 9–23.

18. Erik W. Robelen, "States Suffer Halting Start on Tutoring," *Education Week* (online), September 25, 2002. http://www.edweek.org/ew/ewstory.cfm?slug=04supplement.h22.

19. Christopher Barnes, *What Do Teachers Teach? A Survey of America's Fourth- and Eighth-Grade Teachers* (New York: Center for Civic Inno-

vation at the Manhattan Institute, September 2002). See online version at http://www.manhattan-institute.org/cr_28.pdf.

20. Summarized in my "Design Principles for Accountability" in Williamson M. Evers and Herbert J. Walberg, editors, *School Accountability* (Stanford, Calif.: Hoover Institution Press, 2002).

11

Real
Choice

John E. Chubb

A *Nation at Risk*, published in 1983 by the National Commission on Excellence in Education (Excellence Commission), galvanized attention to low student achievement as the critical issue in America's schools and launched an attack on the problem that has been sustained to this day. In this way, *A Nation at Risk* was a watershed. Never before had schools been asked to focus so sharply on improving student achievement. And never before had policy makers worked so hard to help—or force—schools to deliver. The eighties quickly brought tougher graduation requirements, more academic course taking, higher teacher salaries, and more training for teachers. The nineties added rigorous statewide academic standards, extensive standardized testing, and accountability. In 2002, the federal government mandated testing in reading and math in grades three through eight nationwide.

These are major changes, and, in their sheer focus and commitment to doing education differently, some might even call them revolutionary. But they do not in fact constitute a revolution. For they leave intact a fundamental obstacle to major improvement, which is the system that provides public education in the first place. A *Nation at Risk* clearly believed—and it stated so explicitly—that through good will and hard work, the American education system could deliver on the changes recommended in the report. A *Nation at Risk* did not raise a single question about the capacity of the education system to get the job done. But in the years since A *Nation at Risk*, such questions have been asked with increasing frequency.

Reformers have argued, in particular, that public schools cannot be easily counted on to raise achievement or easily forced to do so. They cannot be counted on because there has traditionally been no effective accountability. Schools that do not deliver better results for kids are almost always, and inevitably, allowed to continue delivering inadequate results. Yet schools cannot be forced to deliver better results either. The very mandates that would be necessary to do so— what to teach, how to teach, how to assess, how to reteach, and so forth—tend to bog schools down, preoccupying them with following rules instead of encouraging them to solve problems and produce results. Reformers are faced with something of a dilemma—to find ways to promote accountability for results without destroying the initiative or autonomy of schools to produce results.

To resolve this dilemma, reformers have increasingly looked beyond the traditional education system for answers. A broad and fundamental reform strategy has taken hold in the years since A *Nation at Risk*. That strategy aims to inject the market forces of school choice and competition into the traditional system, which is based on very different principles—essentially, authority and control. By giving parents the right to choose the school their children attend and forcing schools to compete for enrollment—or risk closure from lack of students and funds—market-oriented reforms aim to improve schools by revolutionizing the system of which they are part. Under a system with market forces at work, policy makers need not micromanage improvement. Instead, they can focus on setting standards, testing for academic progress, and providing parents with information on school performance so that they can make good choices. The market can do the rest. Schools that do not raise test scores will lose students to schools that do. And the innovations necessary to boost achievement will emerge from the competition among existing schools. Those with the best ideas and practices will survive and be imitated.

Of course, the workings of markets are not so simple in practice, and markets come with their own set of challenges. But market-oriented reforms have become important in American education because they offer hope for improvement not constrained by some of the inherent limits of the traditional system. For all of its wisdom, A *Nation at Risk* failed to recognize, or even consider, the possible limits of the traditional system or conceive of fundamental alternatives (or complements) to it. To appreciate the significance of A *Nation at Risk*, we must recognize its bold insights into the traditional ways of schooling, but also acknowledge that it failed to anticipate the remarkable challenge to these traditions in the years that immediately followed.

The Idea of Choice

When A *Nation at Risk* was published, school choice was scarcely more than an academic notion. Milton Friedman, one of the nation's most esteemed economists and a leading conservative thinker, had proposed a system of public education based on vouchers—for use in public or private schools—in a now classic article in 1955.[1] During the federal War on Poverty in the late sixties and early seventies, a number of academics, more liberal in orientation than Friedman, proposed vouchers for economically disadvantaged students, and a modest— and inconclusive—experiment with the idea was carried out in Alum Rock, California.[2] But when the Excellence Commission convened in 1981, it didn't regard the concepts of vouchers and school choice as sufficiently important to even include them among the scores of topics on which it contracted for background research.

This thinking very quickly proved to be shortsighted. In 1982, James S. Coleman, perhaps the most significant academic figure in education policy making in the last fifty years, produced a study, with Thomas Hoffer and Sally Kilgore, that found that students perform better in private schools, and particularly Catholic schools, than they do in public schools, all things being equal.[3] Coleman and his colleagues also showed that Catholic schools, more so than public schools, seemed to approach the "common school" ideal of serving all children equally. Taken together, the findings suggested that on grounds of both effectiveness and equity, policy makers should be open to ideas that would provide public support for private school attendance.

Before the Excellence Commission had even finished its work, the Coleman study was garnering national attention. Coleman had a history of producing iconoclastic yet influential policy research. Less than twenty years earlier, he had led the federal research project that helped justify bussing by showing that the greatest influence on student achievement was that of families and peers—not schools.[4] In the seventies, Coleman inspired more controversy when he found that bussing was counterproductive, for it tended to drive white students out of urban schools while failing to place black students in more diverse environments.[5] When Coleman finally concluded in 1982 that schools, especially Catholic schools, do make a difference, policy makers listened.

Coleman's work prompted a wicked backlash in academia as well as in the policy world. His ideas were anathema to an education establishment that had long opposed vouchers as a threat to public schools. From the public education lobbies in Washington, D.C., to the researchers in university schools of education, Coleman's methods and conclusions were attacked. Yet the idea that private school choice might help students achieve did not go away. Coleman produced a follow-up study in 1987 that reinforced the findings of his earlier work, showing that private school attendees fared better after high school than their public school counterparts, and he attributed the private school advantage to the greater sense of community in private schools, an attribute Coleman labeled "social capital."[6] In 1989 Paul Hill and a team of social scientists from the respected independent research organization RAND concluded that Catholic schools in New York City were succeeding in educating disadvantaged youth who had failed in public schools.[7]

Though the benefits of private schools were to be the subject of continuing debate, the idea of choice is about more than simply helping children switch from public to private schools; it is about changing fundamentally the way in which all schools are governed, rewarded, and controlled. Another major study gave policy makers new reason to think such change made sense. *Politics, Markets, and America's Schools*, by this author and Terry M. Moe, concluded that private schools tend to outperform public schools, all things being equal, because the market environment in which private schools operate is far more conducive to success in education than the political environment in which public schools operate.[8]

The study found that the market forces surrounding private schools systematically promote the very attributes that Coleman and other researchers had been saying were characteristic of effective schools in general, and Catholic schools in particular. It is no accident that private schools seem to outperform public schools: The competitive pressures of the marketplace, where families can take or leave a school, lead schools to organize in whatever ways are conducive to getting results for families. Intentionally or unintentionally, schools subject to market pressures tend to develop clear missions (parents know what the school stands for), focus on academics (parents want to see their children learn), encourage strong site-based leadership (great schools are headed by principals who take charge of student achievement), and build collaborative faculties (great schools make achievement a team effort). Schools that fail to do these things tend to be weak performers, tend not to be favored by parents, and tend to be weeded out via natural selection over time. By contrast, the political forces that surround public schools—particularly public schools in academically troubled urban systems—tend to promote excessive bureaucracy and to impede the development of the qualities that schools need to succeed. School missions get diluted by round after round of school reform; academics get crowded out by new policy goals; principals become middle-managers carrying out the programs chosen by district administrators; and teachers become "labor," fulfilling contractual obligations instead of doing whatever is necessary for the team to succeed. These are only central tendencies, to be sure. Markets tolerate a certain number of lousy private schools, and politics produce many exemplary public schools. But to the extent that politics and markets cause schools to tend sharply in different directions, the central tendencies are extremely important.

Indeed, *Politics, Markets, and America's Schools* posed a quite revolutionary possibility: that the failure of public schools to improve—the failure at the heart of *A Nation at Risk*—was inherent in the way the public system had come to work. Well-intentioned efforts at reform, year in and year out, had imposed so many constraints on schools that they could no longer do the basic things that schools need to do in order to succeed. This being the case, school reform would require fundamental change in the system of public education itself, something more revolutionary than anything envisioned by *A Nation at Risk*. The most effective means of reform, by far, would be to abandon (or sharply curtail) efforts to force improvement from the top down—through bureaucratically administered reform programs—and to promote improvement from the bottom up: Give schools the freedom to organize themselves for effectiveness and give parents the opportunity to choose among competing alternatives. *Politics, Markets, and America's Schools* proposed a new system of public education based on school autonomy, parental choice, equitable financing, and basic accountability requirements—a proposal that was more ambitious than vouchers for private schools, because all schools would be involved, and also more fair, because private schools could not participate unless they played by the same rules.

The study's findings and recommendations caught the attention of policy makers. Perhaps it was the study's publisher, the then-liberal-leaning Brookings Institution, which caused influentials to take notice. Brookings had no history of supporting vouchers or school choice, ideas mostly associated with conservatives. Or perhaps it was the study's extensive empirical base—more than 400 schools and nearly 20,000 students, teachers, and administrators. Whatever the case, the study helped shift thinking about school choice from a strategy to help students escape public schools to a broad market-based reform to improve all schools.

The Politics of Choice

Ideas can be very powerful, but ideas alone seldom change policy. Ideas require advocates with the political wherewithal to win elections and legislative battles. During the eighties the idea of choice attracted powerful advocates and opponents. The Reagan administration and its secretary of education, William C. Bennett, led the charge rhetorically. The Reagan administration had come into office in 1981 opposed to the existence of the recently formed Department of Education. But with the positive reception of *A Nation at Risk*, the administration realized that education could be a winning issue with the public. The idea of vouchers, or, more broadly, of school choice, fit the Republican administration's pro-market, anti-big-government, pro-deregulation orientation quite nicely. And it was an idea that benefited more from "bully pulpit" advocacy of state and local action—advocacy at which Bennett excelled—than from federal legislation, which the divided government of the time would never have passed.

Democrats at the time generally opposed vouchers for private schools and most other forms of school choice as well. As a matter of principle, Democrats have greater faith in government and less faith in markets than Republicans. But Democratic opposition was—and is—also a matter of interest. The most powerful supporters of the Democratic Party—measured in votes and financial contributions— are the national teacher unions, the National Education Association and the American Federation of Teachers (see chapter 6 by Terry M. Moe for a deeper discussion of the teacher unions' ability to block reforms like school choice). The unions are unalterably opposed to vouchers for private schools. They have also worked hard to defeat any public school choice plan that provides meaningful competition to public schools or, more to the point, threatens the jobs of teachers.

By 1990, however, the Democratic Party was becoming just a bit uncomfortable with its antivoucher position. The families who suffer most from poor educational opportunity in America are economically disadvantaged, often minority, inner-city residents—who traditionally vote Democratic. But big-city school systems are where the problems of politics and bureaucracy interfere most with the creation of decent schools. For years, the families served by these schools were promised a better day. Yet over time, urban families saw mostly a series of failed or disappointing initiatives. Black children spent hours every week riding busses to attend schools with white children while white children fled the system of "forced bussing." Meanwhile, their levels of achievement didn't improve. Nor did they improve through federal compensatory aid programs launched during the War on Poverty. By 1990, surveys indicated a high degree of dissatisfaction with local schools among disadvantaged and minority families—and also a high level of support for vouchers and other forms of school choice.[9]

Republicans, though, were not ready to stick their necks out too far for vouchers. The Reagan administration was replaced by the more moderate Bush administration, and Bennett was ultimately succeeded by the thoughtful but less strident Lamar Alexander.[10] The new team advocated for vouchers as part of a broader emphasis on "break-the-mold schools" and invested in a major research and development project for innovative school design called the New American Schools Development Corporation, now just known as New American Schools. The new team's multipronged approach also reflected the ambivalence of many Republicans toward school choice: Suburban schools, where Republicans tend to send their children to school, are not in crisis, and, frankly, they tend to find the idea that those schools might be chosen by inner-city kids a bit unsettling.

Nevertheless, politics had changed a great deal in less than a decade. School choice was being debated in Washington, D.C., as a central school reform strategy, whereas A Nation at Risk had failed even to mention it. Frustration with school performance had grown, especially in the inner cities, despite the country's aggressive efforts to improve schools after A Nation at Risk. Democrats were feeling crosspressured by inner city constituents, and Republicans had taken up school choice—sometimes aggressively, sometimes cautiously—as a pillar of their school reform model. Public opinion reflected these changes. Voucher support achieved majority status with the general public and strong majority status with low-income and minority citizens. Close inspection also revealed that most Americans had not formed very firm views on vouchers one way or the other—no surprise for an issue that was new to the policy agenda. While most people liked the idea of vouchers, they also preferred vouchers with basic government safeguards such as requirements for private schools to use certified teachers, to not discriminate academically in admissions, and to administer state tests.[11] The time was ripe for market-oriented reform, if not for revolution.

Private School Vouchers

The first major event came in 1990. A maverick Democratic state legislator, Polly Williams, and a gutsy Republican governor, Tommy Thompson, teamed to enact the nation's first major voucher program in Milwaukee, Wisconsin.[12] Disillusioned with years of district and

state efforts to improve Milwaukee's poorest schools, Williams demanded vouchers to get black children off busses and into the only
city schools that seemed to be working—small private schools that
had been springing up to serve unhappy families. The Wisconsin
program provided vouchers of $2,500 to children from families eligible
for the federal food stamp program. The vouchers could be used at
only secular private schools and no more than 1 percent of the students
in the Milwaukee school district, about 1,000 students, could participate. Two years later, the participation limit was raised to 1.5 percent.
But the program's most significant change came in 1995, when the
enrollment cap was raised to 15,000 students, the voucher was increased to nearly $5,000, and the program was opened to religious
schools. Because 90 percent of the private schools in Milwaukee were
religious, the original program could never have served large numbers
of students, even without the enrollment cap—at least not very
quickly: It takes time for a market to supply new (nonreligious) private
schools. When religious schools were allowed to participate, enrollment leaped from 1,500 students in the mid-nineties to roughly 10,000
students—and 100 private schools—in 2000.[13]

Milwaukee provided precedent for a second and equally significant
voucher program, for the city of Cleveland, Ohio. In 1995, the state
of Ohio created the Cleveland Scholarship Plan to provide desperately
needed relief for low-income children stuck in chronically poor-per-
forming city schools. Similar to the politics in Wisconsin, the Cleveland plan owed its adoption to Republican leadership and strong grass
roots support from key black leaders in Cleveland. To ensure that
children had ample private choices, from the beginning Ohio included
religious and nonreligious private schools among the schools eligible
to receive the vouchers. Although the voucher was set at only $2,250
and could cover a maximum of 90 percent of tuition (parents having
to cover the rest), the program enrolled 3,900 students in nearly seventy private schools by 2000.[14]

The successful introduction of voucher policies in Wisconsin and

Ohio did not inspire similar success nationwide. Vouchers for private schools remained a highly controversial idea, opposed tooth and nail by teacher unions, supported by grassroots organizations representing the poor, and advocated cautiously by maverick Democrats and conservative, free-market Republicans. Amidst this controversy, five attempts to create voucher programs through state referenda went down to defeat at the polls.[15] In each case, public opinion shifted from supporting the initiatives when they were proposed to rejecting them at the polls, a result of aggressive negative advertising by the public education establishment, particularly the teacher unions.[16] Only Florida, under the leadership of Republican governor Jeb Bush in 1999, was able to legislate a statewide voucher program. It is significantly compromised. The Florida program offers vouchers only to students in schools that qualify as unmitigated failures, and few students have been able to take advantage of them.[17]

However, the continuing strife should not be mistaken for lack of progress. Sluggishness on the policy front led philanthropists in New York City, Washington, D.C., Dayton, and San Antonio, among numerous other major cities, to start programs providing vouchers—called scholarships—to thousands of economically disadvantaged students in cities nationwide. When added to the students served by the Milwaukee and Cleveland government voucher programs, nearly 60,000 students across the United States were attending private schools instead of public schools with public or philanthropic support in 2002.[18] These numbers, while small from a national perspective, are significant. They have created active constituencies for private school choice in a host of major cities. They have encouraged a number of states, including Arizona, Florida, and Pennsylvania, to offer tax credits for contributions to private scholarship funds. And they provide a substantial test of the proposition that private school choice can help students, especially disadvantaged students, achieve academically.

Student achievement, of course, is what A Nation at Risk was all about. The early evidence indicates that private school choice works.

Several of the philanthropic choice programs have been designed to permit thorough evaluations of their effectiveness. Vouchers were awarded randomly, via lottery, to students who applied to the programs. Researchers were then able to compare students who requested vouchers and received them with students who requested vouchers but did not receive them. Because the vouchers were awarded by lottery, researchers can assume that the students selected for the program do not differ from those not selected for the program, in ways that are both observable—say, prior achievement, race, or family income—and nonobservable, like students' motivation to learn or their families' support for education. Known as a randomized field trial and used routinely in medical research, this research design is the best way to determine the effect of a program or treatment. It is rarely used in policy research, however, because government programs are seldom able to allocate benefits randomly. The Milwaukee voucher program, for example, used a lottery to award vouchers when there was excess demand. But in the early years before religious schools provided ample choice, parents did not apply for the vouchers in droves because there were few schools to choose from. Thus, studies using randomized samples, though mildly favorable toward vouchers, were hampered by small sample sizes.[19]

Three of the philanthropic voucher programs did not face such problems and thus provided high-quality random field trials. William G. Howell and Paul E. Peterson, both of Harvard University at the time, led teams that investigated the progress of thousands of students selected for and not selected for private school vouchers in Dayton, New York City, and Washington, D.C.[20] The results were generally consistent and mostly positive. They found that the private schools attended by voucher students, when compared with the public schools that these students would have attended, spent less, offered smaller classes, provided more focused academic programs and better disciplinary climates, expected more homework, and kept in closer touch with families. Parents of the voucher students were much more satisfied with their children's new school than were similar parents with children still in the public schools. Most important, black students saw their test scores rise in private schools more than their counterparts experienced in public school. Finally, there were no major ill effects from the program: In particular, students in the voucher program were neither academically nor ethnically different from students remaining in the public schools and the program neither "creamed" the best students nor exacerbated racial stratification in public or private schools—the most oft-cited fear among voucher opponents.[21]

Whether these findings hold up over time obviously remains to be seen, but there is reason to believe they will. The results are consistent with a great deal of research on the culture of private schools, beginning with that of Coleman in the early eighties. The finding that black students are the prime beneficiaries of the program, in terms of improvements in their test scores, is consistent with research on class-size reduction programs and other studies of public and private school achievement.[22] As Howell and Peterson argue, the finding on black achievement also makes fundamental sense: Black students have suffered the longest and the worst from the inadequacies of the American education and political systems. This is most true when it comes to school choice. Housing discrimination, economic disadvantage, and de jure segregation have combined to limit the educational choices of black children more so than the choices of any other major social group in America. It follows that black students would benefit most from the changes that school choice makes possible.[23]

At the twentieth anniversary of A Nation at Risk, it looks as if the United States may soon have many new opportunities to see whether the early findings about private school choice are valid. On June 27, 2002, the United States Supreme Court upheld the constitutionality of the Cleveland voucher plan. In a decision (Zelman v. Simmons-Harris) that was broad, clear, and unqualified, the Court held five to four that, by providing students the chance to attend religious schools at public expense, the Cleveland plan did not violate the Establishment Clause of the First Amendment. The Cleveland plan satisfied a series of Constitutional tests that the Court had developed over the previous twenty years. The plan was created for the clear secular purpose of improving educational opportunity for the needy students of Cleveland. The plan left entirely to parents the choice of school to attend with the voucher—public, private nonsectarian, or religious. And in a new argument advanced by Justice Sandra Day O'Connor, the state of Ohio offered parents a range of choices, including charter schools (what Ohio calls Community Schools), suburban public schools, and tutoring programs—making the religious schools not the primary recipients of state support for school choice, but one among many. The latter argument was important because it said that a private voucher program should not be judged constitutionally as a policy unto itself but as part of a government's broader school choice policies. That argument helped to render irrelevant the fact that more than 90 percent of the private vouchers in Cleveland were redeemed at religious schools.

President George W. Bush hailed the Court's decision as "historic," comparing it with the Court's 1954 decision in *Brown v. Board of Education* that ended government sanction of "separate but equal" schools for black and white children.[24] Justice Clarence Thomas, in a concurring opinion, took a similar tack, writing, "Just as blacks supported public education during Reconstruction, many blacks and other minorities now support school choice programs because they provide the greatest educational opportunities for their children in struggling communities."[25] Opponents of vouchers promised to fight on in state courts and legislatures where state constitutions sometimes ban aid to private and religious schools. As Robert H. Chanin, the general counsel of the NEA, who argued against the Cleveland program before the Supreme Court, said, "This does not end the legal battle. It simply removes the Establishment Clause from our legal arsenal."[26] But the Court's decision is plainly a major victory for school choice. It removes a barrier that opponents have used time and again to kill choice proposals. The decision also has huge practical implications, because a choice plan for private schools that rules out religious schools would exclude the vast majority of private schools in America from offering students new opportunity. Now it is much more likely that private school choice will be significantly widened—a revolutionary possibility that *A Nation at Risk* could never have anticipated.

Charter Schools

If private vouchers represent the prospect of revolutionary change in public education—markets supplanting politics as the driving force behind the supply of public schools—another approach to school choice represents the prospect of evolutionary change toward a very similar end. Charter schools emerged in 1991 both as a compromise between market advocates and opponents and as an ingenious idea in their own right. Before the idea of charter schools developed, advocates of competition envisioned private schools as the catalyst for educational improvement, the alternative that would offer families new opportunities and force public schools to change. Charter schools provided a mechanism to produce competition and choice in public education without turning to private schools. Charter schools were to be open to all students, accountable to public authorities, and funded entirely with public moneys. Charter schools could not preach religion, exclude students for any reason, charge extra tuition, or do most of the things that worried opponents of private school choice. Yet charter schools held much of the promise of private school choice. Charter schools offered a means for schools not under the control of the traditional school system to educate students at public expense. Potentially, anyone could open a charter school—as long as they could win approval from a public chartering authority. Charter schools were to be free from much of the regulation that stymied innovation and sapped energy in the traditional public schools. Charter schools competing with traditional public schools promised the kind of market-place that might cause all schools to improve.

Charter schools emerged out of the same political pressure cooker that served up private voucher programs, but with a few different ingredients. The idea of charter schools actually enjoyed a measure of support from the toughest opponents of school choice, the national teacher unions. The late Albert Shanker, president of the American Federation of Teachers for more than a quarter century, introduced the idea to the policy world in a speech in 1988. He argued that teachers should be granted charters to run public schools of choice, free from the usual rules and regulations that frustrate teachers, but subject to strict accountability requirements. Shanker, a rare visionary among union leaders, was looking for a bold way for teachers to respond to the escalating demand for radical school improvement. A *Nation at Risk* had spawned a series of influential reports from governors, business leaders, and others calling for more dramatic action than had been in the offing. Charters were Shanker's way of saying that the union could see the virtue of a more marketlike system if it were controlled very carefully and if teachers had a chance to play a central role.[27]

Charters also appealed to the first Bush administration's fascination with "break the mold schools" and innovative school design. Private schools, whatever their claims to effectiveness, were not being touted for their inventiveness. If anything, they were being endorsed for their no-nonsense traditionalism. Charter schools offered something different, the prospect of new approaches to school organization, curriculum, instruction, technology, and more. Charters enjoyed further appeal because they fit with the popular notion of "reinventing government."[28] Charter schools offered a way to improve a government service by making it more entrepreneurial, instead of simply turning the service over to the private sector. By injecting choice and competition into the public sector, charter schools would enable the government—that is, the public education system—to become more efficient and effective.

In 1991, Minnesota became the first state to authorize charter schools. Minnesota had been experimenting with public school choice throughout the eighties—including choice across district lines, the most threatening kind of choice to the education establishment. The state's governor, Rudy Perpich, a Democrat in the state's Progressive tradition, had championed public school choice over union opposition. Two of the nation's most prominent advocates of school choice, Joe Nathan and Ted Kolderie, hailed from Minnesota and helped develop the concept of charter schools into a practical policy. The state, which had a deserved reputation for decent public schools, saw charter schools not as a way to energize a stalled education system, but as a way to bring greater innovation and strength to a successful system. Unlike Milwaukee's voucher program, Minnesota's charter law held broad public appeal, at least rhetorically. Charters were about providing public education differently, not about replacing public education with private education. Charter schools were about strengthening public education, not about challenging its existence. Charter schools were about innovation, not just competition.

Minnesota set an example that was followed rather quickly by many other states. In 1992, California approved charter legislation. In 1993, Colorado, Georgia, New Mexico, Massachusetts, Michigan, and Wisconsin followed suit. By 2002, thirty-nine states and the District of Columbia had passed legislation authorizing charter schools. By offering a mechanism to provide meaningful choice and competition within the public system and by creating the prospect for innovative new schools, charter schools became the most favored approach to market-oriented reform in America.

In the fall of 2002, an estimated 2,700 charter schools were operating in thirty-six states and the District of Columbia.[29] A few states have yet to see their first charter schools open, but across the country this new kind of school, totally unknown to the authors of *A Nation at Risk*, is delivering public education. In a number of states, charter schools have become a major presence: Arizona has 468 charter schools, California 452, Texas 228, Michigan 186, and Florida 232. Enrollment in charter schools has also become significant. At an estimated 575,000 students, charter schools enroll more than 1 percent of all K–12 students nationwide. In just eleven years of operation, charter schools are enrolling 10 percent as many students as private schools—and private schools have a 200-year head start.

So charter schools have clearly caught on. But how are they working? Have they raised the achievement of students attending them? Have they stimulated other public schools to improve? Have they been a source of innovation? And, have they generated any of the negative side effects that opponents have warned about? The simple answer is that it is too early to tell—but the early returns are promising.

The problem with drawing firmer conclusions is twofold. First, many charter school laws have been written to prevent charter schools from realizing their potential. The proliferation of charter laws should not be mistaken for a consensus in favor of them. The education establishment ultimately loathes competition and supports charter schools only as a last resort—to prevent reforms such as vouchers that are even more threatening. When the establishment cannot prevent charters from being adopted, it works to hamstring charter schools with restrictive charter legislation. Charter schools, for example, may require the approval of the local school district to operate—in effect, requiring new competitors to win approval from the local monopoly. Charter schools may be funded at less than the level of the public school competition, by providing no support for their facilities, for example. Charter schools may be required to remain within collective bargaining agreements, limiting the flexibility of the school to organize and reward a staff creatively. Charter schools may be limited in number so they cannot provide too much competition for the status quo. Taken together, these restrictions can weaken charter laws nearly fatally. One widely cited rating system classifies only twenty of the country's charter school laws as "strong," meaning the law has the potential to bring about meaningful education change.[30] Any judgment about the effects of charter schools must control for the limitations that have been imposed upon their potential success. Until more states provide charter schools the full opportunity to succeed, we will be unable to draw firm conclusions about their effectiveness.

The second reason that conclusions about charter schools cannot be drawn with great confidence is that most charter schools have been open for only a few years. A five-year-old charter school is rarity. Schools take time to become established, and students take time to educate. Some charter schools have clearly failed to get the job done, and more than 200 have closed or been closed. Failure, of course, is part of the idea of competition: Schools that do not deserve to operate will cease to exist—a fate that rarely befalls even the worst of the country's traditional public schools. But charter growth has clearly overwhelmed charter contraction. In the eyes of parents, charters are increasingly offering a superior alternative to traditional public schools. It will be some time before we know how charters perform in the eyes of serious researchers.

It will also take time to understand the broader impact of charters on public education. The competitive marketplaces that charters might one day establish are just beginning to be created. Public schools do not know whether to compete or to wait for charter schools to go away. Thus far, the public school establishment has invested more energy in trying to limit charter growth legislatively than in competing educationally.[31] In this environment, families must also grapple with uncertainty: Are charter schools going to be around for the long haul or will they disappear, disrupting their children's education? At this stage in the introduction of charter schools, the market pressures that they might create for all schools to improve are just beginning to be felt.

The early data are nevertheless encouraging. Students who attend charter schools are more economically disadvantaged and racially and ethnically diverse than the national average and are similar in economic disadvantage and diversity to their local communities. There is no evidence that charter schools "cream" the most affluent or successful students from public schools. Parental satisfaction with charter schools is high when compared with parental satisfaction in public schools generally and with parental satisfaction with their prior public school. Although evidence on the innovativeness of charter schools is mixed—and quite subjective—the evidence on student achievement is more positive and compelling.[32]

This is particularly true of the effects of charter schools on public education generally. In a carefully controlled study of student achievement in jurisdictions with high levels of charter school competition, Harvard economist Caroline Hoxby found that charter schools promoted substantial gains in student achievement among traditional public schools.[33] This finding is consistent with findings on the impact of public and private school competition more broadly—that the more competition public schools face from private schools or other public schools, the better the student achievement—and should therefore be taken seriously. It remains to be seen how charter schools themselves perform as a class; the early results range from better than to worse than local achievement norms. But if the presence of charter schools in a community in fact promotes improvement among traditional public schools, it stands to reason that charter schools must gain, too—or lose students and eventually close.[34]

Only time will tell. Opponents of charter schools would like to conclude that charter schools have been given a fair test and failed it. The American Federation of Teachers, having long since abandoned the concept that their former leader introduced, issued a highly critical study in 2002, calling for an end to any expansion of charter schools until the evidence of their success is conclusive.[35] That study, nothing more than a slanted rehash of other critical research, is more a measure of what charter schools have accomplished than what they have not. The establishment continues to fight charter schools politically because charter schools have become a force to be reckoned with educationally. Fair-minded observers will wait to judge the ultimate impact of charter schools and, in the meantime, encourage reforms that give charters a reasonable chance to succeed.[36]

Privately Managed Schools

In 2002, private for-profit firms ran an estimated 370 public schools in the United States.[37] When A Nation at Risk was issued, that number was zero. Why did private management, scarcely an idea in 1983, grow so rapidly?[38] Because the ensuing twenty years created a market for them. This is important to appreciate, for the idea of market-based reform, in large measure, is to create conditions under which the supply of public schools can change. Traditional school reform is about improving the existing public schools; it is about public authorities formulating programs and plans to try to change what schools are doing directly. Market-based reform is very different; it is indirect. It aims to improve schools by creating an environment in which entirely new schools can come into being and existing schools are free to improve—or go under. School choice only makes sense if policy makers create the conditions—ideally a market—that allow for this kind of change. Critics of school choice often ask where students are going to go to school once the "good schools" are all chosen and filled up. Critics want evidence that a market for schools will generate a new and improved supply. Charter schools provide some of that evidence. Private management provides additional and distinctively important evidence.

The rapid growth of private management has essentially two sources. One is charter school policy. Charter schools created a vehicle by which for-profit managers could enter the market for new schools. Although most states require charter holders to be nonprofit entities, states permit charter holders to contract with for-profit firms for various goods and services, including the comprehensive management of schools. For-profit companies can easily enter the market, then, by assembling a nonprofit board to serve as a partner and to acquire a charter. Charter boards also seek out management companies. Opening and running a school can be a daunting task, one that part-time boards have often decided to delegate to professional managers. By 2001, 10 percent of all charter schools were run by for-profit firms, representing two-thirds of all privately managed schools.

But this is only one source of for-profit growth—and in the long run perhaps not the more important source. Private companies are beginning to run schools for public school systems. In the years since *A Nation at Risk*, public school systems have come under tremendous pressure to improve. Competition from charter schools, and in some locales private schools, is forcing public school systems to improve their offerings or lose students and revenue. At the same time, state accountability systems are compelling school systems to raise student test scores or face serious sanctions. Private management companies have responded to these pressures, cultivating demand for their services from systems that, unlike charter schools, do not need help with the basics of school management. Companies have done this by offering much more than basic services. Firms typically offer comprehensive reform packages—involving classroom management, curriculum, instruction, assessment, technology, supervision, and evaluation, and even more—that districts can contract to be implemented in schools that either need major reform or want to try it. The contract might involve a single school or a larger cluster. Contracting enables a school district to introduce new and improved choices for families that might be thinking of switching to a charter or private school—and to do so quickly. Contracting also enables a district to assign schools with particular academic challenges—say, the lowest test scores—to a private manager, while devoting its energies to districtwide improvements.

By offering reform services and helping school systems respond to the pressures that they increasingly face, private management companies have been in increasing demand. Coupled with demand from charter schools, the market has quickly given birth to numerous firms. Forty companies were in the business of education management in 2002. Thirty-six actually managed schools. Many were just getting started and ran only a school or two. But fifteen firms managed at least five schools, and several firms were growing rapidly. The largest by far is Edison Schools, which managed a little over a hundred schools and served 73,000 students in 2001–02.[39] Next in size are Chancellor-Beacon, a merged company with forty-four schools; the Leona Group, with thirty-three schools; National Heritage, with twenty-eight schools; and Mosaica, with twenty-two schools. Together these firms educated 143,000 students in twenty-four states in 2002.

Private management is an important development for school reform, of both the choice and accountability varieties. Private management has the potential to bring to education some of the classic benefits of the free enterprise system, but in completely new ways. Business has long supplied schools with textbooks, computers, software, training, and noneducational services such as food and transportation. Business adds value in these areas that schools or school systems cannot usually produce themselves. The value proposition of private management is that business can add similar or greater value by running entire schools. Business is not bound by the geography that constrains local school systems, and it can achieve economies of scale. A school district cannot easily develop the expertise and systems necessary to launch and manage comprehensive reform models. Business has access to capital that school districts do not, capital that can be used to equip schools and train staff for a completely new start. Business can introduce promotion and compensation systems that enjoy success in the private sector but are seldom even tried in the public sector. Business aims to accomplish these things with the same dollars per-pupil that the district deploys. And business brings the benefits of competition and accountability in its own right. Competition among private managers should drive up the quality of the services that they offer to public education. Private managers are also under contract to produce academic results. If they fail, they can be fired—the ultimate guarantee of accountability and improvement.

As with every market-based reform, it remains to be seen how far private management will go. If chartering authority continues to grow, private management will play a growing role in charter schools. Running schools, particularly over the long haul, is a tough job that not every charter board will want to do alone. District schools are a more complicated story, mostly because politics come into play. The most powerful players in school politics, the national teacher unions, do not favor private management. Officially, the national unions are neutral, but that does not stop their locals from opposing private management when it is proposed in particular districts. This opposition played a crucial role in costing Edison Schools a contract for five schools in New York City in 2001 and helped to reduce the company's historic contract with the School Reform Commission (SRC) in Philadelphia from a proposed forty-five schools to twenty in 2002. On the other hand, Edison Schools has successfully negotiated with union locals in many other districts and even has a formal partnership with the AFT local in Miami.

Unions, however, are not the only force in school politics. Lately, a new force in favor of private management has come into play. State governments nationwide are giving themselves the power to take over individual schools and entire school systems that fail to improve academically. Once they have taken this step, states are contracting with private managers to run and turn around the failing schools. Maryland contracted with Edison in 2000 to operate three low-performing schools in Baltimore. Pennsylvania appointed the SRC, which contracted with four for-profit firms, including Edison, and three nonprofit organizations to run forty-five schools in Philadelphia beginning in the fall of 2002. New Mexico planned to turn over a dozen or more low-performing schools to private managers in 2002. The states insist contractually that private managers improve student achievement.

Achievement is the final variable in predicting the future of private management. Of the crop of companies operating schools in 2002, only Edison had enough schools open for enough years to have a meaningful record of performance. That record is positive, as measured by the gains of its schools against national norms and state standards. RAND is conducting an independent evaluation of Edison's performance that will be published in 2004.[40] Meanwhile, the usual critics lambaste the achievement records of private managers, with studies of little scientific merit. From a policy standpoint, however, the debate over the performance of private managers is academic. State and local clients will judge whether private companies have delivered on their academic promises. For-profit firms that improve student achievement will have their contracts renewed and have a chance to grow. Those that disappoint clients will not. Like other market-based reforms, that is the exciting promise.

Market Essentials

If market-based reform is to realize the potential it has begun to demonstrate in the years since A *Nation at Risk*, policy makers must take additional measures both to promote it and to guide it. Markets are not perfect. Given the chance they can be powerful engines for change, bringing to education the kinds of benefits they have brought throughout the free enterprise system. But markets must be carefully watched if they are to be fair and effective. This is particularly so for a public good such as education, where the government is paying for the service, the benefits are for society as well as for individuals, and the risks of inequity—already so prevalent in public education—are high. Accordingly, policy makers should follow a balanced course, advancing education markets while regulating them for the common good.

The following steps should be part of any such course:

1. States must continue to develop accountability systems for public schools. Such systems should include ambitious and explicit academic standards—for content as well as skills—coupled with standardized tests at every grade level to measure schools' success in meeting them. The federal *No Child Left Behind* law, enacted in 2002, will encourage progress in this direction, but state policy makers should not be satisfied with testing only reading and math as the law requires, nor settling for tests that measure only basic skills, a danger with the tests that are now commonly in use. Accountability systems must also include meaningful rewards and sanctions. *No Child Left Behind* will push states in the proper direction with this challenge as well, but states must find ways to motivate more than just their worst schools, the focus of the federal legislation. Strong accountability systems are vital in a world with freer education markets. If schools are to be freed from much of the top-down control that now frustrates them, they must be held to tough performance standards instead.

2. States must develop information systems to report thoroughly and publicly on the performance of every school. Many states have begun this process with the publication of school "report cards." This practice is essential to the workings of an education system with substantial school choice. Families are more likely to make wise choices among schools if they know fully how schools perform. For every school, states should report standardized test scores, college entrance exam scores, the graduation rate, and student attendance. States should report how a school's test scores and test score gains compare with the scores and gains of demographically similar schools across the state and locally. States should also provide information that might bear on the ability of the school to do a good job—for example, the percentage of teachers with degrees in the subject they are teaching and the teacher attendance rate. Opponents of school choice worry that only savvy

parents will make good choices. States can ensure that all parents can make good choices by providing them with the right information. If schools are totally transparent, they will also be more sensitive to improving their performance.

3. States should take all necessary steps to enable charter schools to compete vigorously and fairly with the public schools run by school districts. States should remove all limits on the number of charter schools that may operate in a state or locale. Let families and the marketplace decide what the right number of charters should be. If traditional public schools are doing their jobs, charters will not grow explosively. States should not give local school systems the ability to veto charter applications within their jurisdictions. States should allow public bodies not tied directly to the education establishment—for example, public universities—to grant charters. States should support charter schools at the full per-pupil level of traditional public schools, including all local, state, and federal aid, general and categorical. And finally, states should provide charter schools with per-pupil capital funds. The biggest impediment to charter school growth is facilities: Most states force charter schools to pay for facilities out of operating funds, a severe disadvantage in their efforts to compete with traditional public schools, which receive capital budgets for facilities.

4. To enable traditional public schools to compete effectively with charter schools, states should relax the regulations governing curriculum, textbooks, teacher certification, staffing, minutes of instruction, and anything else that is substantially relaxed for charter schools. In the end, health and safety regulations, nondiscrimination requirements, and academic standards should comprise most of the state regulatory regimen. School districts can decide for themselves whether to change local regulations. States should lead the way in ensuring that all schools have the flexibility they need in order to innovate and succeed. In opposing choice, tra-

ditional public schools have often argued that the regulations they face make competition unfair. Precisely: Let's give all schools the flexibility to shape their programs in the best interests of their students and compete for their support.

5. Charter schools are an essential component of any publicly financed market-based system of education. Charter schools can be held accountable to state standards, and their charters are ultimately in the hands of public authorities. But any effort to revolutionize American education by putting more power in the hands of parents and less in the hands of system authorities would be foolish to overlook the country's rich resource of private schools. Roughly one in nine students in the United States is educated in a private school. Most of these schools educate a cross section of students and operate for a fraction of what public schools spend. Catholic schools are a prime example. In America's inner cities, private schools offer the only immediately available alternative to district schools. Charter schools will spring up in time. But meanwhile, states should provide vouchers for private schools. The vouchers should be carefully structured to ensure that private schools serve the public interest as effectively as possible. It is a common misconception, promoted by voucher opponents, that vouchers will promote inequity or reward unscrupulous or offensive operators. But the fact is, vouchers can be designed to work however policy makers want them to work. In this spirit, vouchers should be limited to low-income families, since they are the ones who need choices the most. The vouchers should be for use in religious as well as nonsectarian schools, since religious schools predominate and the purpose of voucher policy is to increase the supply of alternative schools. The voucher should be for less than the per-pupil allocation for charter schools—say, 15 percent less— since the objective of the market-based reform proposed here is to promote charter school growth, not private school growth. Pri-

vate schools that accept vouchers should also be required to take them as payment in full for their services: Private schools should not be permitted to discriminate against families unable to top off the tuition with personal funds. Private schools should also be required to administer whatever tests are part of the state accountability system, if a majority of a school's students attend with the benefit of vouchers. Private schools should not, however, be held to any other accountability standards that might apply to charter schools. The state should accept the value of their private status as an alternative arena for school innovation. In an education marketplace brimming with information, private schools will need to convince families of their worth. Private schools should therefore be trusted to provide ample information about their performance on their own.

Conclusion

The kinds of gains in student achievement that A Nation at Risk insisted the country must bring about have obviously not taken place. The reasons for this are many, but among them is the continued reliance of policy makers on the traditional school system to make the gains happen. Meanwhile, policy makers have begun extensive experimentation with an idea—choice—that has the potential to bring about much more meaningful improvement. These experiments are changing the politics of school reform, building constituencies of satisfied families who would be unwilling to return to traditional schools, and creating demand for more choices among those families who are dissatisfied with existing schools but unable to get into the scarce alternatives. They suggest that a revolution may yet be in our future.

Policy makers would do well to heed the recommendations above as they respond to the continuing demand for improvement. They would do well to recognize that market-oriented change takes time and that the reforms enacted over the last decade must be given the time to prove themselves—or not. For these recommendations are not mere *school* reforms. These recommendations promise fundamental change in the way the American education system operates. They promise to strengthen public education by making it more accountable for student achievement, more attentive to the wishes of families, and more innovative in its use of scarce resources. They promote the influence of market forces but keep democratic authority ultimately in control, regulating the market for the public good. And finally, as we reflect on the significance of A *Nation at Risk* and ask whether the gains in achievement that it challenged us to make will eventually be made, the answer will depend less on the progress of reforms that it advocated and more on the progress of reforms it failed to anticipate altogether.

Notes

1. Milton Friedman, "The Role of Government in Education," in *Economics and the Public Interest,* ed. Robert Solo (Rutgers University Press, 1955).
2. On the Alum Rock project, see David K. Cohen and Eleanor Farrar, "Power to the Parents? The Story of Educational Vouchers," *Public Interest,* no. 48 (Summer 1977), 72–97. The most important statement of the liberal case for vouchers is John E. Coons and Stephen D. Sugarman, *Education by Choice, The Case for Family Control* (University of California Press, 1978). A much earlier and less elaborate version of the liberal case is made by Christopher Jencks, "Is the Public School Obsolete?" *The Public Interest* 2 (Winter 1966), 18–27.
3. James S. Coleman, Thomas Hoffer, and Sally Kilgore, *High School Achievement: Public, Private, and Catholic Schools Compared* (New York: Basic Books, 1982).
4. James S. Coleman et al., *Equality of Education Opportunity* (Department of Health, Education, and Welfare, 1966).
5. For a critical discussion of Coleman's findings on bussing, see Gary Orfield, *Must We Bus? Segregated Schools and National Policy* (Washington, D.C.: Brookings Institution Press, 1978).

6. James S. Coleman and Thomas Hoffer, *Public and Private High Schools: The Impact of Communities* (New York: Basic Books, 1987).

7. Paul Hill et al., *High Schools with Character* (Santa Monica, Calif.: RAND, 1989). The superior performance of Catholic schools was later demonstrated in Anthony S. Bryk, Valerie E. Lee, and Peter B. Holland, *Catholic Schools and the Common Good* (Cambridge, Mass.: Harvard University Press, 1993), though they argued that the quality of Catholic schools is not due to the market pressures that those schools face.

8. John E. Chubb and Terry M. Moe, *Politics, Markets, and America's Schools* (Washington, D.C.: Brookings Institution Press, 1990).

9. On public opinion toward school choice and vouchers, see especially Terry M. Moe, *Schools, Vouchers, and the American Public* (Washington, D.C.: Brookings Institution Press, 2001).

10. Lauro Cavasos briefly served as secretary of education between Bennett and Alexander.

11. Moe, *Schools, Vouchers, and the American Public.*

12. Vermont and Maine have "tuitioning plans" dating to the mid-1800s that pay for thousands of students to attend private secular high schools when their towns have no public high schools. While these plans are identical in form to vouchers, they set little precedent—and provoke little opposition—because they produce little competition and do not threaten existing public schools.

13. William G. Howell and Paul E. Peterson, *The Education Gap: Vouchers and Urban Schools* (Washington, D.C.: Brookings Institution Press, 2002), 30–31.

14. Ibid., 31.

15. For a brief recap of those defeats, see "Vouchers on the Ballot," *Education Week* XXXI, no. 42 (July 10, 2002), 24.

16. Moe, *Schools, Vouchers, and the American Public.*

17. Florida also has implemented a voucher program for special education students which, unlike the voucher for students in failed schools, has attracted a large number of participants seeking services they are unable to find in their neighborhood schools.

18. Howell and Peterson, *The Education Gap*, 29.

19. Ibid., 30.

20. Ibid.

21. A thorough review of the empirical evidence on creaming in schools of choice generally is Paul T. Hill, ed. *Choice with Equity* (Stanford, Calif.: Hoover Institution Press, 2002).

22. For a collection of research on the achievement of black students and on programs and policies that have boosted it, see John E. Chubb and Tom Loveless, eds. *Bridging the Achievement Gap* (Washington, D.C.: Brookings Institution Press, 2002).

23. Howell and Peterson, *The Education Gap*, 185–7.

24. Elisabeth Bumiller, "Bush Calls Ruling About Vouchers a 'Historic' Move," *New York Times*, July 2, 2002, A1.

25. Mark Walsh, "Charting the New Landscape of School Choice," *Education Week* XXXI, no. 42 (July 10, 2002), 20.

26. Ibid., 18.

27. The history of charters is best told in Chester E. Finn Jr., Bruno V. Manno, and Gregg Vanourek, *Charter Schools in Action* (Princeton, N.J.: Princeton University Press, 2000), 53–73.

28. See David Osborne and Ted Gaebler, *Reinventing Government: How the Entrepreneurial Spirit Is Transforming the Public Sector* (Reading, Mass.: Addison-Wesley, 1993).

29. Center for Education Reform, "Charter Schools in Operation, Fall 2002," www.edreform.com.

30. Center for Education Reform, "Charter School Laws: Scorecard and Ranking," cer@edreform.com.

31. Bryan C. Hassel, "Charter Schools: Politcs and Practice in Four States," in *Learning from School Choice*, eds. Bryan C. Hassel and Paul E. Peterson (Washington, D.C.: Brookings Institution Press, 1998).

32. The most comprehensive reviews of the evidence are Hill, ed. *Choice with Equity*; and Finn, Manno, and Vanourek, *Charter Schools in Action*. For an opposing review of the evidence, see American Federation of Teachers, *Do Charter Schools Measure Up? The Charter School Experiment After 10 Years* (July 2002).

33. Caroline M. Hoxby, "How School Choice Affects the Achievement of Public School Students," in Hill, ed., *Choice with Equity*, 141–78.

34. Ibid.

35. Ibid.

36. This is the recommendation of the independent RAND study, B. P. Gill

et al., *Rhetoric Versus Reality: What We Know and What We Need to Know About Vouchers and Charter Schools* (Santa Monica, Calif.: RAND, 2001).

37. The material for this section is from internal Edison Schools research, "A Brief Overview of For-Profit Management Organizations," April 2002.

38. For a history of private management prior to the recent period, and from a rather critical standpoint, see Carol Ascher, Norm Fruchter, and Robert Berne, *Hard Lessons: Public Schools and Privatization* (New York: The Twentieth Century Fund Press, 1996).

39. The school count for Edison refers to the number of school buildings it manages, and not, as Edison usually reports, its number of K–5, 6–8, and 9–12 grade groupings.

40. Edison Schools, Inc. *Fourth Annual Report on School Performance*, October 2001.

Index

absenteeism, 89–90, 92*f*

academic skills: advance in skill with advance in processing for, 286, 294–95; content skills in, 285–86, 291–93; dependent on coherence, content of program, and, 293, 299; domain-specific content, reading, and, 286, 296–98; nontransferability issues of mental skills and, 286, 296–98; procedure skills in, 286, 291–93; unconscious/conscious character of, 293; working memory limitations effect on, 287–90

accountability, 13, 136, 146, 186, 188–94, 270, 305–6; by academic subjects, 309, 311*t*, 313*t*; accurate measures for, 15–16; achievement lacking and, 310, 311–13*t*; business leaders backing of, 188–89, 306; centralization of standards for, 308; choice-based education as form of, 196; civil rights groups concern about, 193; computerized feedback for, 317, 327*n*13; consequences of testing, 16, 190–91; contracting, privately managed schools and, 350, 351; curriculum-based external testing for, 315–16; decentralization for operations for, 308, 316; division of labor, competition, and, 315–16; effects from, 316–17, 327*n*13; exemplary standards for, 318, 320; false design of current, 194; goals of, 15; governors' backing of, 189, 306, 307*t*; international competition and, 315–16; of low-performing schools, 192; meaning for, 15, 19–20, 22; NAEP and state's concerns of, 70*n*6; with National Assessment Governing Board, 308–9, 310*t*; No Child Left Behind (NCLB) Act and, 308, 317, 322, 323*t*, 324–25; poor performance of, 190, 191, 194; principles for, 319–20, 321*t*; reform movement for, 186, 188–94, 206–7, 306, 307–8*t*, 308; replacing failed schools from, 16; school quality and, 330–31; states and flawed, 317, 318, 319*t*, 322; states and strong, 316, 317, 318, 319*t*, 322, 325; states for, 70*n*6, 193, 215,